Ian Fleming and the Politics of Ambivalence

Ian Fleming and the Politics of Ambivalence

Ian Kinane

BLOOMSBURY ACADEMIC
LONDON • NEW YORK • OXFORD • NEW DELHI • SYDNEY

BLOOMSBURY ACADEMIC
Bloomsbury Publishing Plc
50 Bedford Square, London, WC1B 3DP, UK
1385 Broadway, New York, NY 10018, USA
29 Earlsfort Terrace, Dublin 2, Ireland

BLOOMSBURY, BLOOMSBURY ACADEMIC and the Diana logo are
trademarks of Bloomsbury Publishing Plc

First published in Great Britain 2021
Paperback edition published 2022

Copyright © Ian Kinane, 2021

Ian Kinane has asserted his right under the Copyright, Designs and Patents Act,
1988, to be identified as Author of this work.

For legal purposes the Acknowledgements on p. vi constitute an extension
of this copyright page.

Cover design: Namkwan Cho
Cover image © Getty Images

All rights reserved. No part of this publication may be reproduced or
transmitted in any form or by any means, electronic or mechanical, including
photocopying, recording, or any information storage or retrieval system,
without prior permission in writing from the publishers.

Bloomsbury Publishing Plc does not have any control over, or responsibility for, any
third-party websites referred to or in this book. All internet addresses given in this
book were correct at the time of going to press. The author and publisher regret any
inconvenience caused if addresses have changed or sites have ceased to exist, but can
accept no responsibility for any such changes.

A catalogue record for this book is available from the British Library.

A catalog record for this book is available from the Library of Congress.

ISBN: HB: 978-1-3501-2896-5
PB: 978-1-3502-3538-0
ePDF: 978-1-3501-2897-2
eBook: 978-1-3501-2898-9

Typeset by Newgen KnowledgeWorks Pvt. Ltd., Chennai, India

To find out more about our authors and books visit www.bloomsbury.com
and sign up for our newsletters.

Contents

Acknowledgements   vi

Introduction: Ian Fleming and the politics of ambivalence; or, From
Jamaica with love?   1

1 Imagined identities and the Black body politic in *Live and Let Die*   53
2 Invasion, animality and bodily transgressions in *Dr. No*   85
3 Mobility, memory and touristic modernity in *The Man with the
   Golden Gun*   125
4 After Fleming: Jamaica on screen   153

Notes   171
Bibliography   199
Index   211

Acknowledgements

I was very fortunate to receive the Everett Helm Fellowship to visit the Ian Fleming archive holdings housed in the Lilly Library at Indiana University Bloomington, where much of the early research for this project took place. I owe a debt of gratitude to the wonderful staff at the Lilly's reading room and especially to Isabel Planton, who has continued to be a source of great help long after my visit. As editor of the *International Journal of James Bond Studies*, I also owe a great deal of thanks to those colleagues who serve on the journal's editorial board, as well as to the contributors, peer reviewers and editors who provide invaluable support and whose work has helped to lay the groundwork for my own. In particular, I would like to single out Monica Germaná, whose work and friendship has been a great inspiration and encouragement. As an Early Career Researcher, I am very fortunate to work in such a supportive academic environment at the University of Roehampton. In particular, my thanks go to Rachele Dini, David Fallon, Alberto Fernández-Carbajal, Dustin M. Frazier Wood, Susan Greenberg, Ian Haywood, Nicki Humble, Kevin McCarron, Clare McManus, Zachary Leader, Laura Peters, Mary L. Shannon, Shelley Trower and Alison Waller for their assistance and support in this project. My thanks, as well, to those friends who share my interest in James Bond and with whom I have enjoyed a good many discussions: Polly Beauwin, Craig Cameron-Fisher, Benjamin George, Gillian Groszewski and Keith Leon. My greatest thanks (and love) to Mam, Dad, Amy, Conor, Kim, Anne, Lolo and, above all, Lizzie – many of whom bore witness to the birth of this obsession, and some of whom, I am sure, are now hoping that I will put it to bed.

Introduction: Ian Fleming and the politics of ambivalence; or, From Jamaica with love?

This book takes as its focus representations of Jamaica and British-Jamaican cultural relations in the literary works of Ian Fleming. That Fleming occupied a rather unusual position as a British writer, living and working part-time in Jamaica in the lead up to, during and in the immediate aftermath of Jamaica's independence from the UK, is significant, I argue, precisely because he is one of the best-placed literary figures of the period to speak to early British-Jamaican social, cultural and political relations. I take the position that Fleming sought, through his writings, to negotiate the deep personal ambivalence he felt towards the prospect of Jamaican independence from the UK, and I argue that Fleming's own personal meditations on the decline of empire shaped complex narratives within Britain concerning Jamaica specifically and Anglo-Caribbean discourses, more broadly – discourses which have continued to influence contemporary race relations and perceptions of migrant identities in Britain today. Fleming's reputedly staunch imperial politics sits uneasily with what I argue to be an implicit resistance within his literary works to 'simple' racism or a reductive imperial rhetoric. To be clear, the book does not make the case that Fleming is anything other than what he was: a casual racialist. However, the assumption that Fleming's writings are vehicles of purely racial or imperial propaganda is without nuance. Such a view overlooks entirely Fleming's deep and abiding love for Jamaica and Jamaicans. As such, this book argues largely for a reconsideration of Fleming's representational politics, engaging readers in a sustained discussion of the complex nuances of representation itself. Throughout his oeuvre, Fleming's literary Jamaica, I argue, increasingly becomes a site of ambivalence. Fleming's ambivalence towards British decolonization, Anglo-Caribbean relations and the Windrush generation's arrival to Britain is tied specifically to his representational politics; Jamaica serves for Fleming as a site for the exploration of a number of imbricated responses to these issues. Fleming's representation of

Anglo-Caribbean relations at large (and British-Jamaican cultural and political relations, more specifically) does not simply reflect British fears concerning issues of race and migration in the post-independence period. Indeed, contrary to the more commonly held critical view that Fleming's texts uphold a prevalently colonial discourse, I argue that much of the critical writing on Fleming's texts are somewhat at odds with the deep ambivalence of Fleming's own representational politics. In short, *Ian Fleming and the Politics of Ambivalence* is the first book-length literary-critical study of the representation of Jamaica in Fleming's work.

Simon Winder has noted that 'the subject of Fleming's relationship with Jamaica is an almost crazily fecund one' and that there is 'a murky link between the collapse of Britain's international position and [Fleming's] private life' (2006: 136). I should make clear at this juncture that the present study is not a historical or biographical one; I am not expressly concerned with Fleming's historical relationship with the island of Jamaica or with his home 'Goldeneye', located in Oracabessa on Jamaica's north coast, though I will certainly touch on this relationship. This work has already been carried out by Matthew Parker in his 2014 book *Goldeneye: Where Bond Was Born: Ian Fleming's Jamaica*, a comprehensive survey of Fleming's time in Jamaica and of the relationships, customs and pastimes he engaged in there. While I certainly agree with Parker's assertion that Jamaica 'offers the key to a fresh understanding of Fleming, Bond and our own strange relationship with this national icon' (2014: 7), I must call into question the extent to which Parker himself engages in a sustained critique or critical analysis of this relationship. Parker's book draws extensively on interviews with Fleming's family, friends and acquaintances; rather than a work of literary criticism, it is largely a work of biography which uses Fleming's time in Jamaica as a framing device. Conversely, rather than simply recounting biographical or historical material (or film trivia[1]), my focus is on the role Jamaica plays within Fleming's complexly ambivalent discourses of representation and the ways in which the signifier 'Jamaica' evolves across the canon of his writings. I argue that, in spite of James Bond's assumed role as a colonial cipher, Fleming's writings actually betray a much more complex ambivalence towards colonial politics and a resistance to imperial rhetoric than has hitherto been examined. I contend that Fleming's three Jamaica-set novels – *Live and Let Die* (1954), *Dr. No* (1958) and *The Man with the Golden Gun* (1965) – evince Fleming's subtle yet pervasive ambivalence regarding British-Jamaican racial politics at the time, an ambivalence that has largely gone unremarked upon in critical discourse, and which has often been misapprehended within popular culture. I argue for a reconsideration of Fleming's Jamaica-set writings not as vehicles of purely racial or cultural propaganda – as they are often taken to be – but, rather, as works of abiding personal concern for evolving mid-twentieth-century British-Jamaican cultural politics and the place of Jamaica therein.

A brief word on the term 'ambivalence'. Colloquially understood as a common psychological state of conflict between mixed positive and negative responses to particular situational stimuli or experiences, ambivalence has long been theorized within clinical psychology and psychoanalytic practice. First employed in psychiatric circles by Eugen Bleuler (1910) to describe contrasting feelings within an individual towards one and the same object or person,[2] the term was picked up by psychoanalyst Sigmund Freud to describe the ambiguity of linguistic signs and the concurrency of both loving and hateful feelings that can reside within the individual towards a single sign (object or person) (Freud 1988: 118–19). Drawing on the work of his long-time collaborator and close friend, Karl Abraham – who had posited in his theories on infantile psychosexual development that ambivalence was a condition of both 'positive and negative instinctual cravings, [as well as] hostile and friendly tendencies' towards the parent-figure (1973: 402) – Freud argued that ambivalence consisted of 'pairs of contrary component instincts' (1988: 256) that are in conflict with one another. In his *Totem and Taboo*, he draws the concept out further, arguing that 'alongside of the veneration, and indeed idolization [in this case, of the totemic sign-object], there is in the unconscious an opposing current of intense hostility' at the same time ([1950] 1961: 49). For Freud's successor Melanie Klein, the concept of ambivalence was endemic to the foundation of her own object relations theory and to her work on the infantile depressive position, which, as Paula Heimann notes, is 'the poignant conflict of ambivalence with guilt and despair for the hatred experienced against the loved object' (1985: 258). More broadly, beyond the remit of clinical psychology and psychoanalysis, the recent turn within philosophy studies towards ambivalence (Razinsky 2016) suggests there is much more work to be done in this area.

But for the purposes of the current study, I wish to focus on ambivalence as a condition of coloniality or, as it is understood in the critical church of postcolonialism, on the dualism inherent in the split cultural identities of those caught within the colonial paradigm. In *The Location of Culture*, Homi K. Bhabha attends to the contradictions inherent in the discursive construction of the colonizer–colonized relationship. He defines this relationship by its very ambivalence, characterized by a bifurcation (or, in his words, 'hybridity') on the part of the colonized subject, who recuperates her/his own cultural identity in the colonial period through a hybridized mimesis of the colonizer's imposed identity in concert with her/his own supplanted identity. Bhabha labels this hybridizing performance 'mimicry', by which he means the colonized other is 'a subject of a difference that is almost the same [as the colonizer], but not quite' and which is always 'constructed around an ambivalence' in self-identification (2006: 122). In appropriating through mimesis the vestiges and cultural apparatuses of the colonizer, the colonized other performs a hybrid cultural identity that succeeds in exposing and undermining through its very performance the 'uncertainty which fixes the colonial subject as a "partial" presence' (123). In other words, 'in disclosing the ambivalence of colonial discourse [mimesis] also disrupts its authority' as a totalizing discourse (126). This hybrid dualism is a condition not only of the colonized subject but also of the colonizer; as Bhabha notes, 'the colonial presence is always ambivalent, split between its appearance as original and authoritative and its articulation [through the mimesis of the colonized other] as repetition and difference' (153). In other words, colonial discourse is itself an ambivalently hybrid discourse, characterized, on the one hand, by mastery, and, on the other, by displacement and fantasy (108).

As I will outline in detail below, Ian Fleming's pseudo-imperial fantasies were played out in his Jamaica-set fiction, in which his personal, psychological ambivalence towards Jamaica's burgeoning nationalism very much replicates the ambivalence of colonial discourse and the ambivalent figure of the colonizer at large. Though Fleming represented himself as nurturing of Jamaican culture, he was certainly exploitative of it too – someone who, to borrow from Anne McClintock, was caught in the 'elusive play of fantasy, desire and the unconscious in colonial contests' (1995: 63). As I will argue, Fleming's political ambivalence, the ambiguity of his positionality with regards to Jamaica and his conflict over the prospect of Jamaican independence from the British Empire, is a significant factor in accounting for the success of the James Bond novels. Unlike Bhabha, who argues that the 'dominant [colonizing] power' is 'shielded from the play of ambivalence' (2006: 64) within the colonial context, my concern, here, is that the white Britisher Fleming constructs a vision both of Jamaica and of himself that is, like Bhabha's colonized subject, caught in the imaginary, an ambivalent space of contradiction and slippage. However, much like Bhabha, the notion of ambivalence is also at the constitutive heart of my analysis (Young 1995: 161). Fleming's writing evidences his simultaneous attraction and disdain towards the prospect of Britain's decolonization of Jamaica, a prospect which hangs spectrally over his Jamaica-set works. As such, it is the 'formal ambivalence of colonial representation itself' (McClintock 1995: 63) within Fleming's work with which this book is primarily concerned, and the ways in which Fleming elects to fashion his own political, social and cultural ambivalence through James Bond's Jamaican adventures.³

Before we proceed, and in order to further contextualize the present study, I want to first turn to a September 2018 *Times* review of Idris Elba's directorial film debut, the largely Jamaica-set *Yardie* (2018). In the review, journalist Janice Turner ponders, 'Why are there so few films about Jamaica? India is a movie staple; but millions of Britons have roots in the West Indies. When was the last time we saw Kingston on screen? The Bond film *Dr. No*?' (2018: 24). Turner's comment, here, raises a number of interrelated critical concerns regarding cultural and political representation which converge in the present study and which will be outlined, here, by way of introduction. The first of these concerns is implicit: that is, the representational gap that exists between *Yardie* and the audience at whom the film is primarily targeted, the Black Britons who are, according to Turner's review of the crowd's response to the film, 'delighted to see their childhood on screen, to hear the music of their teens, to enjoy a recreation … of a 1980s Jamaican grandmother's flat, [and] to chuckle at the quaint colloquialisms no one uses any more' (ibid.). Unaccustomed to seeing the intimate cultural life of Jamaica represented on British screens, the delight of this screening's particular audience, according to Turner, is predicated on the pleasure of recognition. The novelty in viewing scenes of domestic Jamaican life (many instances of which will be familiar to the audience, whose members, perhaps, may not have participated in the daily customs of Jamaica since first coming to Britain) is a source of collective jubilation for the crowd. It is novel (as in: not usual) and therefore enjoyable to see such experiences attended to in British film. But Elba's film is also novel in the sense that, for many, the representation of Jamaican cultural life in film is still in itself a thing of relative newness.⁴ The film's novelty, that which provokes its audience's delight, is also that which implicitly underlines the paucity of authentic and sustained representation of Jamaican cultural forms available in the mainstream to Jamaican and Black British communities within Britain. Indeed, Turner describes the film's largely Black British audience with whom she shared the screening as 'hungry' (ibid.), a word that, at once, puts the reader in mind of a *body* of people whose personal, social and cultural livelihoods can be said to be *nourished* and *sustained* by the film, whilst simultaneously belying the idea that the same audience has also hitherto been *deprived* and *starved* of such material. So, in terms of the first significant takeaway from Turner's article, it should be noted that there is a representational gap between the experiences of Jamaican customs, histories and sociocultural practices and those modes and frames of representation (film, television, literature) which mediatize such practices. In this representational gap, films such as *Yardie* remain, on the whole, novel – both unusual and forever delightful in their newness; their very newness prohibitive, in a sense, of their cultural normalization.

The second, compounding concern raised by Turner's article is the means by which the apparent triumph of minority cultural representation (which, in this context, *Yardie* represents) is diverted into self-conscious, benevolent appreciation by the writer herself, modified by the dominant culture's framing of this representative experience as self-reflective. The film's newness is not simply a condition of the under-representation of Jamaican practices and cultural conditions in Britain; in this case, the film is presented as enlightening precisely because it happens to be new to Turner herself. '*Yardie* took me somewhere I haven't been,' she notes (ibid.), at once commenting on her own lack of familiarity with Jamaica and, in that same instant, activating the gaze of the tourist: she is metaphorically transported away.[5] Turner's own appreciation of Jamaica (as something to be seen, something with the aura of newness) is placed alongside the appreciation of the Black British and Jamaican audience for their ancestral country, an appreciation that is based in a mixture of authentic cultural recognition, nostalgia and lived experience. But the power of the film, as the framing of Turner's article suggests, resides not solely in the effect it has on the Black British and Jamaican audience but in the effect it has on Turner herself, who is watching the audience. The film *moves* her (the tourist who is transported, again), but not so much as she is moved by the experience of watching the audience. She says, 'It is electrifying to watch a film among people so delighted' (ibid.). There is, I think, more than the hint of self-satisfaction, here, as the Black Britons' and Jamaicans' experience of the film is sublimated into the author's own appreciation of a spectacle she has borne witness to. So, the second takeaway from Turner's article, then, is the extent to which Black British and Jamaican cultural experiences, and the reportage of those cultural experiences in representation, can be framed in particular ways that reflect less the experience of minority culture(s) and more that of the reporter or writer.[6] If there exists a representational gap between authentic minority cultural practices and the modes and forms by which those cultural practices are mediatized, then it follows that those minority communities are divested of the ownership (and authenticity) of their own cultural representation. In the case of Turner's article, here, this divestment is directed through the touristic gaze of extant, racializing power dynamics that prioritize an almost ethnographic delineation between the mediator (Turner herself) and the film's Black audience. We can see this in

Turner's attempt to divert her readers away from any suspicions of unsavoury cultural appropriation on her part, when she announces at the start of the article that the *Yardie* screening took place at the Brixton Ritzy (on Windrush Square and right beside the Black Cultural Archives), a place she describes as 'more likely to be full of white hipsters' but which, for that particular evening, was populated by 'a hungry black audience' (ibid.). Here, Turner's (apparently unconscious) use of adjectives skirts discomfitingly close to those atavistic discourses of cannibalism which, of course, largely defined British fears, mainly in the nineteenth century, of the consuming threat of the Black body.[7]

The third and final point of significance to be noted in Turner's article is, of course, her guesstimate that, prior to *Yardie*, the last time Kingston, Jamaica, was seen on British film screens was in the first James Bond film, *Dr. No* (1962).[8] Turner's point is important for the present study for two main reasons. Firstly, she underlines the almost symbiotic relationship within the public imagination between Ian Fleming, his character James Bond and the island of Jamaica, on which Fleming wrote all of the Bond stories and upon which a number of the popular spy's adventures took place. Secondly, and more significantly, by calling to mind the film *Dr. No* in the context of an event marking *Yardie*'s production and release, Turner implicitly draws a correlation between Fleming, Bond and Jamaica, on the one hand, and the politics of representation, race and (to a certain extent) class, on the other. Moreover, it is in this point, here, that my first two observations about Turner's article coalesce. Ian Fleming lived and worked in Jamaica for the spring months every year for the twelve years prior to his death. He set many of his James Bond novels in Jamaica. He wrote about Jamaican people and locales, often dressing real people and occurrences up in his fiction. He professed a love for Jamaica and for Jamaican people, and he considered the island his adopted home. It was also in Jamaica that Fleming laid down the blueprint of his literary style – what we might judge by today's standards as inflammatory, essentialist and racialist 'empire fiction' framed within a discourse of adventurous heroism. Thus, Fleming is the very epitome of a writer whose work has institutionalized the representational gap between Jamaica's customs, histories and social, political and cultural conditions – which are tendered in his fiction ostensibly with loving appreciation and an objective authoritativeness – and the intended audience for whom that work is primarily written: white, British, 'warm-blooded heterosexuals in railway trains, airplanes, or beds' (Fleming qtd in Zeiger 1966: 110). Such representations are encoded with and license a particular set of racial, sexual and political responses that are grounded in ethnographic spectacularization. In spite of the author's adherence to local geographical history, Fleming's Jamaica is an overwhelmingly representative topography, a space reflective at once not only of the 'real' Jamaica but also, and predominantly, a space that is – much like Turner's reportage of her experience at the *Yardie* screening – sublimated within the author's own touristic gaze and framed within the parameters of similar ethnographic power dynamics. There is much of the 'real' Jamaica to be found in the pages of Fleming's work, but it is Fleming's deliberate framing of Jamaica as a self-reflective spectacle, as something he has borne witness to in the guise of magnanimous cultural interlocutor, which further enhances the representational gap between reportage and cultural authenticity. To be clear, I am not suggesting that Fleming does or should strive towards representing an 'authentic' Jamaica (whatever that is); rather, I wish to underline the point that, like Turner's vision of Jamaica, Fleming's Jamaica is an ideologically infused signifier through which certain ethno-cultural representations have been collapsed upon and folded within the author's own experiences. While it might be argued that cultural ethnography is not necessarily (if ever) the purview of fiction, Fleming's works – exoticist travel narratives, for the most part – make competing claims on the reader's attention. On the one hand, Fleming's writings signal their own outrageousness, their departure from cultural, political and literary realism evidently marked in their many absurdities. On the other hand, Fleming's writings insist on returning the reader to the 'real' Jamaica which the author purports to know very well.[9] Fleming's insistence on appraising Jamaica and Jamaican culture either through his own *subjective* experience or by recourse to other works of *fiction*[10] suggests that his writings are not simply fiction but, rather, can be read as works of 'impure' or 'pseudo' ethnography through which Fleming tasks himself with 'translating' Jamaica for his British readership – most of whom, it should be remembered, are encountering Jamaican people for the first time as a result of large-scale migration from the Caribbean to Britain's shores, and whose preconceptions of such immigrant communities were often informed through such ethnographic fictions.

Of course, Fleming's act of literary 'translation' is also an act of omission. In attempting to convey to his British readership at least some of the nuances and minutiae of Jamaican culture, Fleming invariably selects which elements of the 'real' Jamaica are to be included in his pseudo-ethnography and which are to be excluded (and which can reasonably be accommodated within the parameters of the particular genre in which he is writing). Representation necessarily entails a selective accommodation of the material to hand, and, as such, all representation is a form of omission. With respect to those discourses of representation informed by colonialism's inherent structural power imbalances (in which representation itself is used purposefully as a tool to sustain dominant hegemonic relations[11]), Fleming's pseudo-ethnographic construction of Jamaica is part of a much more dated tradition within British imperial history. The Caribbean region has long been cast in the historical imagination of the Anglophone West as a geo-imaginary location, an unreal *topos*. Mimi Sheller has argued that 'although the Caribbean lies at the heart of the western hemisphere and was historically pivotal in the rise of Europe to world dominance, it has nevertheless been spatially and temporally eviscerated from the imaginary geographies of "western modernity"' (2003: 1). Sheller suggests that one of the reasons the Caribbean region has been absented from Britain's national, cultural and historical narratives in particular is that, for the late eighteenth century and for much of the nineteenth century, the Caribbean constituted in the British imagination a fearful place of racial hybridity and miscegenation, 'a special zone open to the re-mixing of previously separate populations and "racial" substances' (ibid.: 111). The racially-ambiguous Caribs were seen to represent a threat to the purity of Anglo-Saxon genetics, and the Caribbean became, in the British imagination, a scientific testing ground upon which European theories of racial miscegenation were scrutinized. The British greatly feared the intermixing of disparate races, and there was much debate over the potentials of genetic cross-breeding. Fears of potential devolution in the British genetic strain through intermixing 'drove many Europeans to insist upon the fundamental difference of races and to attempt to reinforce and shore up racial boundaries by systems of inequality, discrimination, and segregation' (ibid.). Thus, Sheller argues, 'the imagined community of the West has no space for the islands that were its origin' and that 'despite its indisputable narrative position at the origin of the plot of western modernity, history has been edited and the Caribbean left on the cutting-room floor' (ibid.: 1). Sheller's use of the term 'on the cutting-room floor' to describe the process by which the Caribbean region has become abjected from the cultural imagination of the Anglophone West should reorient the reader's attention towards those modes and frames of representation I mentioned above with respect to Turner's article on the screening of *Yardie*. Sheller uses the language of film machinery to suggest that, like a piece of film that has been cut, the Caribbean region has seemingly been edited out of the cultural imagination of Western historical modernity. Here, Sheller calls attention to the processes of mediatization by and through which history becomes reified only once it has passed through and has been recorded in text, within and by a particular medium.[12] She also inadvertently draws attention to the agency at play behind such processes: the work of those individuals whose creative endeavours produce these texts and who select certain textual 'realities' which prioritize a particular political or ideological vision of history – the 'hands' of the film editor (to expand on this analogy) who makes those incisions and cuts, and whose careful deliberations dictate and largely shape the interpretive possibilities of the finished film.[13]

Fleming's Jamaica is part of the very same geospatial construct which Sheller outlines above. The Jamaica upon which Fleming operates and which is subject to use in his writings is not simply that which appears in 'tourist brochures, or in occasional disaster tales involving hurricanes, boat-people, drugs barons, dictators, or revolutions' (ibid.); it is not simply reality (or *a* reality) invested with fiction. Rather, Fleming's fictions deliberately draw upon and augment the processes by which the Caribbean has always been made use of in the British cultural and historical imagination: as a geo-imaginary location, a geography annexed to the imagination. As we will see, Fleming invests in his writings the view that Jamaica has 'long been metaphorically consumed through colonial and imperial travel narratives, fictions, and artistic depictions' (ibid.: 107); his incorporation or consumption of Jamaica within the framework of British colonial history, and his simultaneous reconstruction of the 'real' Jamaica of his own experiences, is actually central to the representational strategies of his Jamaica-set novels. By casting himself as cultural interlocutor, Fleming creates a 'new' Jamaica for his British readership, a Jamaica that is at once ahistorical (in that Fleming ignores or attempts to compensate in his writings for the historical realities of Britain's loss of empire and global influence) but also one that is firmly rooted in *a* specific history (the Jamaica known specifically to Fleming during a particular moment of the island's history). Fleming's use of Jamaica in his novels is predicated on the strategic denial of the island's geo-historical realities and on an investment in his own personal myth of the erasure of decolonization. As Sheller observes of the erasure in the Western cultural imagination of the Caribbean region, 'having washed its hands of history, the North can now present itself as the hero in the piece, graciously donating democratic tutelage, economic aid, foreign investment, military advisers, and police support' (ibid.: 1). So too with Fleming. Having 'washed his hands' of the historical realities of British-Jamaican geopolitical relations in the lead-up to and in the immediate aftermath of Jamaica's independence from Britain in 1962, Fleming's fiction affords him the opportunity 'to construct an imaginary world in which the *Pax Britannica* still operates' (Richards 2001: 136). As I will demonstrate below, Fleming's colonial cipher (James Bond) allows him to play the role of Jamaica's beneficent benefactor, while his fiction (inadvertently or otherwise) promulgates de facto British political influence on the island during the historical period in which British rule in the Caribbean was beginning to lose its foothold. As such, Fleming's fiction has not always been strictly accountable to history. While Britain's declining influence and its gradually diminishing role in global geopolitics can be traced through each of Fleming's successive Jamaica-set works (*Live and Let Die*, *Dr. No* and *The Man with the Golden Gun* – which take place throughout those periods of Jamaican history prior to, during and in the aftermath of the independence movement, respectively), Fleming's writings can nevertheless be read as aberrations of history; they are cognizant of the new and changing realities of British-Jamaican colonial relations while at the same time belying something of an ambivalence towards the effects of these changes.

The *Pax Britannica* which Fleming reinstitutes in his later fiction, then, is one of tension between the historical and political realities of Jamaica's independence from Britain and an imaginary Jamaica, Fleming's geo-imaginary and geopolitical fantasy annexed from its developing national history. This strategy is as much literary as it is political. The Caribbean in Fleming's fictive universe functions not simply as a spatial analogue to the author's unresolved postcolonial anxieties; it also operates on a number of semiotic levels. For Vivian Halloran, the Caribbean performs an important structural function as a 'physical foil to James Bond' (2005: 171). Taking much the same position as Mimi Sheller on historical Anglo-Caribbean relations, Halloran argues that the 'racial and geographical hybridity and intermixing' which Bond encounters in the Caribbean (particularly in *Live and Let Die* and *Dr. No*) must necessarily 'be deciphered and read in conjunction to a European framework of long-standing prejudices' (ibid.).[14] If Bond serves reciprocally as a foil for the Caribbean region (in Halloran's terms), and if British conceptions of the Caribbean are to be read through Western modernity's historical fears of racial miscegenation, it follows that a productive reading of the Bond icon must also incorporate a study of Jamaica not as it was but *as it was perceived* by Fleming and within the British cultural imagination of the time. Fleming's mediatized Jamaica, I argue, is a topographically hybrid construct, forged in equal parts from the author's local experiences of the island (Jamaica as it was; the past) and his concerns, anxieties and desirous projections for its future (the Jamaica of Fleming's geopolitical fantasy; the future). Halloran refers to Fleming's hybrid Jamaica as an 'ambiguously geographic ethnoscape … a meeting point for Old and New Worlds as well as a place from which to articulate a hybrid cultural identity' (ibid.: 176). While I am disinclined to agree with the assertion that Fleming's treatment of Jamaica and of mixed-race Jamaicans in his fiction articulates in any politically resonant fashion the nuances of hybrid Jamaican cultural and racial identities (Fleming's novels are expressly unconcerned with problematizing and resolving in any meaningful sense issues of racial hybridity), I do concur with Halloran that Fleming's Jamaica is a 'meeting point for Old and New worlds'. However, whereas Halloran views this as the conflation of 'England's colonial past' and the 'specters of international communism' (ibid.), I see Fleming's Jamaica more accurately as a merging of Jamaica's colonial past (history, reality) with the author's own geopolitical reimaginings of that colonial past within an emergent post-colonial context. In a sense, the 'new' world of Fleming's Jamaica is not really new at all; it is merely the colonial logic of the old order preserved and reconstituted, as Fleming attempts to grapple with the changing world order brought about by the gradual dissolution of Britain's empire.[15] Halloran's use of the phrase 'ambiguously geographic ethnoscape' is suggestive of precisely such a dissolution. Britain's eventual concession to various independence movements from within the Caribbean (Jamaica being the first Caribbean country to attain its independence in the post-war period, in 1962[16]) meant that firm national territorial lines became unstuck as world geography was redrawn. With Britain's waning imperial influence in the era of decolonization, geographical borders came into flux and national geographies were ambiguously redefined. The geographic ethnoscape of Fleming's literary Jamaica, then, is also ambiguous precisely because Fleming's topography is not a simple mimesis of the island's historical geography but a compound imaginative territory upon which Fleming plays out certain concerns over fluctuating British-Jamaican cultural and political relations, and in which Jamaica functions for Fleming as an indicative testing-ground for reimagining Britain's (and his own) imperial past.

According to Halloran, Fleming's Jamaica-set fiction is explicitly concerned with the notion of 'doubleness' (ibid.: 172) or with the double nature of this particular regional sphere within Fleming's imagination. Jamaica and the Caribbean are certainly landscapes to which Bond is often sent by M in punitive dismissal or exile, but they are also spaces of exotic plenty and sensuous ease for Bond to enjoy himself. It is in terms of doubleness, too, that Alex Adams reads the Bond novels. As he sees it:

> Bond expresses our [Britain's] complicated relationship with our past, and our empire – at once a little bit proud, a little bit ashamed, and forever aware that our 'greatest days' are behind us. It is this complexity, born in the Jamaica of Fleming's time, that gives continued life to James Bond and projects an image of Britishness that makes us likeable to ourselves, and to the rest of the world. (2017: 321–2)

Adams articulates well the connections between Jamaica and Fleming's ambivalence with respect to Britain's colonial project. Much like the blend of shame and pride felt within the modern British consciousness over the atrocities and 'glories' of empire, it is clear to Adams that Fleming's ambivalence regarding Britain's colonial past and its impending postcolonial future is tied to the author's beloved Jamaica. Because of Fleming's perceived connection to the island, and because of the interstitial space he occupied as a part-time British expatriate who lived on and wrote a great deal about Jamaica, it is through Jamaica that Fleming can be said to problematize the history of British imperialism within the Caribbean region, and through which he negotiates his reaction to Britain's anticipated withdrawal from local governance following Jamaica's independence. Adams suggests that it is precisely Fleming's ambivalence over the issue of British rule in Jamaica which 'gives continued life' to the fictional icon, James Bond. This seems on the surface to be quite a large claim. While I do not agree that Fleming's ambivalent but nevertheless often problematic relationship to British colonial politics fashions in Bond 'an image of Britishness that makes us likeable to ourselves, and to the rest of the world' (a sentiment which smacks of the discomfiting expiation of colonial guilt), I do think that part of the success of the Bond icon can be traced back to Fleming's ambivalent cultural and social politics, particularly with regard to British-Jamaican relations.

Fleming, Bond and British-Jamaican relations

The period in which Fleming was writing (1952–64) certainly coincided with a great number of tumultuous political, social and cultural changes in Britain and to British-Jamaican relations that were to have a considerable effect on Britain's international standing as a major world power.[17] *Casino Royale*, the first James Bond novel, was published on 13 April 1953, two months before the coronation of Queen Elizabeth II (2 June 1953), while the final James Bond novel, *The Man with the Golden Gun*, was published on 1 April 1965, two months after the death of beloved statesman and former prime minister Sir Winston Churchill (24 January 1965). James Chapman has noted that Britain's 'exclusion from the Common Market when French President Charles de Gaulle vetoed Britain's application in 1963, left Britain isolated in Europe and increasingly dependent on the patronage of the United States' ([1999] 2007: 28). Alex Adams has also commented that 'when Fleming published *Casino Royale* in 1953, Britain was rationing food in conditions of postwar austerity and reeling from major decolonisation in India and Palestine, and when he finished *The Man with the Golden Gun* in 1965, Britain had undergone further decolonisations in Kenya, Cyprus, Uganda, Sierra Leone and many other places, including Fleming's beloved Jamaica in 1962' (2017: 143). Fleming purchased his Jamaican home Goldeneye in 1946, two years prior to the docking of the SS *Empire Windrush* in Essex, on 22 June 1948, which carried to Britain the first generation of immigrant workers from Jamaica, Trinidad and Tobago and other Caribbean islands – those who later became known as the Windrush generation. Thus, James Bond's literary career coincided with (indeed, was framed by) the Windrush period, which lasted from 1948 until 1971. At the dawn of modern British multiculturalism, with the first of Britain's incoming migrants arriving from Jamaica, Ian Fleming was writing on and about Jamaica, about British-Jamaican cultural relations and, most significantly, about British perceptions and cultural misapprehensions of Jamaica and Jamaican people. Lisa M. Dresner has argued that, as opposed to the more traditional view during this period that the Bond novels were responsible for 'accelerating the collapse of Empire' (see Lindner 2003: 80), Fleming's writings actually increasingly began to 'reflect a response to the *consequences* of Empire' (2011: 282, italics in original). Between 1952 and 1955, the number of Jamaicans who had migrated to Britain rose from two thousand to seventeen thousand (Parker 2014: 146). As the Jamaican journalist and Fleming's friend Morris Cargill notes, 'hundreds of thousands of Jamaicans [had] gone to England to live, thereby setting many difficult social and other problems for English people – a situation which has not exactly increased [Jamaican] popularity' (1965a: 23). Jamaican journalist Evon Blake also wrote that 'Britons made [emigrant Jamaicans] feel like the uninvited they were' (qtd in Parker: 146), and, in 1955, in response to an evergrowing unrest towards Jamaican migrants, Winston Churchill's Conservative election manifesto promised to 'Keep Britain White' (Parker 2014: 146) – a promise which the later Commonwealth Immigration Act of 1962 (which introduced stringent immigration controls in Britain) proposed to deliver on. As Dresner notes, Fleming's Bond novels 'appear about five years into the surge of immigration' of (mainly) Windrush migrants into Great Britain (2011: 282). Fleming's fiction, then, can be seen to offer British readers at the time a supposed conceptual framework to contextualize burgeoning British-Jamaican relations; Fleming's representational politics – the way in which Jamaica and Jamaicans were first presented to his British readers – can be said to be central to the birth of British multiculturalism during the Windrush.

According to Christine Berberich, Fleming sought to wilfully ignore the fact that Britain was, from the 1940s onwards, turning into a multicultural society.

She points out that *Live and Let Die* and *Dr. No* are 'particularly indicative of [Fleming's] message of not only white but also Anglo-Saxon supremacy'. In both of these novels of race, there is the 'constant juxtaposition of the "natives" of Jamaica and their white British counterparts' (Berberich 2012: 25). Chapman has noted that James Bond is 'an essentially conservative hero, a defender of the realm' ([1999] 2007: 29) whose job it is to maintain order within Britain's colonies and foreign territories and to dispense punishment to those in contravention of that order. Britain's colonial governance of Jamaica, of course, legitimated Bond's role as 'global policeman' (Baron [2003] 2009: 145) and afforded him both economy of movement and authority of law within that colony. This is very much the case in the first of Fleming's Jamaica-set novels, *Live and Let Die*. In the build-up to Jamaican independence from Britain, however, Bond's right to rule in Jamaica became less assured as Fleming became increasingly ambivalent in his response to decolonization – as can be seen in the second of Fleming's Jamaica-set novels, *Dr. No*. Bond's role evolved from that of righteous policeman to defender of the faith, whose task it now was 'to vindicate a myth of Englishness which [had] been put into question by the tide of history' (Bennett and Woollacott 1987: 110) and to offer conciliatory assurances of Britain's staying power in a time of increased racial and cultural miscegenation. By the time Fleming's third and final Jamaica-set work, *The Man with the Golden Gun*, was published posthumously in 1965, Bond's role had evolved once more. Jamaica was now independent of British rule and so Fleming could not reasonably expect to extol in his writings the values of British colonialism. Instead, Bond functioned in Fleming's later work as a symbol of 'the best aspects of the British national character that have persisted, survived, through the profoundly bruising victory in the Second World War and the trials of decolonisation that followed it' (Adams 2017: 143). Bond became an emblem of the British will to survive, a figure who evidenced Britain's ability to sustain even the collapse of its global empire; Bond's return to Jamaica following British decolonization of the island was symbolic of Fleming's own regard for the island and for his desire for continued British-Jamaican diplomatic relations. By charting the development of Bond's political function across each successive Jamaica-set novel, it becomes clear that the character functions as a means for Fleming to negotiate his own response (and to direct the response of his readership) to changing British-Jamaican political, cultural and social relations. To borrow a phrase from Michael Denning, if 'the spy novel is in a sense the war novel of the Cold War', then Ian Fleming's Jamaica-set Bond novels represent 'the cover story of an era of decolonization' (1987: 92). In effect, Fleming's James Bond novels (particularly those later entries such as *Dr. No* and *The Man with the Golden Gun*) attempt to 'cover up' the loss of Britain's empire and to assuage anxieties about Britain's decreasing geopolitical relevance in the modern world. Within Fleming's fictive universe, though, Britain's decolonization of Jamaica is, curiously, both increasingly resisted or denied and accommodated by the author; Fleming seems altogether much more ambivalent in his responses to Britain's loss of Jamaica than cursory readings of his ostensibly imperial rhetoric might first suggest.

Ernest Cuneo, a lawyer and author who was close friends with Fleming,[18] has noted that the 'twentieth century marked the conflux of divergent forces, and a number of these forces converged with Ian Fleming' (1984: xi). It would, perhaps, be appropriate to extend this and to further suggest that a great many of the forces which characterized twentieth-century Britain's changing global identity converged with the island of Jamaica, specifically. As Matthew Parker notes, 'the relentless attention to race, the aching concern with the end of Empire and national decline, the awkward new relationship with the United States, even the Cold War – all these roads lead back to Jamaica' (2014: 6). Indeed, the history of the James Bond novels is in many ways the history of British-Jamaican relations. James Bond was 'born' in Jamaica.[19] To his own question, 'Would these books have been born if I had not been living in the gorgeous vacuum of a Jamaican holiday?' Fleming answers resoundingly, 'I doubt it' (1965: 12). He told the *Sunday Times* weekly review in 1963, 'I write all my books in Jamaica. I can't really write anywhere else – because there's a vacuum there and I can only write in a vacuum' ('World of Bond' 1963: n.p.). It was in Jamaica that Fleming appropriated the name 'James Bond' from the author of a work of Caribbean ornithology, *Birds of the West Indies* (1936), which he found lying around his home Goldeneye. In three of Fleming's major novels, Bond returns to Jamaica. Somewhat fittingly, Fleming's final James Bond novel, *The Man with the Golden Gun*, sees the eponymous spy return to Jamaica for the final time. Parker further notes that 'imperial, then post-imperial Jamaica contributes a vivid setting for three of [the] novels and a number of short stories, as well as cropping up referenced in almost all of Fleming's other books' (2014: 6).[20] It becomes clear throughout his oeuvre that Fleming purposefully returns Bond to Jamaica at a number of significant junctures in both the character's and his own history. In 1956, during a period of ill health in which he began to suffer badly from sciatica, he decided to be done with Bond. In a letter to Raymond Chandler, whom he had always admired, Fleming confided that he was 'very fed up with Bond' and that it had 'been very difficult to make him go through his tawdry tricks in "From

Russia with Love"' (1956a: n.p.). It is at the end of this novel, of course, that SMERSH operative Rosa Klebb kicks Bond in the shin with a poison-tipped blade concealed within her shoe, and the novel concludes irresolutely with Bond slumping to the floor as though dead. Following a public outcry over the fate of James Bond, though, Fleming decided to resurrect the character in his sixth novel, *Dr. No*, which is set predominantly in Jamaica. Bond also returns to Jamaica in *The Man with the Golden Gun*, after he has been brainwashed by the KGB at the end of *You Only Live Twice* (1964). It is clear that, within the structural economies of the Bond novels, Jamaica functions as a site of resuscitation – both for the character Bond and for the writer Fleming. In *Live and Let Die*, for instance, Bond 'undertakes a fitness regime ... combined with abstemious living' while he is in Jamaica; he submits to Quarrel's exercise programme and strengthens his body in preparation for his battle with Mr Big (Parker 2014: 94). Jamaica is the site upon which such physical transformations take place. Equally, it is a space of mental and spiritual reparation: in both *Dr. No* and *The Man with the Golden Gun*, Bond is 'sent by M to Jamaica in part to recover from a previous physical and mental trauma' (ibid.). Not only is Jamaica a space upon which Bond is afforded time to recover and to heal, it is also, according to Vivian Halloran, 'the only fit testing ground for Bond to atone for the sins he has committed on the European continent' (2005: 173). In *Dr. No* and *The Man with the Golden Gun*, Jamaica is where Bond is sent in order to regain M's trust (after having nearly been killed while on an assignment in *From Russia with Love* (1956) and after nearly murdering M himself at the beginning of *The Man with the Golden Gun*). Jamaica is also the place where Fleming himself professed to enjoy 'the most healthy life I could wish to live' (qtd in Parker 2014: 93). Indeed, Fleming's close friend Noël Coward referred to the island as 'Dr Jamaica' on account of the natural health benefits derived from the tropical climate and the simple living there. Fleming himself notes that the island was both restorative and creatively inspiring: in Jamaica, he says, 'there is peace and that wonderful vacuum of days that makes one work ... it is the peace and silence and cut-offness from the madding world that urges people to create here' (1965: 12). Thus, Jamaica serves for Fleming as a site of reincarnation and creation; it is in Jamaica that Bond figuratively lives, dies and is resurrected. It is clear that when Fleming is unsure of his footing as a writer, or when he does not know quite what to do with Bond, he returns the character to the Jamaica he knows and to the landscape in which such a character best functions. Jamaica makes Bond relevant; his sojourns in Jamaica re-enliven Britain's imperial legacy in its Caribbean colonies and, in turn, Jamaica's colonial history re-enlivens Bond's role as postcolonial policeman. Thus, the vitality of Bond as a character (and Fleming as a writer) is inextricably tied to Jamaica.

Fleming's fascination with the island began in July 1943, when he was sent in his capacity as assistant to the director of naval intelligence (at the time, Sir John Godfrey[21]) to Kingston, Jamaica, to attend an Anglo-American naval intelligence conference at the Myrtle Bank Hotel. The central theme of this conference was to plan how best to mitigate the spike in British and American warships that had been torpedoed by German U-boats (McCormick 1993: 111). Accompanying Fleming was his old school friend, Ivar Bryce,[22] who was a Secret Intelligence Service (SIS) agent operating out of Latin America at the time. Bryce and his wife Sheila owned the Bellevue, one of Jamaica's grandest 'great houses', which had once hosted Fleming's childhood hero, Horatio Nelson. Fleming's biographer Andrew Lycett has noted that 'Ian was enthralled by the potent combination of Bellevue's magnificent situation high in the hills, overlooking the ocean, the memory of Nelson, and the sad sound of the torrential rain, dripping through the tropical trees' (2008: 144). On his return flight to London via Washington, Fleming is said to have remarked to Bryce: 'you know, Ivar, I have made a great decision … When we have won this blasted war, I am going to live in Jamaica. Just live in Jamaica and lap it up, and swim in the sea and write books' (qtd in Lycett [1995] 2008: 144). While Fleming's quaint romantic interest in the island certainly comes through here, Donald McCormick recognizes in this decision a much more cynical motivation, one perhaps born of Fleming's years in the intelligence services:

> While planning his Jamaican retreat Fleming was also giving serious thought to his future. In one sense the choice of a site for the retreat was linked with this. He had no doubt that from now on Britain would have closer ties to the United States than ever before and that he needed to visit the Western world regularly to keep in touch with his numerous new-found friends there – in the United States and the Caribbean. (1993: 113)

It is somewhat telling that, in McCormick's reading of Fleming's global outlook, Britain is no longer included in the geopolitical make-up of 'the Western world'. Given the seismic shift in Britain's political influence during and in the aftermath of the Second World War, this is, perhaps, unsurprising.[23] Fleming's choice of Jamaica, though, McCormick implies, is largely predicated on the island's proximity to the American continent. For Fleming, the 'greatest threat to the British Empire lay in American support for the rising nationalist movements among colonised people' (Parker 2014: 98). Ronnie D. Lipschutz has speculated that both Fleming's selection of Jamaica and his subsequent creation of the character James Bond can be traced to his disaffection for the United States. He argues that 'Fleming could not forgive the United States for having shouldered aside the British after World War II. Bond was Fleming's revenge, forever saving Americans from both their clumsiness and the Russians' (2001: 53). Fleming's proximity to the United States while in Jamaica allowed him close contact with and access to the North American continent; Jamaica (and the islands of the Caribbean, at large) served as something of a middle territory between Britain and the United States, one a declining empire and the other an emerging superpower flanking the Atlantic Ocean. As an island state agitating for self-governance and independence from Britain, Jamaica was, for Fleming, 'a productive space to think about and plot how a British agent might work with American personnel and forces, while negotiating a Cold War context shaped by anxieties about communist insurrection; the influence of Cuba, China, and the Soviet Union; and the resource and strategic potential of the British Caribbean' (Funnell and Dodds 2017: 7).

Fleming's interest in the Americas (aside from those personal friendships with Ivar Bryce and Ernest Cuneo which he maintained there) is distinctly political, and Jamaica is configured in Fleming's conceptual imaginary as both a retreat from the 'blasted war' and an extension of his own intelligence network into the Americas. Indeed, as Lycett notes, when Goldeneye was built in 1946, it 'looked barren and forbidding, like an itinerant district commissioner's lodge in some distant colonial land' ([1995] 2008: 173). To Fleming, Goldeneye certainly seemed to function as a microcosmic colony of sorts, over which he exerted an almost obsessive control. Before Fleming had settled on the name 'Goldeneye' for his Jamaican retreat, he had rejected a number of other suggestions. One was 'Rum Cove'; another was 'Shame Lady'. Reportedly, the name 'Shame Lady' had been considered due to the extensive overgrowth, on the site, of a local Jamaican plant by the same name. Its name derived from a particular feature: when the leaves of this plant were touched, they curled up as though in shame. There is, however, another story. Apparently, when Fleming first visited the plot of land that would eventually become Goldeneye, he peered down over the edge of the cliff and saw 'the most beautiful naked Negress' bathing in the waters below (Zeiger: [1965] 1966: 90; see also Bryce 1965: n.p.). Impressed by what he saw, and since the whole site was covered in the Shame Lady plant, Fleming felt that the name held considerable appeal. Of course, this anecdote only further underlines the idea that Jamaica represents for Fleming his own personal colonial outcrop; Fleming's purchase of the land is uncomfortably transposed within this anecdote with his desire for and appraisal of the Black female body, and the supposed naming of his estate after this particular event augments the politics of desire and mastery which conditions Fleming's personal colonization of Jamaica. Claire Blanchard, a former girlfriend of Fleming's, noted that she was against the name 'Goldeneye' because it 'reminded [her] of golden eye ointment'. She said that, together, she and Ian 'went through an awful lot of names – most of them with a Regency flavour to them' (Blanchard 1965: n.d.). Given the extent to which Fleming sought mastery, order and control over his own Jamaican colonial outcrop, it is little wonder, then, that he desired a name with monarchic overtones.

Fleming, Jamaica and power

In order to understand the topopolitics (Waterman 2018) of Fleming's writing and the ways in which Jamaica's ethnoscape has come to be represented in his fiction, one must understand Fleming's relationship to power. For Fleming, Jamaica was all about power – Britain's loss of it and Jamaica's gain. If Fleming's fiction provided British readers with a supposed conceptual framework to interpret British-Jamaican relations in an emergent postcolonial context, then it is also clear that Jamaica is the fictive topography upon which such negotiations take place, and upon which Fleming's orientalist poetics operate. Power, of course, is simply the desire for control and influence made manifest. Through the representational discourses of his orientalist fiction, Fleming assumed the position of power broker – that is, his work largely informed and shaped his British readership's cultural perceptions of Jamaica at the time and augmented a particular vision of British-Jamaican cultural and racial power relations. His books certainly played into Britain's fears of Jamaican migration, racial miscegenation and multiculturalism, while at the same time addressing British misapprehensions over Jamaican self-governance and national independence. On the one hand, Jamaica represents for Fleming a retreat from life in England, a place he was greatly charmed by, and, by many accounts, a place he was greatly in love with; on the other hand, though, with the British Empire 'dying of its wounds, suffering a haemorrhage of its capital as well as its blood' (Benson 1984: xi), Jamaica represents a space for the reinforcement of pre-war narratives of British triumphalism where the order of the old world is preserved and the comfort of Britain's imperial position is maintained. As Cynthia J. Miller notes:

> Fleming's Britain of the early 1950s still bore the scars of war … Readily-identifiable enemies of nation and hearth had been overcome, but not eradicated,

and the Cold War era carried notions of new global predators forward in the public consciousness. With a new young Queen on the throne, the country was undergoing a generational shift, from old guardians of the empire to new, while the world around Great Britain remained heavy-laden with suspicion and unrest. (2011: xiv)

Fleming's Jamaica-set fiction, then, made manifest his desire for control of Britain's (and his own personal) wayward colony; his literary Jamaica became a psychogeography shaped not only in his own image but also in the image of an imperial Britain that was determined to stave off the realities of its diminishing global influence.

The effects of the representational discourses embedded in his Jamaica-set fiction are, in turn, measured by the impact Fleming's fiction had on the cultural imaginary, and the extent to which the particular political ideologies underpinning his writings were seized upon by the global power elite. Certainly, Fleming was no stranger to a number of major political players of the twentieth century. Winston Churchill, twice prime minister of Britain (1940–5, 1951–5), was a close friend of Fleming's father, Valentine Fleming, a fellow Conservative member of parliament and military captain who was killed while serving in France in 1917. Churchill wrote Valentine's obituary in *The Times* (25 May 1917). Fleming was also good friends with Allen Dulles, the American lawyer and first civilian director of the Central Intelligence Agency (see Moran 2013); he also struck up friendly relations with John F. Kennedy, then a senator for Massachusetts, and later president of the United States, when he was introduced to him by Marion Leiter, a mutual friend (and another of Fleming's contacts whose name he appropriated for one of his characters). Though there was not much physical contact between the two men, they were much in sympathy with one another, and, according to Parker, 'Fleming worked the Kennedy connection hard' (2014: 261). Henry Brandon, the *Sunday Times* correspondent in Washington, noted that

> there was something about Ian which definitely appealed to Kennedy. And intrigued him too. They shared many interests, particularly in sex, in expertise, in good living, in travel. And apart from all this Kennedy was fascinated by the element of fantasy in Ian – how much a sobre mature sort of man could have such an element of total fantasy in him.[24] (1965: n.p.)

Finally, Fleming also associated with the Greek shipping magnate Aristotle Onassis, one of the twentieth century's richest men, who would later marry Kennedy's widow, Jacqueline Kennedy, in 1968 (Fleming 2015: 194, 330). It is clear that Fleming cultivated a good number of his political connections, particularly his relationships with those in government. Moreover, it is evident that Fleming's world view, articulated through the character of James Bond, was endorsed by this powerful coterie of men. In a March 1961 *Time* magazine article, then president John F. Kennedy declared that 'Fleming was one of his favourite authors, that he always had one of his books on his bedside table, and that *From Russia with Love* was one of the ten works he would save from a possible atomic catastrophe' (Tornabuoni 1966: 17).[25] The fact was not lost on many that, with his charm, vitality and good looks, Kennedy 'certainly imitated [Bond] to a degree no President has even remotely approached before' (Cuneo 1984: xii). The playboy Bond found life in the playboy president. Indeed, as Cuneo notes, 'President Kennedy's death duel with Cuba's Castro has James Bond overtones' (ibid.). It may even be argued that, in *The Man with the Golden Gun*, which is set in Jamaica and follows Bond's efforts to suppress a campaign of pro-Cuban agricultural terrorism by a syndicate of American gangsters and Russian KGB agents, Fleming is paying homage to Kennedy's battle against Cuban communism and against Castro specifically. It is certainly no coincidence that, in August 1961, only five months after Kennedy's endorsement, Albert R. Broccoli and Harry Saltzman optioned the film rights to the Bond novels (Rosenberg and Harlemann Stewart 1989: 7). Moreover, Fleming's success in the American literary market increased exponentially as a result of Kennedy's favour. In 1983, to celebrate the first two decades of James Bond's success on the big screen, Thames Television in England produced a documentary assessing the impact Fleming's character had had on the popular imagination. Among those interviewed for the production was the fortieth president of the United States, Ronald Reagan, whose participation, much like Kennedy's endorsement twenty-two years before, augmented Bond's (and Fleming's) status as a global political entity. Indeed, as Cynthia J. Miller has noted, with the naming of 'Asteroid 9007 James Bond' after Fleming's literary invention in 1983, James Bond is 'no longer a property of the British national imagination'; rather, 'Bond belongs to the world – to the universe, in fact', and his 'cultural resonance has been felt not only across national borders, but across genres and media, as well' (2011: xv).

So, it is apparent that Fleming sought out power in the form of political influence and, moreover, that the character of James Bond was the vehicle through which Fleming attained a great deal of influence and public sway, certainly in matters of Anglo-American interest. Fleming's desire for political dominion culminated in his selection of Jamaica as his own veritable colony, whereupon he could entertain imperial fantasies of becoming 'the absolute ruler of a country where everybody was crazy about [him]' (Fleming 1959: n.p.). Jamaica's history proved a source of fascination for Fleming, who saw in himself much of the qualities of those historical leaders and men of empire who had previously settled on the island. It was, of course, Christopher Columbus who 'discovered' Jamaica within the European imagination in May 1494, on his second journey to the West Indies, 'reporting it to be "paradise", "the fairest island that ever eyes have beheld; mountainous and the land seem to touch the sky"' (Parker 2014: 17).[26] As I mentioned above, Fleming's hero Nelson, who had once lodged at Bellevue, also held great romantic appeal for Fleming (115–16). More contemporarily, Jamaica had become something of a retreat for a number of high-profile British political figures and business leaders. These included Lord Ronald Graham, the son of the sixth Duke of Monstrose, who retired to Jamaica in 1940 after his pro-Nazi views became an embarrassment; Peregrine Brownlow, lord-in-waiting to Edward VIII; and millionaire businessman Sir Harold Mitchell, who 'created a plantation-style set up pretty much from scratch' (24). Men such as these, having refurbished the old Great Houses, 'saw themselves as inheritors of [Jamaica's] old plantocracy' (23). It has also been pointed out that Fleming himself became something of a plantocrat. John Pearson, Fleming's first biographer, refers to him as 'a sort of eccentric Jamaica[n] squire' and to Goldeneye as 'Flemingland', a place where Fleming's 'Scots landowning instincts asserted themselves' (Pearson n.d.: n.p.). Goldeneye functioned as a gateway of sorts for landed aristocratic creatives between the malaise of post-war Britain and the sunny redolence and hedonism of the tropics. Winder has pointed out that 'it cannot be coincidence that two of the most influential and interesting apologists for traditional Britain, Fleming and Noël Coward, should have been close neighbours on Jamaica's north shore' (2006: 136). Parker adds that 'it is striking that two such influential defenders of the Britain of its empire days were close neighbours and friends in Jamaica ... as the country moved from imperial throwback all the way to independence' (2014: 74). It was claimed in 1951 in the *Daily Gleaner*, Jamaica's local newspaper, that thanks to pioneers like Fleming and Coward, Jamaica was undergoing a 'remarkable development' along its coast, from 'Frenchman's Cove and San San estate in the east to Tryall in the west' (ibid.: 82). Indeed, Fleming was one of a number of Britons celebrated locally in Jamaica on account of the economic redevelopment of the island that had come about as a result of the interests of wealthy property buyers and developers from Britain. In a pecuniary sense, Fleming can certainly be said to have contributed to the boom in pleasure tourism which the island enjoyed in the aftermath of the Second World War.[27] Goldeneye hosted a wide array of literary and artistic types, including Cecil Beaton, Truman Capote, Lucian Freud, Graham Green, Patrick Leigh Fermor, Rosamund Lehmann, Peter Quennell and Evelyn Waugh (Fleming 1965: 12). Thus, Fleming kept company with quite the assortment of influential expatriates. Parker has noted, however, that Fleming's response to Jamaica's increase in popularity was something of a paradox: on the one hand, Fleming was championed as something of an unofficial ambassador for Jamaica and for Jamaican tourism; on the other hand, he was 'ambivalent about this invasion of the decadent jet-set'. In his ambivalence he 'had much in common with a number of Jamaicans watching with despair the rapid changes happening to their island' (2014: 87).[28]

But it was the sojourn at Goldeneye of beleaguered Conservative prime minister Anthony Eden that firmly aligned Fleming's Jamaica with power in the form of British governance. In November 1956, Eden was suffering through severe exhaustion during the Suez Canal crisis[29] when his wife Clarissa, a good friend of Fleming's wife, Ann, and godmother to the Flemings' son, Caspar, suggested to her husband that a private retreat to Goldeneye would be beneficial for his health.[30] The Edens approached the Flemings through Alan Lennox-Boyd, who was, at the time, secretary of state for the colonies and a personal friend of the Flemings (Pearson 1966: 290). Fleming's ambivalence towards the prospect of hosting the Edens was characteristic: on the one hand, he saw it as a patriotic duty to Britain as well as a personal duty to his wife's friend, Lady Eden. Furthermore, he was overjoyed by the prospect that 'the myth of Goldeneye was about to enter history' (ibid.: 292). Fleming's own personal colonial fantasy writ large was about to be writ even larger in the history books of the nation; he had, in John Pearson's words, 'won ascendancy again' (ibid.: 294). Moreover, he had harboured cynical hopes that the prime minister's visit to Goldeneye would do something to boost the sale of his novels in the American market – which, as it transpires, is exactly what ended up happening (ibid.: 293; Benson 1984: 15). On the other hand, though, Fleming was deeply ambivalent about Eden's political leadership and critical of his handling of the Suez Canal crisis, which he called 'asinine': 'In the whole of modern history I can't think of a comparable shambles created by any single country' (qtd in Pearson 1966: 294). Politically, it was, for Fleming, somewhat hazardous to be seen to host the divisive Eden. Though Fleming was not himself present during the Edens' visit to Goldeneye, he would forever be memorialized as a political sympathizer to the prime minister – which, strictly speaking, was not the case.[31] Fleming was also irritated by some of the arrangements undertaken at Goldeneye without his prior consent: he noted that the Jamaican Government turned my little gazebo on the western corner of the property into a direct teleprinter link with Number 10 Downing Street. The police guards cut 'God Bless Sir Anthony and Lady Eden' into the bark of my cedar trees. The detective, sleeping in the back room, shot at the bush rats, beloved by my wife, with his revolver. (1965: 13)

Having 'won ascendancy', in his eyes, through the association of his precious Goldeneye estate with the British political elite, Fleming was altogether much more ambivalent about his home being transformed into government offices from which the Suez Canal crisis was being managed and from which Britain was, in his estimation, still being misruled. That Eden was ousted from power only three weeks after his stay at Goldeneye would seem to suggest that his retreat to the Caribbean during one of the most fraught periods of twentieth-century British history was a misstep. Indeed, a *Spectator* article published on 7 December 1956 suggested that 'Jamaica [had] done more damage than Suez to Sir Anthony's standing in his party at Westminster' (qtd in Parker 2014: 210).

Aside from the lack of confidence shown to him by his own political party, though, the question of Eden's leadership came into question during his stay at Goldeneye in a coincidental and unexpected manner. When word had come through that Eden and his wife would be arriving, Florence Foot, the wife of the governor-in-chief of Jamaica, Sir Hugh Foot, who was organizing the prime minister's visit through Government House, insisted to Blanche Blackwell, Fleming's neighbour (and later lover), that Fleming's Jamaican housekeeper Violet leave the estate. When Blackwell refused to pass the message on, Lady Foot told Violet that 'your Queen would like you to [do] this for her Prime Minister' – to which Violet replied, 'I still don't care, lady. I obey the Commander' (Blackwell 1965: n.p.). Fleming was known to elicit a fierce loyalty from his staff, who referred to him with fondness as 'the Commander', an epithet which recalls Fleming's rank in the Royal Naval Reserve but which also simultaneously underlines Fleming's own cultivation of power and ascendancy on the island. The significance of Violet's refusal of Lady Foot's request cannot be missed. For a short period of time in 1956, Goldeneye was the de facto location from which Eden governed Britain. Violet's deference to Fleming, though, rather than to the request of Lady Foot, who claims in this instance to speak on behalf of Queen Elizabeth herself, suggests that Goldeneye is configured in this exchange as the site of an ambiguous confusion of power relations. Between a weakened Eden, whose presence transposes the premiership of Britain's governance onto Fleming's Jamaican estate, and an absent Fleming, whose status as commander of the household (and of Violet's loyalty) seemingly supplants even the power of prime minister and queen alike, Fleming emerges as the de facto commander of Goldeneye. In characteristically wry fashion, Winder captures some of the ambiguous blurring and splicing of political power dynamics at Goldeneye when he notes that, but for Fleming's absence, Eden's visit to Jamaica would have been 'the perfect cross-over between the political world (which in Eden's case was substantially a mad fantasy) and the world of mad fantasy (which in Fleming's case said so much about real politics)'. Winder further notes with irony that, 'at the zenith of [British] national incompetence, the architect of that incompetence stays at the very house in which the greatest reassurance and palliative, the Robin Hood of British imperialists' darkest hour, was created' (2006: 131).

So it should be clear, by now, that Fleming's Jamaican psychogeography is representative of the author's will to power.[32] Fleming's desire for mastery over his Jamaican environment can be seen in his non-fiction writing, in which he assumes the role of Britain's cultural interlocutor for Jamaica. In 1947, a year after building Goldeneye, Fleming wrote a mood piece on Jamaica for Cyril Connolly's *Horizon* magazine, an article tailored to the tourist trade written as part of the 'Where Shall John Go?' series, an advice column of sorts for young émigrés and holidaymakers. In the article, Fleming provides a lucid summation of Jamaica's various touristic sights, geographical landmarks and the numerous flora and fauna that were to be found on the island. He describes Kingston as a 'tough town' and warns his readers off the local 'stews' (gatherings), noting that 'they would provide you with every known amorous constellation and permutation' (qtd in Lycett [1995] 2008: 175). He is full of praise for Jamaica's 'delicious food, exotic drinks and music, which he describes as a variation of Trinidadian calypso' (Lycett [1995] 2008: 175). Indeed, Fleming's writings can be said to contribute in no small part to Jamaica's boom in tourism and to the increasing numbers of expatriate Britons relocating to the island. Lycett notes that 'Ian's public relations exercise in *Horizon* had clearly been read. The gloom of war had finally lifted and people with money were flocking to the island, which had the added advantage of being in the sterling area' (194). Fleming would later reproduce the article in 1965 by way of an introduction to a collection of essays on Jamaican cultural life put together by his friend Morris Cargill. Although Fleming only contributed the introduction, that Cargill titled the entire collection *Ian Fleming Introduces Jamaica* is further indicative of the synonymity between Fleming and Jamaica within both the Jamaican and the British cultural imaginations of the period.

When Cargill first approached Fleming, it was clear that he did so because he wanted, in Fleming's words, 'a book written about Jamaica by Jamaicans and by those who, while not Jamaicans, had lived there and had like him learned to love the country' (1965: 5). As far as Cargill was concerned, Fleming loved Jamaica and enjoyed warm relations with the local Jamaicans. He notes that:

> Ian was a gregarious person and liked to meet all the local tradespeople … There's no doubt that Ian did genuinely like Jamaicans, whom he saw as 'full of goodwill and cheerfulness and humour'. … However, according to the great-niece of Fleming's housekeeper Violet, Fleming was "integrated" into Oracabessa [the parish where Fleming lived] life by Violet … But, like almost all white expatriates, most white Jamaicans and certainly all tourists, Fleming did not have any real, equal-status black Jamaican friend. (1965a: 161)

Fleming considered his relationship with Jamaica and with the Jamaican people to be on good terms. He has spoken of 'the friendly embrace of Jamaica and of the Jamaican way of life' (1965: 14) and went so far as to suggest that, in Jamaica, he 'learned about living amongst, and appreciating, coloured people' (12) – a comment which is, on the surface, a simple expression of practised condescension towards the Jamaican and which, more subtly, can be read as an awkward attempt by Fleming to expiate his own colonial guilt. Parker refers to this particular comment as 'Fleming's proudest boast' (2014: 160). Whether Fleming's sentiment, here, is simply boastful, or whether it belies a sincere desire on his part to integrate within the local Jamaican population, it nevertheless represents precisely the difficulties in interpreting the ambivalence of Fleming's representational politics. There is much debate as to the extent to which Fleming actually did integrate himself within Jamaican life, and as to the manner in which he sought to represent local Jamaica. While his friend Cargill describes Fleming as 'a great friend of Jamaica' and as someone who 'did more perhaps than any other single person to give [Jamaica] extensive and favourable publicity abroad' (qtd in Parker 2014: 307), Sir Jock Campbell, an old friend of Fleming's from Eton College, asserts that 'Ian never really got involved in Jamaica. This was why he never used to upset the real Jamaican writers' (1965: n.p.).

Fleming's attitude to Jamaica's colonial administration was, by and large, much less ambivalent. By all accounts, Fleming loathed the snobbery of Britain's expatriate community living in Jamaica and the formal politics at play, although he did consider Jamaica to be the 'middle way between the Lethe of the tropics and a life of fork-lunches with the District Commissioner's wife' (Fleming 1965: 15). In other words, Jamaica for Fleming represented the best of both worlds: he could enjoy the luxury and status afforded him by his role as a wealthy ex-naval expatriate passing his winters in the tropics, but he was removed enough from the social politics of the island's colonial culture so as to not be concerned with it. Fleming did not consider 'island politics [to be] a grave danger' to expatriates, and although he acknowledged that 'there will always be a racial simmering and occasional clashes between coloured and white vanities', he espoused the value of 'liking [one's] neighbours' (19–20). With respect to local politics, Fleming is at once seemingly dismissive of Jamaica's 'desire for self-government' (Parker 2014: 60) but, equally, he is cognizant of the Jamaicans' rights to 'a greater share (or all) of the prizes which England got from the colony, for motor-cars, race-horses (a Jamaican passion), tennis clubs and tea parties and all the other desirable claptrap of Europeans' (Fleming 1965: 19). Though he considers Alexander Bustamante and Norman Manley to be 'two great Jamaican leaders',[33] he is also dismissive of local politics: he considers it old-fashioned rather than a 'grave danger' to the 'liberality and wisdom of our present policy' of *Pax Britannica* (qtd in Parker 2014: 60). He believes the island's then governor and colonial secretary, Sir John Huggins and Sir Hugh Foot, respectively, have held 'wise and successful sway' (Fleming 1965: 19). Though Fleming was 'appalled by the tea-and-tennis set atmosphere' of Kingston (qtd in Parker 2014: 105), he was also much enthralled to the governor's wife, Molly Huggins, whom he praises for 'wrestl[ing] with the Colonial Office about the rights and concerns of all the women of Jamaica' (ibid.). Fleming's praise for Molly Huggins and her accomplishments within local Jamaican life must also necessarily be couched in an understanding of Molly's social and racial inclusiveness: Molly was very forthright in her defence of racial equality, her support of which Fleming seemed to endorse. Molly herself has said that 'we rather startled Jamaica in the early days by having coloured Jamaicans to play tennis, as this really had not been done very much in the past. But we [she and her Governor husband] had decided from the beginning that we would have no colour prejudices of any kind' (qtd in Parker 2014: 28). Furthermore, Fleming was also the chairman of the Publicity Committee of the Jamaica Relief Fund, which raised upwards of £100,000 to support local Jamaicans whose livelihoods had been ravaged in Hurricane Charlie in 1951 (Fleming 1951: n.p.). In a letter to William Stephenson (the Canadian intelligence officer who is reputed to be the inspiration for James Bond), Fleming even warmly welcomes the prospect of British decolonization in the Caribbean when he notes with congeniality that 'England is in the process of slowly sinking beneath the waves. She had a very good run and I only hope she does her sinking gracefully' (qtd in Fleming 2015: 290). Thus, on the whole, much of Fleming's private correspondences and publicly expressed opinions prior to Britain's decolonization of Jamaica suggest a deeply ambivalent personality that is, on the one hand, equitable, philanthropic and socially progressive but, on the other, mired by traditional political indifference and a laissez-faire racialism.

Fleming, orientalism and the Jamaican exotic

In his 1965 reproduction of the *Horizon* article for Cargill's collection (which was published three years after Jamaica gained its independence from Britain), Fleming calls attention to the seismic shifts that had occurred in British-Jamaican relations on the island in the intervening eight years, emphasizing that 'in this long span of time everything [in Jamaica] has changed and yet nothing' (1965: 11). Jamaica, he says, has

> flirted with Federation and then broken off the engagement, she has gained her Independence and Membership of the United Nations, bauxite and tourism have changed her economy, emigration to the United Kingdom, with all its problems, brings around £7,000,000 back into the island every year, the West Indian cricketers have become the darlings of the Commonwealth, and a Jamaican girl has been chosen Miss World. (ibid.)

However, the more implicit tenor of his introduction is to signal to the British holidaymaker that they need have no fear of a post-independent Jamaica; Fleming himself can testify that 'everything [on the island] has changed *and yet nothing*' (ibid., my italics). Of the revised edition of his article on Jamaica, Fleming notes that 'I have made very few alterations in the light of my experience of Jamaica since it was first written. But these few alterations are only in facts; the mood remains unaltered' (ibid.: 15). He offers his assurance that while life on the island may be demonstrably different from before (in the wake of independence), his mood, his feelings and his own thoughts about the island remain largely unchanged. This admission is significant precisely because it suggests that Fleming does indeed draw a distinction between the geopolitical history of Jamaica (which has changed considerably in the wake of the island's independence movement) and the geo-imaginary topographical fantasy of the island he has annexed from a particular social, cultural and political history. Even though Jamaica has undergone momentous political changes since he first wrote the article for *Horizon* magazine in 1947, Fleming does not judge it necessary to reflect within the Cargill collection upon such contemporary changes. Rather, his dismissal of the 'mood' of post-independent Jamaica (he says, implausibly, that it 'remains unaltered' from before) is a strategic one which suggests in its rhetoric that Fleming himself views the Jamaica of post-independence entirely in the context of its colonial heritage. In other words, as Sam Goodman notes, 'Fleming's *perception* of Jamaica *remains* an essentially pastoral, picaresque one that no amount of post-war industrial development can entirely remove' (2016: 148, my italics).

Of the changes to Jamaican cultural and political life which he does acknowledge, Fleming notes that 'Jamaica has grown from a child into an adult' (1965: 11). His choice of metaphor connotes a particularly uncomfortable image: that of England as the proud, benevolent parent-figure to Jamaica, who is configured rhetorically as the fledgling adolescent. The implication, here, is that while Jamaica's independence has, indeed, brought about great changes in British-Jamaican political relations, the fearful Briton can take comfort in the knowledge that Jamaica has received the 'right kind' of schooling from Britain and that in its cultural and social practices the island will remain a 'good child' of England.[34] Fleming insists to his readers that there is much to recognize in this 'new' Jamaica and still less to be feared by it. British-Jamaican cultural and social life and the de facto order, he implies, remain unchanged; the island is still very much a place to be enjoyed, and not feared, by Britons. Fleming deliberately employs within his fictional writings a particular rhetorical technique which is designed to secure the interests (and assuage the anxieties) of his British readership – that is, what Charles W. Mills classifies as Fleming's 'characterization of the kindly, childlike Jamaican' (2010: 107). Fleming deliberately casts a number of his Jamaican characters as childlike in order to ameliorate British racial fears and concerns about the 'unruliness' of the local Jamaican populace and to justify (post-)imperial British perceptions of Jamaica as a space in need of continuous colonial parentage. Further to this, a number of other entangled dichotomous pairings emerge: if England is parental it is also white, civilized and possesses a right to authority; and if Jamaica is childlike it is also seen in terms of its Blackness, its savagery and its powerlessness.[35] Indeed, these dichotomies seem to play out in Fleming's construction of his Jamaican ethnoscape, which is, in Parker's words, 'stuck in a comfortable time warp where imperial and social structures remained virtually unchanged from a hundred years previously' (2014: 26).

Such rhetorical strategies undoubtedly call further into question Fleming's aforementioned ambivalence towards Jamaican independence and British decolonization. Though Fleming sought to present Jamaica authentically, his fictional writings are replete with an exoticist rhetoric designed to orient the reader's touristic gaze. Fleming's literary Jamaica was 'neither Croydon with jacarandas, nor [a] Conradian tropical nightmare where moral disintegration was inevitable' (Lycett [1995] 2008: 174). Rather, Fleming embellished the 'hypnotic whisper' and 'tropic luxury' of the island (Fleming 1965: 15, 20), couching British fears of racial otherness and the disintegration of British civilization in the comfortable, familiar language of grand tourism. Fleming's evident fascination with Jamaica (in particular with its flora and undersea life[36]) became embedded within his literary practice as a form of cultural exoticism; his writings became invested with what Bruce A. Rosenberg and Ann Harlemann Stewart identify as the fascination with 'the exotic' that 'has often accompanied English interest in colonial peoples and those in the far reaches of the Empire' (1989: 119; see also Cawelti and Rosenberg 1987: 96). Jamaica was, for Fleming, a *topos* of cultural and racial other-worldliness, and it is clear from his fiction that the politics of the exotic have come to pervade and unify his formal style. As Vivian Halloran notes, Fleming's exotic vision of Jamaica is entirely 'shaped by the social forces of displacement, repatriation, immigration, defection, and decolonization', as well as by the 'reconfiguration of the geopolitical map in the post-World War II period' (2005: 158). Fleming's Jamaica, then, is not an organic reproduction of the island he knew well, and nor can it be said that Fleming's perspective is that of the entirely naturalized expatriate. On the contrary, Fleming's psychogeography is a compound vision of Jamaican otherness framed (in part) as culturally authoritative travel writing. Fleming's Jamaica is not a 'natural' vision of West Indian socio-economics but a reactionary response to the displacement of Britain from its position of influence in the geopolitical *polis* as well as to the processes of colonial repatriation and West Indian migration to Britain that were taking place during the period of Britain's decolonization. To read Fleming is to read about otherness – not the extreme kind one is likely to encounter in Joseph Conrad, for instance, but a somewhat 'sanitized' exoticism which entices and excites the reader, rather than provoking and repelling them. As Anette Pankratz notes, while the 'white man's burden' took place in 'far-off, uncomfortable jungles', Fleming's hero engages Britain's racial threats 'on the beaches and skiing slopes of attractive holiday resorts, in casinos and hotels' (2007: 133). The James Bond novels and short stories perform a certain 'disciplined exoticism' (Zeiger [1965] 1966: 99–100): that is to say, 'the exotic' is narratologically centralized through the descriptive economies of Fleming's writing. This is certainly the case in his Jamaica-set works, as we shall see, but this 'disciplined exoticism' also extends to his non-Jamaican stories. Fleming's fascination with the exotic is, in part, a negotiation of his own complex national politics, and the psychogeography of his literary Jamaica serves as a correlative to dear old England[37] – which he refers to in *On Her Majesty's Secret Service* (1963) as 'this little atoll of ours' (Fleming [1963] 2012k: 273). Fleming's disciplined exoticism is intimately linked to his regard for Britain, which is configured in this metaphor not as a mighty empire but as a clustered ring of islands. The discourse of exoticism which underpins much of Fleming's writing cannot simply be said to perform the rhetorical work of empire; rather, in rhetorically reconfiguring Britain itself as one of the tropical atolls of its own empire, Fleming seeks to collapse upon itself Britain's 'insular mentality' and its 'spirit of Empire' (Pankratz 2007: 130) by highlighting the conceptual fallacies of that mentality. As a cluster of islands, Britain is no less geographically assailable than the many tropical islands and atolls under the jurisdiction of empire. Fleming's use of the term 'little atoll' is a concession to the very fragility of empire and to the potential vulnerabilities of Britain's island stronghold. In recreating the political, social and cultural strata of Britain's 'little atoll' in the psychogeography of his literary Jamaica, Fleming is not just 'fusing "Little Englandisms" with the ethos of imperialism' (Pankratz 2007: 131), he is also conceptually aligning the islands of Britain and Jamaica. James Bond has always been the vehicle through which Fleming sought to negotiate his spliced British-Jamaican political, cultural and social identities. As Pankratz notes, Bond is 'enmeshed in a tight web of cultural negotiations, set against several "others" positioned in overlapping cultural spaces and thereby acting as elements in polyvalent mappings of Britain – from insular and Imperial England to a global consumer society' (130). Pankratz makes clear that, for Fleming, 'Britain' is not an isolated signifier but a polyvalent concept, a nexus or amalgamation of imperial cultural spaces. Fleming's Britain, then, is both insular and global; it is at once bound by its island geography and unbound in the colonial imagination, enmeshed as it is in multiple global territories and spaces. It is, perhaps, for this reason that the character Bond is shown to be somewhat uncomfortable whenever he is in Britain. In Fleming's third novel, *Moonraker* (1955), the only one of Bond's adventures set entirely in Britain (between London and Kent), the reader is told that 'Bond knew there was something alien and un-English about himself. He knew he was a difficult man to cover up. Particularly in England. He shrugged his shoulders. Abroad was what mattered' (Fleming [1955] 2012c: 44). Within the popular consciousness, the figure of James Bond has always been synonymous with Britain and with Britishness. However, by his own admission, Bond feels (and is) 'alien' to Britain, and 'un-English'; when in Britain, he is othered as 'a stranger on a strange island' (Pankratz 2007: 129).[38] Once again,

Fleming calls Britain's insular mentality into question: the 'little atoll' of Britain is also a 'strange island' to its own inhabitants (in this case, Bond). For Bond, 'Englishness' is a matter of ambivalence; his identity – and thus the political function of the character at large – is best understood in the context of Fleming's politics of the exotic. Fleming tells us as much: 'abroad was what mattered'. Thus, any understanding of Bond's 'Britishness' and Fleming's polyvalent concept of 'Britain' must necessarily take into account the author's orientalist politics.

In 1957, Fleming wrote in a letter to Michael Howard (his editor at Jonathan Cape) that the connecting theme of his writings was 'that the world is still a very exciting place in spite of aeroplanes and suchlike and that just because some types of adventure are old-fashioned that doesn't make them any less exciting' (qtd in Fleming 2015: 183). Fleming's fondness for 'old-fashioned' adventure narratives almost certainly had its genesis in those works of children's fiction written during the high-imperial age that he read in his youth. His childhood favourites included Johann David Wyss's *The Swiss Family Robinson* (1812), Robert Louis Stevenson's *Treasure Island* (1883), H. Rider Haggard's *King Solomon's Mines* (1885) and Anthony Hope's *Prisoner of Zenda* (1894).[39] In his adolescence and throughout adulthood, Fleming favoured the work of Dornford Yates, E. Philips Oppenheim, William le Queux, Sax Rohmer (whose infamous Dr Fu Manchu provides the inspiration for the eponymous villain of *Dr. No*), 'Sapper' (the pen name of H. C. McNeile), John Buchan, Mickey Spillane, Raymond Chandler, Dashiell Hammett, Chester Himes, Georges Simenon and Geoffrey Household.[40] Fleming's favourite novels as an adult were all about race and slavery: these included Herbert de Lisser's *White Witch of Rosehall* (1929) and Hugh Edwards's *Sangoree* (1932) and *All Night at Mr Stanyhursts* (1933) (Parker 2014: 120). Such works can be said to espouse the values of British imperialism and augment visions of the non-anglophone world as primitive and degenerate. Within his own travel writings, though Fleming was characteristically attentive to much local detail, his work often performed a scurrilous – and, from a journalistic standpoint, irresponsible – orientalization of his ethnographic subjects.[41] When the *Sunday Times* sent Fleming to the Seychelles in April 1958, the resulting article was 'part travelogue, part mystery story and part paean to a romantic outpost on the rim of the British Empire' (Fleming 2015: 193). This particular literary and formal practice is one which Fleming had been developing in his fictional writings for a number of years and which can be said to define the writing style of his Jamaica-set novels: an enthrallment to the exotic often dressed up as journalistic objectivity. Andrew Taylor has noted that such exoticism 'must have given the [Bond] books some of their early appeal for British readers, for whom foreign travel was a luxury because of the punitive tax regime after the war' (2012: xi–xii). But Richard Gant has claimed that many local Jamaicans, too, 'read and read again [Fleming's] books and recognise in the adventures of James Bond the local touches, the small scenes, and know themselves the roots which grew into many stories' (1966: 5). In his efforts to assert Fleming's close connections with the indigenous Jamaican people, Gant fails to recognize the orientalist politics at play within Fleming's writing and the extent to which Fleming does not so much incorporate the local Jamaican experience as he does sublimate the real Jamaica within the psychogeography of his own creation. Such racial and cultural scripting informed, in turn, the cultural imagination of Fleming's British readership, who were, at the time, experiencing large-scale immigration from Caribbean ex-colonies and Jamaica in particular. Fleming's representations of British-Jamaican social, cultural, political and economic relations coincided with the birth of British multiculturalism and formed part of the earliest cultural discourses on race and race relations in Britain during the Windrush.

Cynthia Baron's article '*Doctor No*: Bonding Britishness to Racial Sovereignty' is one of the first to address in a sustained manner the issue of Bond's orientalism, the discourse of which, I argue, largely underpins the topopolitics of Fleming's literary Jamaica.[42] Baron is correct in her assertion that the James Bond phenomenon 'illuminates aspects of a "modern" British identity that emerged in opposition to "colonial" Others who had come to England to find a home' ([2003] 2009: 153). Of significance, here, is Baron's admission that the national consciousness of present-day Britain is still enthralled to such orientalizing discourses. Baron notes that Fleming's orientalist approach 'represents a popular and very troubling British response to the unprecedented immigration from the West Indies, India, and Pakistan' following the dissolution of empire (157). Much like the cultural anxieties which came to define the Britain of the mid-twentieth century, during the period in which Jamaican migrants first sailed to British shores, Baron argues that Fleming's orientalist politics have continued to inform much larger discursive cultural and national narratives within the twenty-first century concerning Britain's racial, cultural and socio-economic identities.[43] Such narratives, Baron contends, simultaneously '[identify] Britishness with racial sovereignty' and with 'natural, undisputed ascendancy' (154) while deliberately misrepresenting or in some way falsely representing non-anglophone cultures as 'Otherized'.[44] Of course, the most significant and problematic element of Fleming's role within these representational discourses is that, with respect to his literary representation of Jamaica and its cultural and socio-economic discourses, the 'truth was not [Fleming's] primary concern. It was enough that he believed it [himself]' (Pearson 1966: 148). In other words, Fleming was not so much concerned with accurately representing Jamaican culture and British-Jamaican relations as he was in imparting his own beliefs about these issues to his readership. Fleming's imperializing framing approach to Jamaica was very much bound up in his romantic interest in the island; through the exoticist rhetoric he employed in his writings, he sought 'to weave a spell around his own environment' (McCormick 1993: 116–17) and to recreate within Goldeneye the 'details of his dreams' (Pearson 1966: 136).

James Bond, of course, is 'the ultimate Orientalist', whose very presence in Jamaica 'polices the boundaries of Britishness' and whose imperial gaze (the visual and descriptive economies at work in the novels) 'reactivates the power of the British Empire' (Baron [2003] 2009 : 136).[45] As John Pearson notes, 'James Bond becomes for Fleming a means of observing the world around him and of making it more glamorous, more exciting, more truly his than ever it has been before' (1966: 217). Pearson's description, here, underlines the discomfiting nature of Fleming's desire for visual mastery of the world around him. Fleming's need to 'possess' the world – to make it 'more truly his than ever it has been before' – can be seen in the language of the exotic which he employs to frame and contain Jamaica within his writings. Fleming's fondness for the exotic, then, is not apolitical: he is a thorough orientalist. His books are concerned not with Jamaica in actuality but with the *idea* of Jamaica as an imperial ethnoscape. As Halloran notes, 'Fleming's repeated references to Nassau, the Cayman Islands, Haiti, Cuba, and Jamaica in the Bond fiction, as well as [to] the [Caribbean] region's history of European colonialism' underline his historically orientalist outlook. The Caribbean (in general) and Jamaica (more specifically) are conscripted within the 'competing ethnic and national claims [of Fleming's Jamaica-set works] to authenticity and/or validity' (2005: 159) activated in narrative as psychogeographic articulations of Fleming's own ambivalent (albeit frequently problematic) world view. It is for this reason I must disregard Daniel Ferreras Savoye's claim that 'the representation of cultural and/or race conflict in the James Bond universe has become more nuanced' (2013: 69). Bond is a strategic orientalist; it is erroneous to suggest that the fictive universe he occupies (and commands) has become increasingly nuanced to the politics of race when the structural framework of the ongoing film series continues to be mired in essentialist, racialist doctrine. One only has to look at the disposability of a great number of Bond's non-Caucasian allies for evidence of the series' lively and ongoing problems with race.[46] Equally, I am not in sympathy with

Ferreras Savoye's view that the inclusion within the film franchise of a female M or a Black Felix Leiter 'offsets the strength of the [franchise's] original message [of political incorrectness] by diluting its apparent traditional white male ideology into a certain ambiguity' (ibid.: 70). The 'black James Bond' debate[47] that has raged in recent years is a smokescreen: the filmic James Bond has always been (and will continue to be) concerned with the politics of whiteness, irrespective of the race or skin colour of the principal actor. Credible evidence of the franchise's apparent nuancing of race and gender conflicts is not really be found in the casting of Judi Dench as M (who served for the whole of Pierce Brosnan's tenure and for the first three Daniel Craig Bond films) or in the fact that the current Felix Leiter is played by the African-American actor Jeffrey Wright (in *Casino Royale* (2006), *Quantum of Solace* (2008) and *No Time to Die* (2021)). The inclusion of these actors does not, as Ferreras Savoye claims, dilute traditional white male ideology (they are at all times subsidiary to Bond, a character who represents the very personification of that ideology); rather, their inclusion serves as a concession to liberal sensibilities.[48] However, I am more in sympathy with Ferreras Savoye's assertion that the 'subtle negotiation between the [gender and racial] ideology inherent in the Bond universe and its adaptation to a more politically correct receiver often results in ambiguous or even contradictory messages' (2013: 69). In its attempts to remain relevant in an era of increasingly visible political activism by and on behalf of women and minority communities, there is little wonder that the James Bond franchise, which has historically promulgated a violently masculinist ideology, often at the expense of women (sexism) and people of colour (racism), is politically ambivalent and ill-defined.

Addressing Fleming's ambivalence: James Bond's critical heritage

Contrary, perhaps, to traditional understandings of Fleming's work, critical opinion has largely been divided over Fleming's position on a number of issues – most prominently, his sex and gender politics, his racial politics and, of course, his representational politics. It is with the latter that this study is most concerned, and which I will focus on most predominantly. In order to approach the political and racial ambivalences at the heart of Fleming's Jamaica-set works, though, I want, firstly, to point out the critical ambivalence towards Fleming as a writer that has largely characterized academic approaches to Bond. My goal in this is to suggest a more nuanced understanding of some of the political ambiguities at the heart of the Bond canon. Much of the critical consensus on Fleming would suggest that I am too concessionary in my approach, and perhaps far too generous as well. Indeed, some have argued that Fleming is a 'mediocre writer' and that his work is 'preposterous, ludicrous, and not to be taken too seriously' (Rosenberg and Harlemann Stewart: ix).[49] However, I disregard Rosenberg and Harlemann Stewart's view of Fleming as a writer who is 'barely interested in the conditions of his world' (86). Rosenberg and Harlemann Stewart suggest that Fleming did not take seriously the decline of Britain's empire and that, rather than addressing the politics of decolonization and Britain's imperilled national mythology in his works, Fleming 'preferred to write narratives that blended farce and melodrama, fictions that wove lists of fact into situations and plots that were ridiculous' (ibid.). But Fleming's Jamaica-set works are entirely – and, moreover, overtly – concerned with the politics of empire; farce and melodrama are precisely the vehicles through which Fleming sought to navigate the sociopolitical ruptures of empire and his own ambivalence towards these issues. Rosenberg and Harlemann Stewart's claim fails to take into consideration one of the basic tenets of Fleming's writing: that is, the ideology of empire which underpins virtually all of his work, and which undergoes a sizeable shift in those works published from the early 1960s onwards, following Jamaica's eventual independence from Britain. While Fleming himself has confessed that his writings 'have no message for suffering humanity' and that his books 'do not aim at changing people or making them go out and do something' (qtd in Zeiger [1965] 1966: 110),[50] it would be a misstep to argue that Fleming's often farcical and melodramatic formal style belies anything other than a deep (and, at times, deeply philosophical) anxiety about the condition of postcolonial Jamaica and British decolonization. The critical disregard for Fleming that I have noted, here, is typical and indicative of a good deal of scholarship on Bond.

More nuanced in his defence and consideration of Fleming is the much-respected Italian novelist and critic Umberto Eco, who has argued that Fleming writes deliberately ambiguous texts for 'those who take them as the gospel truth and those who see their humour' ([1965] 1966: 46). Eco's discussion of Fleming's deliberate ambiguities is concerned with the formal and structural properties of his writings: he notes that Fleming 'blends his narrative elements with an unstable montage, alternating Grand Guignol and *nouveau roman*' in a style that fuses together these elements 'to produce an unstable patchwork, a tongue-in-cheek bricolage' (53, 55). Thus, on a formal level, Fleming's literary works are defined by their structural ambivalences. As I will demonstrate, this is the case on the level of narrative too. Fleming's writings can be read far more ambivalently than previously thought precisely because, in Lisa M. Dresner's words, the James Bond novels and short stories are themselves inherently 'mixed, boundary-crossing, eliding documents' (2011: 282) which derive from Fleming's fundamentally confused politics. For example, critics have long been divided on the question of whether or not Fleming was an actual racist and on whether his books can be read as accurate reflections of his own politics on race. For some, it is clear that Fleming was an out-and-out racist: Rosenberg and Harlemann Stewart are insistent that 'whether by gratuitous insult or unflattering stereotype, Fleming's books single out individuals because of their ethnic heritage and describe ethnic groups and nationalities in mindless ways that do not consider individual merit but merely condemn' (1989: 92). They claim that it is not simply the case that Fleming's work reflects the public mood of Britain during the 1950s (though it is not much of a stretch to suggest that Fleming's racial biases were consistent with much of his readership at the time). Rosenberg and Harlemann Stewart dismiss Nigel West's claim that Fleming's racism expressed the biases of 'polite society' and that the bigotry present in the novels reflects the bigotry of the 'right' kind of people (qtd in Rosenberg and Harlemann Stewart 1989: 87). Rather, they argue that Fleming's racial prejudices are deeply embedded within and reified through his writings as a means of categorizing and assimilating social, cultural, political and racial otherness. They argue that his prejudices are indicative of his paranoia regarding the ascendancy and superiority of the British race and that racial prejudice 'saved him from the mental strain of having to evaluate each person on his own merits' (Rosenberg and Harlemann Stewart 1989: 104–5). For Fleming, the racialism which underpins much of his writing is part of a strategic orientalism, itself a not unproblematic aspect of the Bond canon specifically designed not only to excite and thrill the reader but also to emphasize the 'hierarchy that underlies every prejudicial system: [that] the English were the chosen race' and that 'the English were the noblest and best' (105).[51] Significantly, however, Rosenberg and Harlemann Stewart do question the extent to which Fleming actually believed in the racist ideation perpetuated within his writings: 'if it occurs in the pages of his books with such consistency,' they query, 'for whom did he think he was writing?' (92).

Perhaps surprisingly, there is also a great deal of academic criticism written in defence of Fleming's perceived racism, and on a number of grounds. I must reiterate, here, that it is not my intention to defend Fleming against claims of actual racism but to draw attention to the ambivalence of his representational politics and to question the extent to which a good many critics have overlooked the more complex representational politics to be found in his writings. Rosenberg and Harlemann Stewart argue that defenders of Fleming's work usually fall into one of two ideological camps: either they argue that Fleming's race politics are not to be taken seriously because, as the likes of Raymond Durgnat and Mordecai Richler have claimed, Fleming himself is not to be taken seriously as a writer,[52] or, somewhat more problematically, they argue that such attitudes are to be considered appropriate within the context of the period Fleming was writing (ibid.: 93). Kingsley Amis, one of the most vocal members of the intelligentsia and a vanguard of Fleming's work, argues that the James Bond novels and short stories are less expressions of Fleming's personal prejudices than they are vehicles through which Fleming has 'made national prejudices *knowledgeable*' (1965: 76, italics in original). In other words, Amis sees the James Bond novels not as symptomatic of Fleming's inherent racism but as critical commentaries upon the racialist attitudes and assumptions which characterize British nationalism, for which James Bond serves as a wry and ironic mouthpiece. Amis counters the notion that Fleming's work promotes racial prejudice in actuality on the grounds that 'to use foreigners as villains is a convention older than literature' and that Bond's xenophobia is 'undifferentiated' (166). Amis argues further that Fleming is equally sympathetic in his presentation of many other races (particularly the peoples of the Caribbean) as he is in the white Anglo-Saxon Briton.[53] Though Amis's *The James Bond Dossier* is often lauded as the first critical work on Ian Fleming's writing, O. F. Snelling's *Double O Seven James Bond: A Report* predates it by a year (and is, dare I say, a superior work). Snelling and Amis are much in sympathy with one another. Snelling argues that the 'most intimate' of Bond's friends and allies in the novels – Quarrel in *Live and Let Die* and *Dr. No*, Darko Kerim in *From Russia with Love*, Marc Ange Draco in *On Her Majesty's Secret Service* and Tiger Tanaka in *You Only Live Twice* – are all non-Caucasian (1964: 188).[54] Another of Fleming's defenders is Umberto Eco, who argues that Fleming is racist *only* 'in the sense that any artist is one if, to represent the devil, he depicts him with oblique eyes; in the sense that a nurse is one who, wishing to frighten children with the bogeyman, suggests that he is black' (1979: 161–2). For Eco, at least, it is clear that Fleming is simply Manichean: his novels very much reflect his view that the world is made up of both good and evil forces in conflict with one another which just so happen to align with notions of race.[55] While Eco does concede that 'it is difficult ... to maintain that Fleming is not inclined to consider the British superior to all Oriental or Mediterranean races', he is also adamant in his defence that Fleming is 'profuse in his acknowledgement of the new African races and of their contribution to contemporary civilisation' (1966: 59). In other words, it is not simply the case that Fleming is dismissive of the non-Anglo-Saxon; he entertains a healthy respect for them, too. As Raymond Benson has noted of Mr Big, Bond's opponent in Live and Let Die, 'in choosing a black man for his villain, Fleming wasn't necessarily making a statement about blacks'. While Benson acknowledges the exaggerated stereotyping underpinning Fleming's presentation of Big, he also points out the fact that Bond and the narrator seem enthralled to him: 'Mr. Big himself is quite brilliant. (SMERSH would never pick a man with no brains to run such an important operation for them, whether he was black or white.) Mr. Big is meticulous ... [he] speaks slowly and distinctly, and knows exactly what he wants' (1984: 97). Similarly, Paul Anthony and Jacqueline Friedman argue that the presentation of Big 'was not true racism', which they contend would have been thoroughly unacceptable even to Fleming's contemporary audience in the 1950s. They argue that Fleming was very much aware of the fact that 'his racial content would be questioned more sharply when it involved [Black people]', which is why, they assert, he goes to great lengths in his presentation of Mr Big to 'show us that his racial feelings are note hostile' and that 'possessing a great villain is no reproach unto a people' (1965: 93).

The most intriguing comment on Fleming's racial politics comes from Gerald Early, an African-American critic who, in his youth, read Fleming against the race relations novels of Richard Wright and who argues that Fleming 'opened up' for him the political ideologies at the heart of White's writing:

> What reading Wright simultaneously with Fleming did was make me more impressed by Wright's idea that blacks, rightly angry over having the nature of their humanity questioned by whites, respond by creating an ideology to prove their humanity to themselves which only more deeply traps them in their throes of their self-consciousness. (1999: 152)

Early notes that he felt 'liberated' from his self-consciousness as an (racial) outsider in America through his readings of Fleming, and through his understanding of the racial paradigms at play in Fleming's work. As Vivian Halloran asserts,

> Early does not judge Fleming's portrayal of black characters by the American standard, the one-drop rule as the determining factor in black racial identity. Instead, he treats Fleming's fiction as a supplement to his reading of African American literature as a young man ... As a teenager, Early developed a new understanding of the national domestic racial dynamic within the black community in America through his reading of James Bond's adventures as the defender and enforcer of the British Empire. (2005: 163)

Most intriguingly, Early is not as vituperatively denigrating of Fleming's racial politics as he might be. Of both *Live and Let Die* and *Dr. No*, arguably the two most problematic of Fleming's novels when it comes to issues of race relations and representation, Early says the following: 'both books might be dismissed as the usual sort of racist claptrap, although it seems to me they are, in fact, less racist, or shall I say *far more interestingly racist*, than the films they later spawned' (1999: 152, my italics). Early's concession, here, to the ambivalence at play in Fleming's representational politics is most telling. He does not simply dismiss Fleming as a racist, as his comparative reading of Richard Wright's politics of Black empowerment might lead him to conclude; rather, he recognizes the capacity within Fleming for a critical dialogue regarding the 'far more interestingly' racialist elements of Fleming's work and the potential for critical dialogue to be had between (and which incorporates) Fleming's representational discourses and other writers of colour concerning the politics of race and otherness. What Early allows for, really, is the potential for reading critical disparity into Fleming's representational discourses.

If we are to read Fleming with any degree of seriousness (which, I think, we must), then we need to read seriously the ambivalence inherent in the responses of Fleming's critics towards the particular discourses of representation to be found within his work. Considerations of Fleming's racial politics have largely tended towards the reductive; rather than acknowledging the many ambivalences present within his work regarding British-Jamaican political and cultural relations, and regarding the fluctuating structural relations between Fleming's Britishness and his 'Jamaican-ness', responses to his Jamaica-set works, in particular, have been fairly uniform in decoding Fleming's racism. Defenders of Fleming, such as Amis and Eco, may themselves be unaware of their own privilege – indeed, they may very well have shared in some of Fleming's ostensible prejudices. (As for myself, I cannot but be aware of the caution that must be heeded by a white academic claiming to write authoritatively about such matters.) But more than a cursory glance at Fleming's Jamaica-set work is enough to suggest that we cannot simply dismiss the representational politics of the James Bond novels as a matter of Black and white. There is nuance and subtlety to Fleming's presentation of his Jamaican psychogeography that necessitates a much more complex engagement with the politics of representation itself. It is for this reason that I tend to agree with Joyce Goggin, who notes that Fleming's 'depiction of racial divides, be they white/mixed race, or the harder, supposedly more clearly defined white/black divide, gets muddled' in Fleming's fictional universe, where racial dichotomies are 'being thrown into question and rethought by an author who may have been struggling with these issues himself' (2018: 149). Goggin's assessment of Fleming as someone who was struggling with his own fluctuating personal, cultural, social, national and political views on British-Jamaican relations is far more consistent with the content of his books than is accommodated by the dogmatically dichotomizing views of either Rosenberg and Harlemann Stewart or Amis and Eco. It must be acknowledged that 'Fleming's approach to ethnicity was more complex than some passages in his works might imply' (Black 2005: 12). Mordecai Richler has argued that 'it was Fleming's most brilliant stroke to *present* himself not as an old-fashioned frothing water-hog, but as an ostensibly civilized voice which offered sanitized racialism' (1972: 81, my italics). Though Richler is by and large harshly dismissive of Fleming's fictional enterprise, his choice phrasing suggests that there is a certain distinction to be drawn between Fleming's narrative voice and Fleming himself. Fleming elects in his Bond novels to *present* a certain vision of himself through which British racial prejudices of the day are given voice. Fleming's concern with the James Bond novels was always to make money, and lots of it. His books, therefore, are suitably tailored for Britain's particular market readership whose prejudicial make-up finds reassurances in the 'sanitized racism' of his writings. Incidentally, the term 'sanitized racism' is a neatly ambivalent one: on the one hand suggestive of the cultural normalization of racism to be found within Fleming's writings, on the other suggestive of the 'clean', innocent or non-pernicious form of stereotyping which Fleming certainly enjoys. As Robbie B. H. Goh notes, James Bond 'operates as an icon of popular culture by directing consumer desires onto a racist and sexist plane of disparagement and conquest'; racial hatred, he argues, 'justifies the consumer pleasures into which Bond initiates the reader' at the time and 'provides [a] psychological and moral satisfaction' to Fleming's contemporary readers (1999: 35). Goh's focus, here, is largely on the consumer, the mid-twentieth-century readership whom Fleming, he argues, consciously apes in his writings. As with Anthony and Friedman, Goh, too, asserts that issues of race certainly were prevalent during the period in which Bond was first produced; indeed, Goh acknowledges that, following the Second World War and the Suez Canal crisis in 1956, Britain's declining global position meant that 'Britain's racial homogeneity was placed under the greatest pressure it had ever faced' (ibid.:31). Immigration from the Caribbean, India, Pakistan and the African continent, as well as a number of race riots (Notting Hill and Nottingham in 1958), suggested that race was not simply a cultural, political or historical issue for Fleming but a profitable one, too. Fleming's books are largely concerned with (and certainly stoked) British fears of racial miscegenation and the threat of incursion that was feared from the Windrush and a number of other British immigrants.⁵⁶

While it is certainly the case that Fleming sought to navigate great financial gain through the exploitation of these fears, it is not quite so certain that he shared in them. James Chapman asserts that Fleming was 'equivocal' in his writings about the changes that were occurring in the racial and political landscape of British society following immigration. On the one hand, Fleming despised the consequences of these changes ('the stories are replete with assertions of national pride and with references to decline'), but, on the other, he embraced them (Chapman [1999] 2007: 28). For Andrew Lycett, Fleming's writings captured the zeitgeist of 1950s and 1960s Britain precisely through their 'attempt to reflect the disturbing moral ambiguity of a post-war world' ([1995] 2008: 221) in which racial sovereignty was encroaching with fearful certainty upon a British cultural consciousness that was ill-prepared for the dissolution of empire. Though largely disparaging of the administrative capabilities of the Colonial Office in Jamaica, Fleming nevertheless believed that Britain owed a duty of care to its former overseas possession once Jamaica attained independence, even after, and in spite of, Britain's sufferance of political defeat (Parker 2014: 247). Finally, Paul Anthony and Jacqueline Friedman point out that, though he 'insists that the British Empire was necessary, [Fleming] does not go so far as to claim that it was just' (1965: 23). This latter point is significant. Though the character of James Bond may be said to convey much of Fleming's personal sympathies with respect to issues of race and British-Jamaican cultural relations during the transition from colonial rule to the postcolonial period, Fleming's presentation of Bond within this paradigm is not without implicit (self-)censure.⁵⁷ If Bond is the fictive embodiment of Fleming's neocolonial vision of British-Jamaican relations, then he too is an ambivalently conceived one.

Fleming's confused ideological vision of Bond's fictive universe, though 'carefully sanitized', is also a 'long journey into the wilds of moral ambiguity [and] political doubt' (Wark [1991] 2006: 6) in which Fleming strives to consolidate his own understanding of shifting global politics and to shore up his confused political, national, cultural, social and personal identities. At once, Bond is both 'avenging angel of the free world' as well as 'an instrument of state-sponsored terrorism, killing on command to insure the interests of a singular political agenda'; he is a reflection of the concerns of 1950s Britain as well as an 'embodiment of the glory, honor, and refinement of pre-war Britain' (Miller 2011: xiii–xiv). According to Lisa M. Dresner, Bond is a figure of 'displacement, miscegenation, and boundary crossing' defined precisely by his indefinability and his blurring of national, economic, political and racial boundaries (2011: 271). For Praseeda Gopinath, Bond occupies a similar 'middle space of transition' between a number of polarities, most particularly the 'disinterestedness of imperialism [and] a more contained domestic, welfare state' (2013: 144). Here, Gopinath acknowledges Bond's disinclination towards imperialism, a comment which sits in contravention to much Fleming criticism but which nevertheless underlines the epistemic ambiguities at the centre of Fleming's post-imperial writings. Similarly, Joachim Frenk and Christian Krug acknowledge the 'multiplicity' at the heart of the Bond icon, noting that Bond is 'both a signifier of Britain's imperial past – without seeming old-fashioned – and the agent of a cutting-edge present – without becoming a victim of the *Zeitgeist*' (2011: 2). Such a view must necessarily be nuanced.[58] Arguably, Bond very much presents an archaic and reactive form of heroism – though Raymond Durgnat asserts that the question of Bond's historical timeliness is a moot one (1970: 151). Nevertheless, Frenk and Krug are correct in pointing out the significance of the character's multiplicity. Bond is not simply one thing or another; rather, the very liminality at the heart of the character affords the politics of Fleming's writings a much more complex ambivalence.[59] Bond is, in the now infamous words of Tony Bennett and Janet Woollacott, a 'mobile signifier' (1987: 42). Through his narratives' many ambivalences, Fleming succeeds in situating the reader within a framework of 'doubleness' (Halloran 2005: 167) wherein certain ideological polarities within the texts are brought into convergence with one another, the result of which is a deliberate conflation of complementary political meanings and potential interpretations.

Redressing Fleming's ambivalence: new critical directions

Many earlier critics (Amis, Eco, Harlemann and Stewart, for example) have commented at length on Fleming's attitudes towards race and Jamaica, but too often has the postcolonial contexts of Fleming's writings been either overlooked or improperly regarded by those writing in the immediate context of post-war, post-imperial Britain – and very rarely have the postcolonial contexts of Fleming's work been considered alongside the jarring political and ideological ambivalences which underpin those James Bond novels set in and around Jamaica.[60] I suggest that critical discussion of Fleming's work is undergoing a shift from simple considerations of Fleming's racialism within the immediate post-imperial period to an engagement with Fleming's representational politics and the politics of ambivalence – those deliberately provocative approaches he adopts in his writings towards questions of race and representation. Certainly, in the case of the Jamaica-set novels, Fleming's ambivalence is acutely political, concerned as it is with fluctuating British-Jamaican political, cultural and socio-economic relations and Fleming's own unstable ideological position. Cynthia Baron, for one, recognizes the extent to which Fleming simultaneously 'invites [the reader] to re-examine British strategies of self-definition in the post-colonial era' following the dissolution of empire – a period of necessary reinvention in the aftermath of Britain's defeat in the Second World War – while nevertheless 'implicitly [attacking] the older generation's "liberal" complacency and inveterate mismanagement' of the colonial empire ([2003] 2009: 153-4). Fleming's political outlook, Baron contends, is both retrospective and prospective; he bemoans the soft liberal tendencies of successive conservative governments for Britain's declining political influence on the global stage whilst simultaneously advocating in his fiction for a reinvention of British cultural and political norms. Christine Berberich has decried such an ambivalent political outlook, denouncing it as a 'rather problematic call for a new sense of identity that shows an awareness of waning British influence in the world while also trying to maintain the myth of British – and here, particularly English – superiority' (2012: 14).[61] Moreover, Berberich has pointed out some of the further ambivalences at the heart of Fleming's fictional enterprise: she dismisses as 'superficial' the novels' 'celebration of violence, sex, and consumerism' and argues that the character James Bond is a 'façade' behind which hides a man *'both at ease and at odds with his time*: a man steeped in Victorian values of duty, yet at the same time celebrating the (especially sexual) freedoms that came with the more permissive post-war decades' (ibid., my italics). Rather than simple parables of adventure, hedonism and sex, Berberich contends that Fleming's James Bond novels more accurately 'reflect the confusion of a time of widespread and rapid change' (ibid.). Much like the age in which he was writing, Fleming's politics, too, are confused.

Perhaps more than any of his contemporaries, David Cannadine has been most vocal about the inherent contradictions and ambivalences to be found within Fleming's work. Cannadine argues that Fleming's political ambivalences derived largely from the climate in which he was first writing. He notes, on the one hand, that the Bond novels are 'quite extraordinarily patriotic' and that they 'fervently' embody a belief in the 'greatness and innate moral superiority' of England (1979: 47) – an observation which makes sense given the fluctuating instability of post-imperial Britain in mid-twentieth-century global geopolitics. On the other hand, Cannadine contends that Fleming was far less abiding in his adherence to traditional forms of British national, cultural, political and social identities and moral standards.[62] Cannadine notes that Fleming's novels 'not only depicted [Britain's moral decline in the post-war period] graphically, but evidently welcomed it, and may indeed have helped encourage it'. Indeed, he argues, the James Bond novels can be read as a 'sustained attack on conventional morality', particularly that of the mores around sex and sexual conduct which were gradually loosening.[63] (48–9) Cannadine iterates a number of times Fleming's ambivalence with respect to Britain's fluctuating moral and social climate: he notes that 'while in some ways [Fleming's] response to internal, moral "decline" was to urge further progress forward, in others he was anxious that the clock be put back'; and 'while, in one sense, Fleming's reaction to the moral "decline" of post-war Britain was that of welcome encouragement, in another, he profoundly regretted it and sought to return to the more wholesome, public-school moral climate he had known as a boy' (50, 52). In his later book, *In Churchill's Shadow: Confronting the Past in Modern Britain* (2002), Cannadine doubles down on his claims regarding Fleming's ambivalence, concluding that 'Fleming's attitude towards Britain's domestic decline was genuinely equivocal'.[64] It is scarcely surprising to him, then, that Fleming's books were 'praised by some for being "entirely wholesome" and condemned by others for being "morally repugnant", with equal conviction and plausibility' (2002: 303).

Finally, and perhaps most significantly, Vivian Halloran calls explicit attention to the question of ambivalence within Fleming's writings. Popular opinion holds it true that Fleming is an out-and-out racist and that his books perpetuate a xenophobic vision of the non-anglophone, non-Anglo-Saxon world. In actuality, however, as Halloran notes, Fleming's writing 'always deconstructs any notion that racial whiteness signifies any particular cultural identity in his novels' (2005: 163). Halloran calls attention to the hybridity or 'doubleness' of the Bond character, once again; she argues that Bond's 'mixed Scottish and Swiss heritage and his upbringing abroad mark him as much of a hybrid figure as any of the villains he encounters in his assignments'. Furthermore, she asserts, 'his dual Scottish and Swiss heritage situates him, at least partially, as a colonial subject – he is not English, although his father's Scottish blood qualifies him as British' (164). While I concede the point that Bond's mixed heritage certainly complicates those racial binaries which are traditionally acknowledged as underpinning Fleming's work, I am much less convinced by the idea that Bond himself is a colonial subject; such a view seems, to me, to overlook the iconicity of Bond as a distinctly historicized British subject.[65] However, I take Halloran's concluding assertion – that 'by simply writing James Bond off as a racist icon, we risk misunderstanding how a changing world requires the development of new rules for interaction and understanding across difference' (171) – as foundational to the current project. I contend that the ambivalences at the heart of Fleming's representation of British-Jamaican cultural and racial relations suggests that we cannot simply dismiss Fleming as an outright racist – and, moreover, that Fleming's representational politics demand to be read in the context of the many ambivalences that have been identified with respect to issues of British-Jamaican political, racial and sociocultural relations within his works.

To this end, I propose to critically examine the 'propagandist allegories' of Fleming's Jamaican psychogeography, as well as the 'explicit practices and representations' of that landscape on a meta-discursive level (Waterman 2018: 185). By this I mean that I will explore the ways in which the signifier 'Jamaica' has come to be understood and employed as a psychogeography within Fleming's fictional universe. It is my intention to build up a complete picture of Fleming's Jamaican topopolitics – that is, the ways in which Fleming's literary Jamaica has been textually crafted as both a real and a symbolic space. To that end, I propose to follow something of Jason Dittmer's approach to the study of Jamaica in his article 'Ian Fleming's Jamaica: Spaces of Legitimation and the Bond-age of Popular Culture'. Dittmer is concerned with Fleming's material, imaginary and artistic conceptions of Jamaica – that is, the ways in which Jamaica is spatialized within the text, the ways in which Jamaica is imagined within the text and the ways in which Jamaica is reified as a representational space through the text, respectively (2008: 17). Much like Dittmer, I too am concerned with ways in which the complex politics of British-Jamaican relations are imagined (or reimagined) through the material practices of space and through representation within Fleming's fiction. Finally, while I also concur with Dittmer's assertion that Fleming's Jamaica-set fiction functions as a space of 'legitimation' configuring particular British-Jamaican race relations, I depart from Dittmer's assumption that this space of legitimation serves simply or solely as a 'reinforcement for the dominant assumptions of the neo-imperial order' (18). As I argue, Fleming's fiction does not simply reproduce the rhetoric of either imperialism or neo-imperialism; rather, as my examination of Fleming's various literary and communicational networks demonstrates, the concept-signifier 'Jamaica' is part of a much more ambivalent infrastructure employed by Fleming in his approach towards British-Jamaican colonial and postcolonial relations. My principal contention is that an analysis of Fleming's topopolitics reveals a much more complex and ambivalent attitude towards British-Jamaican colonial politics than has hitherto been examined.

In the first chapter, 'Imagined identities and the Black body politic in *Live and Let Die*', I take as my focus the first of Fleming's works set in Jamaica: *Live and Let Die*, published in 1954, during a period in which campaigns for Jamaica's independence were increasingly being mobilized and when Britain's hold on its territories in the Caribbean basin was gradually loosening. In this chapter, I propose to examine the significance of Fleming's ambivalence towards issues of race in the pre-independence period in Jamaica. I argue that *Live and Let Die* is divided along a number of competing ideological strands which the text itself proves unable to reconcile or resolve – largely because of Fleming's attempts to negotiate his own conflicted instincts with respect to the politics of race. On the one hand, the novel certainly contains many questionable assumptions about race and African Americans, in particular; but on the other hand, I argue that the novel evidences Fleming's accommodation for a particular 'blurring' or harmonizing of racial conflict and racial identities through Bond's meditation on the condition of race and on the politics of Black power which underpins the narrative. It is simply just not the case that *Live and Let Die* can be dismissed as a work of racism. The figure of the zombie plays an important role in the novel and, I argue, is an especially important symbol for Fleming, precisely because it connotes resurrection. In certain Caribbean Voodoo practices, the figure of the zombie is resurrected by another for whom the zombie carries out orders. I contend that the zombie is a potent cultural metaphor for Britain's colonial subjugation of Jamaica and that Fleming's use of this metaphor (resurrection, reawakening, etc.) is part of the novel's complex and ambivalent ideologies concerning Jamaican nationalism and Jamaica's desire for independence from Britain. Furthermore, that Mr Big plans to flood the American market with gold coins ostensibly recovered from Captain Morgan's sunken treasure is also significantly linked to the motifs of rebirth and resurrection that Fleming employs through his use of the zombie within the narrative. That Mr Big seeks to destabilize the American economy through the introduction of what amounts to reparation finances is also part of the complex racial politics of the novel, in which the white saviour denies the Black 'transgressor' his inherited right. Bond's defeat of the villain then, I argue, while often seen as the fait accompli of any Bond story, problematizes the neatly paradigmatic moral vision (and moral certainty) of Fleming's novel as a 'good versus evil' narrative. Overall, I argue that the narrative pattern of 'suppression–resurrection' is important for an understanding of the novel's (and Fleming's) complex racial politics.

In the second chapter, 'Invasion, animality and bodily transgressions in *Dr. No*', I focus on the period of Jamaican history immediately preceding the country's independence from Britain. The primary text I examine, here, is Fleming's second Jamaica-set novel, *Dr. No*, published in 1958. I argue that Fleming's interest in pan-Caribbean cultural and racial politics of the time, and his decision to place Jamaica's political situation within the context of other existing British colonies in the Caribbean, represents part of Fleming's persistent ambivalence towards Britain's impending decolonization of the island. Much of my argument in this chapter centres on the prevalence within *Dr. No* of a number of interrelated themes and motifs – most prominently, that of transgression. In the period of increased British-Jamaican political agitation, Fleming's writings are almost entirely replete with images of penetration, invasion, boundary-crossing and incursion. I argue that this imagery is resonant of Fleming's (and Britain's) increasing fears of Jamaican nationalization. Moreover, I contend that the anxieties over physical invasion and incursion which the novel peddles are not simply connotative of British fears of Jamaican migrants and the arrival of the Windrush to British shores, but that Fleming's employment of these images is tied to his own consideration of Britain's colonial shame. In his reconsideration of physical, temporal and spatial boundaries within the novel, Fleming employs a series of trans-corporeal metaphors designed to characterize the great upheaval of Jamaica's impending independence as well as the transcendence of political territories which this was seen to represent. Fleming's use of animal imagery and other related motifs of animalism, I argue, convey a great deal of anxiety over changing geopolitical relations. By way of the figurative language Fleming uses to connote the character's trans-human state, Bond himself, in his actions and in his duty, is positioned as a transgressor of certain unspeakable lines. Finally, I argue that, through his consideration of Honey Rider as an ambivalent colonial subject, Fleming calls into question the trans-materiality of his Jamaican psychogeography as a site of colonial ruination.

In my third chapter, 'Mobility, memory and touristic modernity in *The Man with the Golden Gun*', I take as my focus the last of Fleming's Jamaica-set novels. Though it is a vastly inferior work to much of Fleming's output, the posthumously published 1965 novel *The Man with the Golden Gun* nevertheless offers an unfiltered (largely unedited) insight into Fleming's conception of

British-Jamaican relations in post-independence Jamaica. Like the previous two chapters, I contend that *The Man with the Golden Gun* is structured around a number of interrelated motifs through which Fleming attempts to navigate the geopolitical shifts that have occurred since he first began living and writing in (and about) Jamaica. Much of the novel, I argue, is concerned with the interplay between moments and images of dynamism (or movement) and stasis, between restriction and freedom. Bond's erstwhile role as an imperial agent who is unhampered in his traversal of the globe is further called into question in this novel (specifically through the aforementioned interplay) as Fleming attempts to reorient Bond's new, postcolonial identity within the economic and sociocultural contexts of Jamaica's emergent self-governance. The Jamaica of this novel, I contend, is a vastly different one to either *Live and Let Die* or *Dr. No*, but Fleming is no less characteristically ambivalent in his approach to its representational politics. The novel is filled with images of ruins and buildings in disrepair or (re)construction. On the one hand, Fleming seems to suggest that this is representative of the faded splendour of a Jamaica that, under British rule, enjoyed a much more robust economy; on the other hand, and against these particular motifs, the novel also plays with the idea of a pre-British Jamaican history, of a time prior to Britain's occupation of the island. I argue that the novel represents an intersection between a nostalgia for colonial rule (Fleming's attempts to reinscribe British relevance; Bond's assistance in building the Scaramanga's hotel as a neo-imperial enterprise) and the pre-memory of Britain's occupation (Fleming's meditations on Bond's function in a postcolonial period; Tiffy's overgrown bordello, reclaimed by the landscape). Throughout the novel, Fleming never quite manages to reconcile his love for Jamaica with the cultural politics of imperial Britain. Given that Bond functions generally as a cipher for conservative, national British interests, Fleming's choice to repeatedly return his hero to Jamaica is, I contend, part of the author's complex politics of representation and his (unsuccessful) attempts to come to terms with the postcolonial transformations of British-Jamaican cultural relations, Jamaica itself and with his own literary creation, James Bond, who, unlike his earlier visits to the island (in *Live and Let Die*, for example), has become altogether out of place within the embryonic culture of national Jamaica.

Finally, I will conclude with a look at a number of the Eon-produced, Jamaica-set Bond films, including *Dr. No* and *Live and Let Die*. The former was released in October 1962, only two months after Jamaica was officially granted independence from Britain in August 1962. By way of comparative approach, I examine the literary and cinematic incarnations of Bond's fictive universe. That the film producers should elect to film and release *Dr. No* as the very first Bond film is not an apolitical decision, I argue. Fleming's Jamaica is the cornerstone upon which the cinematic Bond franchise is built and, as such, I consider the ways the island is employed as a representative landscape in the post-independence period and in more contemporary audiences' conceptions of Jamaica and British-Jamaican relations.

1

Imagined identities and the Black body politic in *Live and Let Die*

In this chapter, my focus is the first of Ian Fleming's Jamaica-set novels, written in spring 1953 and set during a period of increased nationalist agitation in Jamaica, when independence movements were becoming mobilized as Britain's hold over its imperial territories within the Caribbean basin began to slip measurably in the post-war period. The novel is set, predominantly, between Harlem in New York and Jamaica. In its conflation of Harlem and Jamaica as racialized topographies, *Live and Let Die* represents Fleming's attempt to grapple with the changing face of race relations within the western hemisphere at large. *Live and Let Die* can be said to articulate Fleming's burgeoning anxieties and increasing ambivalence over issues of race and racial politics in Jamaica, as well as his growing awareness of the effects of race on the political landscape of Anglo-American relations in the aftermath of the war, during the period of America's geopolitical ascendancy. Fleming was also keenly aware of the decline of Britain's geopolitical influence and of his country's devalued role in international politics. His response to these issues, in his writings, is often thought of as reactionary – what Lars Ole Sauerberg refers to as Fleming's 'forced sobriety mingled with an inclination to continued nationalistic inebriation' (1984: 150). In actuality, Fleming does much to situate James Bond and his Jamaican psychogeography within the nuanced politics of British decolonization. Jeremy Black has argued that 'there is a misleading theme [within certain British historical circles] of [Britain's] gradual and inevitable descent from imperial status, and the emphasis is on Britain's willingness to concede independence and on the generally peaceful nature of the process' (2004: 295). Although countries such as India, Burma, Ceylon and Palestine had been granted independence from Britain prior to Jamaica, their 'loss was not seen as part of an inevitable process of imperial withdrawal' (ibid.). As Black asserts, while Britain granted independence to certain countries, there were actually attempts made in the Caribbean and in other regions to 'strengthen both formal and informal empire' where it was believed that certain other 'colonies were far from ready for independence' (ibid.). Fleming's focus on the Caribbean context, then, according to Black, represents an attempt to '[locate] empire in the wider context of British strategic interests' with specific 'reference to the West's position in the Cold War' (ibid.: 296). Black further notes that Bond's status as defender of the empire is to be defined largely 'in terms of the struggle with the Soviets' (ibid.: 295), a struggle in which Britain had become engaged during a period of heightened political agitation and fears of the potential ramifications of communism. But Fleming is not simply reacting to Britain's changing geopolitical status; he is engaging with issues of political nationalism and his own ambivalent regard for the dissolution of empire during the period in which such issues were becoming increasingly negotiable. Indeed, as Jason Dittmer has argued, the 'stark racial geography' of *Live and Let Die* 'connects to "real" geopolitical events' at the time and to Fleming's 'anxieties … as a Briton living on the island' during the lead-up to Jamaican independence (2008: 24).

Many critics and commentators have argued that *Live and Let Die* evidences Fleming's racism, and that the novel belies an unsettling and pernicious racial politics. For Dittmer, 'the dearth of actual Jamaicans in this story … illustrates a general racism of omission'. The island of Jamaica, he argues, is further 'abstracted from its own local people and culture, framed exclusively as part of the British Empire and as a Cold War battlefield' (2008: 22). Dittmer is, presumably, referring to the fact that none of the principal characters in the novel are Jamaican nationals and that none of the principal action of the novel takes place in Jamaica. Sam Goodman also highlights the 'unenlightened' and 'repellent attitudes towards colonial subjects [and] towards colonial space' which the book ostensibly promotes: he argues that *Live and Let Die* is populated with 'bestialised natives attempting continually to undermine (white) British authority' (2016: 147). Who these 'bestialised natives' are, though, Goodman never makes clear. He can hardly be referring to the indigenous Jamaicans within the novel, since very few of them actually appear at all in the course of Bond's mission (Dittmer's point, above); and certainly, none are regarded in these terms. The novel does not disparage Jamaicans as 'bestialised natives'; it is Goodman himself who makes this false equivalence. Furthermore, this equivalence itself suggests a relationship between 'bestialised natives' and African Americans, about whom the racial politics of *Live and Let Die* might more accurately be said to concern. With the native Jamaican, Goodman seems to conflate a group of African-American gangsters. The points of comparison are, for many reasons, unjust. This mischaracterization of Fleming's attitudes towards native Jamaicans is part of the much wider discourse of false equivalences often drawn between the James Bond novels, Fleming's racial politics and Jamaica. Eldridge Cleaver's assertion that James Bond offers 'whites a triumphant image of themselves [that many] want desperately to hear reaffirmed: *I am still the White Man, lord of the land, licensed to kill, and the world is still an empire at my feet*' ([1968] 1970: 81, italics in original) certainly encapsulates a particular – if not perfectly just – ethnocentric critique of Bond. It does not, however, speak to the complexities of Fleming's own ambivalence towards white triumphalism precipitated by the dissolution of Britain's empire. Even Fleming's first biographer, John Pearson, fails to accurately appraise Fleming's Jamaican writings: he argues that '*Live and Let Die* is notably free from the gloom, the fears of fleshy decay and imminent disaster which creeps into the later books. Here Fleming seems to have few doubts about himself and James Bond' (1966: 221). Pearson's reading of *Live and Let Die* is largely fallacious, as the novel is actually saturated with images of death and bodily decay. The greyish tint of Mr Big's skin is continuously described in terms of fleshy decay; the myth of the Voodoo Baron Samedi which Big employs to strike fear into the hearts of his subordinates is one characterized by death and bodily revivification; more generally, the novel is actually replete with images of skulls and ruins. Here, we might think of the image of Mr Big's fleshless skull ravaged by barracuda at the novel's conclusion and the uninhabited ruins of the Great House within the Beau Desert property at which Bond and Quarrel sojourn before their assault on the Isle of Surprise, Mr Big's hideaway. Thus, with its anxious imagery of literally decaying flesh, *Live and Let Die* can be said to belie a great deal of Fleming's apprehension concerning the Black body politic.

With respect to issues of race, the Jamaica-set James Bond novels might be thought of, in more productive terms, as 'anxiety novels' rather than works of dismissive racism. Indeed, as I will argue, *Live and Let Die*, in particular, can be read as an example of Fleming's attempts to negotiate his own fluctuating ideation with respect to the politics of race in the context of both the emerging Black Power movement within the United States and fledgling multiculturalism within Britain. It should be stressed that Fleming's anxieties over such emerging political contexts are not in and of themselves racist in orientation, and that *Live and Let Die* actually navigates an ambivalence regarding race that is much more characteristic of Fleming than perhaps many of his critics would allow for. Contrary to popular opinion, Fleming himself often questions such attitudes and values, entertaining within his fiction an ambivalent lack of resolve over these issues. It is my contention that a more thorough investigation of the narrative fissures within Fleming's Jamaica-set works reveals Fleming's far more probing and less simply racialist views than has previously been considered. Matthew Parker, for one, places a great deal of emphasis on the fact that, in the novels and short stories, 'Fleming – and Bond – [look] down on pretty much *everyone* who [is] not British' and that they '[perceive] people of all colours in terms of negative stereotypes of race and nationality' (2014: 157, italics in original). While such traits are hardly laudable, Parker does stress the point that Fleming's prejudice is indiscriminate and that it is neither directed at nor centred on any one racial or cultural group, in particular. Parker doubles down on his argument, noting that the Bond texts actually make it quite clear on a number of occasions that 'when any characters in the novels mistreat a black person, they get their comeuppance' (158), a point which certainly complicates the perceived simplicity of Fleming's and the novels' racial politics. Fleming's reputation as a racist has become an enduring – if not central – component of his image within the British cultural imaginary, and one which has (not entirely fairly, in my estimation) become augmented by the very ambivalence to the issues of British-Jamaican racial politics with which he grapples in his writings. If critics insist on reading the character James Bond as Fleming himself (as some do), and if Fleming's reputation as a racist is contingent upon the attitudes and values espoused by his central character, then it does not follow that Fleming himself is to be read simply as a racist, given that Bond is also shown to embody complex and ambivalent attitudes towards other races and cultures. The false equivalences drawn between the character Bond and the author Fleming are useful to contemporary readers in so far as these equivalences (i.e. Fleming is probably a racist because Bond exhibits some questionable attitudes towards race, or vice versa) maintain something of a structural distance between modern-day readings of these texts and the historical period in which Fleming was writing. In other words, such equivalences afford the modern reader licence to appreciate and even enjoy the anachronistic world view of James Bond whilst simultaneously assuaging any potential discomforts by reinforcing the notion that Fleming's ambivalence around issues of race and British-Jamaican race relations is necessarily a discomfiting thing of the past. That Fleming's ambivalence towards issues of British-Jamaican racial, cultural and political relations has been misconstrued as racism in toto is troubling precisely because it suggests that the modern reader is uncomfortable with her/his own unresolved ambivalence over issues of race – or, at the very least, uncomfortable with the idea that one might, in the specific historical context of mid-twentieth-century Britain, entertain political ambivalence towards such issues. It is, potentially, easier to dismiss Fleming as a racist and to think of Fleming's racism (as well as racism more generally) as a thing of the past than it is to engage with the less than palatable notion that such attitudes were indeed commonplace within British culture during the period. The false equivalence that is often made between Ian Fleming and his creation James Bond, then, is part of Britain's cultural and national enterprise in managing racial guilt: it is somewhat more comfortable, it seems, to dismiss as racist Bond's creator than it is to consider the implications of racial ambivalence within the Bond icon. Thus, while *Live and Let Die* is characterized by political conflict certainly configured through race, I do not concede to Margaret Marshment's view that the *entire* 'moral universe of the [novel] is defined clearly in terms of black and white' (1978: 335). There are actually few moral absolutes within the Bond universe, and this view all but erases the deliberate and pervasive politics of ambivalence at play within Fleming's writings.

It is worth noting that, though Jeremy Black considers Fleming's approach to ethnicity in *Live and Let Die* a product of Black–white racial tensions in Cardiff, Wales, during the mid-twentieth century (2005: 12), Vivian Halloran observes that Fleming actually shies away from presenting within his entire canon of James Bond stories any Black–white racial conflict *within* Britain itself (2005: 161). Given that the Windrush generation had been settling in Britain for up to ten years before he started writing *Live and Let Die*, that Fleming should elect not to portray Britain's internal racial conflicts between white Britons and Black Caribbean migrants is an important point. That is to say, while Fleming never presents the effects of racial *tensions* in Britain, he also elides any mention of the effects of racial *integration* in the post-Windrush period. These omissions are noticeable, particularly when considered in context and alongside Fleming's popular reputation as a racist. His decision to situate Black–white racial tensions within *Live and Let Die* not in Britain but in North America suggests a resurgent imperializing narrative of colonial management (which largely defined Britain's relationship to its colonies, including America itself, for much of the period of empire) that has been transposed anachronistically onto contemporary Anglo-American geopolitics. In an era of Britain's declining global influence, during which the United States was economically ascendant, Bond's management of America's 'racial problem' suggests that it was much easier for Fleming to write in this context than it was to contend with the relatively newer profile of Britain's fledgling multicultural ethnoscape. That Fleming chose not to contend with Britain's internal racial politics within his writings further suggests that such issues were, even for Fleming, too close to home to engage with – which is, really, an implicit denial of, or simple disregard for, the changing ethnic landscape of modern Britain. Fleming's treatment of race and racial issues are very much consigned to the margins of Britain's empire (and Bond's world); much like Bond's admission in *Moonraker*, for Fleming, too, it seems that 'abroad was what mattered' (Fleming [1955] 2012c: 44). As such, America's 'racial problems' in *Live and Let Die* are presented as separate and distinct from the burgeoning multiculturalism of mid-twentieth-century Britain, to which Fleming makes almost entirely no allusion.

Blurred lines: James Bond's imagined identities

Perhaps more than any other of his novels, *Live and Let Die* demonstrates Fleming's complex politics of desire with respect to race and to African-American culture, more specifically. Nowhere is this more noticeable than in the Harlem scenes of the first third of the book. Having been assigned to the United States by M to investigate suspected Soviet financing of American underworld activity by treasure stolen from the Jamaican hoard of pirate Henry Morgan, Bond and his counterpart in the CIA, Felix Leiter, arrive in Harlem to investigate 'The Boneyard', one of the nightclubs owned by Mr Big, the Haitian-born communist agent with ties to Soviet counter-intelligence agency SMERSH. Fleming's appraisal of Harlem's nightlife in these scenes is replete with contradictory images of Black culture, which is presented in the text as a source of both fearful regard and, largely, as something desirously fascinating, as Fleming's initial inclinations towards trite racial cliché gives way to a more nuanced representational politics. Certainly, we may note with discomfort Fleming's undeniable inclination towards casual racism: Bond's inability to discern between individuals ('the lighting made it impossible to distinguish features unless they were only a few feet away' (Fleming [1954] 2012b: 67)) suggests, troublingly, that the inhabitants of the club are to be viewed as one amorphous body or as a homogenized people. The analogy made between the Black profile and a 'drowned corpse' (68) explicitly aligns Blackness with death and deathliness, a point which, I contend, takes on further significance through the myth of the undead Voodoo Baron Samedi, which I will address below. And the reference to El Greco ('the whole scene was macabre and livid, as if El Greco had done a painting by moonlight of an exhumed graveyard in a burning town' (ibid.)) seemingly reinforces images of racial disfigurement through its implicit contrast in light- and dark-coloured skin tones. Moreover, Fleming's choice use of simile and metaphor throughout this scene suggests a rhetorical palette limited in its consideration of African-American culture. The phrase 'packed in like black olives in a jar' (ibid.) suggests compression and, again, homogenization; the word 'feral' (ibid.) – always an uncomfortable racial epithet – suggests a certain animalism which chimes with Bond's later appraisal of Big's henchmen as 'clumsy black apes' (ibid.: 83), while the 'jabber' (ibid.: 68) of noise throughout the scene implies a speech pattern that is nonsensical and incomprehensible.

However, it must be said that the most pernicious considerations of Black culture in these scenes come not from Bond but from Leiter. Whereas Bond is cautiously circumspect in his approach to Harlem's Black community, Leiter, a white American in Fleming's books, curiously fashions himself as an authority on Black culture – what Gerald Early calls a 'negrophile' (1999: 153). Leiter tells Bond, 'Fortunately ... I like the negroes and they know it somehow. I used to be a bit of an aficionado of Harlem' (Fleming [1954] 2012b: 50–1). Leiter's condescension, here, smacks of the misguided assumption that his patronage of Harlem's Black community is welcomed and appreciated; his 'expertise' on Harlem really only extends as far as Dixieland jazz music, a topic on which he has published and which – he claims absurdly – licenses his affiliation with the Black community. Leiter's expertize on Harlem is analogous to Fleming's expertise on Jamaica: the authority of each is drawn largely from what *they have said about* these cultures, respectively (i.e. Leiter's publications on Dixieland jazz and Fleming's own writings). Leiter's seemingly cheery regard for Black culture belies a barely suppressed racial prejudice that is a good deal more pronounced than Bond's. Leiter notes that Harlem is a 'jungle' (ibid.: 50), a term which is recalled in Bond's use of the word 'feral' and which further implies an animalistic vision of the Black community. Leiter also considers Harlem the 'capital of the negro world', a place with 'plenty of stinkeroos' (ibid.: 51). He also notes of an African-American couple he overhears in Sugar Ray's (one of the bars he and Bond patronize in their search for Mr Big) that 'they're straight out of "Nigger Heaven"' (ibid.: 56). Here, Fleming is drawing on the controversial title of Carl Van Vechten's 1926 novel, a work that has become an informal (and much maligned) literary guide to Harlem and the Harlem Renaissance. While the term 'Nigger Heaven' refers historically to the church balconies which segregated members of different racial communities from one another in the nineteenth century, subsequent critical discussion of the novel has focused on the ambivalence of Van Vechten's choice of title. As a white man, Van Vechten's use of the pejorative term 'Nigger' was seen as offensive and deliberately inflammatory. The novel itself, though, is actually a passionate and reverent celebration of

Black culture that seeks to dispel disparaging imagery of Harlem: its world is populated by middle-class, intellectual, ambitious, politically motivated and aspiring African Americans who contest racial segregation and race-based violence. Thus, while the novel was intended as a celebration of Black culture, the title itself introduces to the politics of Van Vechten's writings a complex – and unresolved – ambivalence (Sanneh 2014: n.p.). Fleming's incorporation of Van Vechten's novel (both are white men writing about Black culture in Harlem) poses some intriguing interpretive possibilities for his own treatment of race and racial issues within *Live and Let Die*.

It is not insignificant that Fleming chooses to place the novel's most objectionable statements concerning race in the mouth of the American agent, the effect of which is to somewhat inoculate Bond from such controversy by insisting that the novel's racial problems are America's rather than Britain's.[1] It should be noted that Bond does not actually share in Leiter's derision of the young couple in Sugar Ray's, and that the positive adjectives which Fleming uses to describe them underline his appreciation for African-American aesthetics and style: the man is 'handsome', 'expensive' and 'languid'; the woman is 'sexy', 'sensual' and 'sweet' (Fleming [1954] 2012b: 56–7). Fleming's fascination with (and evident delight in) African-American culture pervades the scene, often to the point of narrative superfluity. Indeed, Andrew Taylor has noted:

> Fleming devotes three pages to describing the couple's appearance and their conversation ... The episode has no relevance whatsoever to the story. The recording of the speech patterns [of the couple] and the attempt to render the sound of the conversation phonetically have a bizarrely sociological quality to them. Fleming included the passage in the book solely because it interested him. (2012: xiv–xv)

The couple's conversation, which Fleming relays phonetically, is neither sensationalist nor extraordinary; it is a simple but passionate exchange between two lovers about the nature of jealousy. Of the couple, Bond notes with admiration to Leiter that 'they're interested in much the same things as everyone else – sex, having fun, keeping up with the Jones's'; and on the topic of the couple's sexuality Bond is most ebullient: 'Thank God they're not genteel about it' (Fleming 2012b: 59). Here, Fleming's regard for the pleasures of sex comes through. Fleming himself was a sensualist, an advocate of sexual reform in Britain, and a staunch critic of Victorian sexual mores, which he believed hampered Britons' natural lustful instincts. Monica Germaná has argued that Bond's appraisal of this couple overtly racializes them and that it 'fetishize[s] certain physical qualities'

(2019: 78). Actually, African-American sexuality is not orientalized, here, but celebrated for its frankness, its lack of shame and for its contrast to conservative British tastes; Bond's unrestrained appreciation of the couple's sexual languor evidences Fleming's own desire which is, here, unhindered by the politics of race.

So too with the scene in The Boneyard nightclub where Bond watches the floor show by the exotic dancer G. G. Sumatra. When Sumatra begins her striptease, Bond is transfixed by her 'small, hard, bronze, beautiful' body and by the 'shuddering jerks' her body gives in response to the rhythm of the bass drum, which 'kept its beat dead on the timing of the human pulse' (Fleming [1954] 2012b: 71–2). In turn, Bond's own body responds to this erotic stimuli: 'He felt his own hands gripping the tablecloth. His mouth was dry' (72). While the politics of desire and the politics of race may be said to intersect in this scene, they are not necessarily entwined; as Germaná notes, 'the racial politics of [this scene] are not so clear-cut' (2019: 81). It is clear that Sumatra's body-performance is not bound to the imperializing gaze of the white interloper: her performance is not, in narrative terms, a strictly orientalized one, and nor does she dance for Bond's pleasure. Rather, her body becomes the site for the cultural expression of a shared African-American sexuality that excludes Bond. As she gyrates, shudders and spasms her way through the dance, accompanied by the 'hurricane of sexual rhythm' on the drums (Fleming [1954] 2012b: 72), Sumatra's audience are coaxed from silence and 'quiet growls' to 'panting and grunting' and the 'delighted howls' of a simulated orgy. As the dance reaches its climax, Fleming notes that 'the audience began to shout at her: "Cmon, G-G. Take it away, Baby. Cmon. Grind Baby, grind"', (ibid.) an invocation which unifies the experiential pleasures of both dancer and audience – and which, more significantly, implicitly undermines Bond's (and the reader's) totalizing imperial gaze. Like an earlier scene in the nightclub, where Bond observes that, before Sumatra's appearance, 'from time to time a man or girl would erupt on to the dance floor and start a wild solo jive', and where 'there would be a burst of catcalls and whistles [and] cries of "Strip, strip, strip," "Get hot, baby!" [and] "Shake it, shake it"', (ibid.: 68). African-American sexuality is presented as a spontaneous and collective cultural experience, and not as a racialized performance for the benefit of the white observer. Paul Anthony and Jacqueline Friedman have argued that Sumatra 'endanger[s] James Bond by her dancing because it is performed in service of her Negro master' (1965: 105), but this is not quite right. The scene suggests that Sumatra's body is neither in the throes of Voodoo possession nor possessed by Bond's imperializing gaze; she shows no awareness of Bond at all, or any particular care for his personal stimulation.

In actuality, the scene resists readings of the Black female body as penetratively colonized by the imperial male gaze; as Germaná notes, 'such manipulation of the male/colonial gaze' that takes place in this scene undermines 'the power dynamics traditionally associated with patriarchy/colonialism' (2019: 83). In this scene, Fleming presents Black female sexuality as a culturally empowering, collective experience over which Sumatra herself presides; for it is Sumatra who dictates the terms of her striptease's concluding reveal, the removal of her final garment of clothing. As she stipulates, she will only complete the final reveal 'with da lights out' (Fleming [1954] 2012b: 73). Of course, the switching off of the club's lights is the ruse by which Bond and Leiter are captured, as, in the darkness, the table at which they are seated descends through a trapdoor in the floor into the underground vaults below, where they are met by Mr Big's henchmen. Nevertheless, Sumatra's stipulation further reinforces Fleming's ambivalent racial politics: in refusing to remove her underwear in anything but darkness, Bond and the reader are denied the visual pleasure of the totalizing imperial gaze, the sight of her body rendered entirely naked. Fleming makes it clear in this narrative sequence that Sumatra's body is not for Bond's eyes only; rather, her body is part of the shared sexual economy of the African-American cultural experience presented in this scene, which necessarily excludes (or is not simply written for) the orientalizing gaze of Bond (and the reader). Indeed, this is underlined by the fact that, at the dance's climax, the anticipated moment of erotic jouissance is deferred: the final reveal for the reader is not the desirously bared female body but the menace of the multiple Black bodies who receive Bond and Leiter below the trapdoor.

Bruce A. Rosenberg and Ann Harlemann Stewart have argued that Fleming's 'racial others are, for the most part, not objects of envy' (1989: 120). However, it is clear from the above scene that Fleming does indeed envy the expression of African-American sexuality. As Parker notes, 'Bond admires these characters' lack of hypocrisy' when it comes to matters of sex (2014: 159), which Fleming sees as a major deficit in the British national character. Bond is shown to enjoy the 'spontaneity, the physicality and what he would see as the sexy exoticism' of the performance, which Fleming himself holds in high regard (ibid.). Parker's comment – that '[Bond's] affection [for African Americans] is genuine, then, but based on what we would now see as racist clichés' (ibid.) – is, perhaps, one of the most significant observations to be made about Fleming's writings. There is, in fact, a much more nuanced and complex representational politics of race at work, here, and Fleming's writings must be read more closely against the fluid politics of ambivalence at play within them. Martha Mary Daas, for one, is clear in her defence of Fleming's use of African-American cultural rhetoric: she notes that, in *Live and Let Die*,

> the worlds of Harlem and Jamaica are foreign to Bond and his CIA counterpart Felix Leiter, but they are never demeaned. To the modern reader, Fleming's use of dialects for people from Harlem and Jamaica may be perceived as less than satisfactory. However, this can be attributed to the time period in which the book was written rather than to a racist attitude on Fleming's part.[2] (2011: 165)

O. F. Snelling is also convinced that Fleming's 'handling of urban negro dialect is … completely convincing' (1964: 120).[3] With respect to Harlem in particular, Daas notes that Bond shows a 'certain amount of respect and also trepidation … He knows he doesn't belong, so his attitude is one of careful observation' (2011: 167). This is very clear from the text, when, walking down Harlem's Seventh Avenue, Bond observes that he and Leiter 'were trespassing. They just weren't wanted' and that he 'felt the uneasiness that he had known so well during the war, when he had been working for a time behind the enemy lines' (Fleming [1954] 2012b: 60). Rather than dismissing it derogatorily, Fleming makes clear to stress Bond's healthy appreciation of and respect for Harlem's African-American culture. As Umberto Eco observes, 'Fleming is profuse in his acknowledgement of the new African races and of their contribution to contemporary civilisation' ([1965] 1966: 59). Anthony and Friedman are much more critical of what they perceive as Fleming's concessionary approach to Black culture, asking, 'When has Fleming ever gone so far to appease any other race?' (1965: 105). However, Gerald Early, a vehement critic of Fleming's (and an African American), does note that Fleming, for his frequently brash offensiveness, is just as likely to be accused of racism towards non-African-American characters as he is towards African-American characters, specifically (1999: 154).

The critical ambivalence towards Fleming's work with respect to issues of race, then, suggests that Fleming's racial politics are open to doubt. This point is given further credence when we explore the complex blurring of racial identities with which Fleming experiments in the novel: more specifically, the play on Bond's own imagined racialized position. Throughout the narrative of *Live and Let Die*, Fleming can be said to negotiate the politics of Bond's whiteness through a particular alignment that is made between Bond and the African-American community. This alignment is predicated on the visual economy of surveillance: that is, on the threat of being seen or observed. For Mr Big's enterprise in Harlem, surveillance culture, manifested through the literal policing of his business by Bond and the CIA, represents a threat to his operations and to his livelihood. For Bond, being seen for who he really is (in other words, being unmasked as a spy) carries the very real possibility of death at the hands of Mr Big's criminal network. For both Mr Big and Bond, then, the threat of being observed or looked at by the other becomes grounds for an intricate form of identification, a form of mutual recognition and sympathy with one another which Fleming affects through Bond's complex (and, again, imagined) assimilation of African-American racial identity. When, at the beginning of the novel, Bond arrives at Idlewild Airport (now John F. Kennedy International Airport), he muses on the diplomatic processes put in place by the United States' health, immigration and customs services for ushering agents of allied intelligence services through airport security. Here, Fleming recounts in brief the machinery at work within the diplomatic service to ensure Bond's expedient transition, noting the 'hasty traffic' that would be taking place on the communication networks between the Federal Bureau of Investigation (FBI) and the CIA to clear his passport (Fleming [1954] 2012b: 2). However, Bond also acknowledges discomfort at the thought of his information being accessed by American government agents:

> He disliked the idea of his dossier being in the possession of any foreign power. Anonymity was the chief tool of his trade. Every thread of his real identity that went on record in any file diminished his value and, ultimately, was a threat to his life. Here in America, where they knew all about him, *he felt like a negro whose shadow has been stolen by the witch-doctor*. A vital part of himself was in pawn, in the hands of others. Friends, of course, in this instance, but still ... (ibid.: 2–3, my italics)

Here, Fleming achieves a number of things. Firstly, the elliptical end to the final sentence does much to convey the implied distrust of American authorities which Fleming's works decidedly cultivate. By explicitly naming as 'friends' Bond's ostensible American allies, and by seeming to casually dismiss the prospective threat of the United States' potential misuse of Bond's personal information, Fleming succeeds in insinuating from the beginning of the novel the fraught nature of contemporary Anglo-American geopolitics. The implication, here, is that it is in Britain's political interest to appear to curry close relations with the economically ascendant United States.

Of far greater significance, though, is the simile which Fleming uses to convey the relative lack of anonymity Bond feels on US soil: Fleming tells the reader that Bond felt 'like a negro whose shadow has been stolen by the witch-doctor'. Here, Fleming explicitly links Bond's fears of maintaining an effective cover within the United States to the plight of the 'negro' upon whom some black magic or Voodoo has been performed. While the reference to black magic and to the figure of the witch doctor can be said to effectively foreshadow *Live and Let Die*'s major leitmotif (the occult Voodoo which Mr Big employs in the guise of the Baron Samedi to maintain his subjects' fearful loyalty), the analogy is also a much more purposeful one. The grounds for this particular racial comparison – while undoubtedly questionable – speak to issues of cultural marginalization in the United States. In this imagined assumption of a Black racial identity, through this particular analogy, Fleming positions Bond in sympathetic alignment with the African-American community; this alignment functions in terms of the novel's geopolitics to orientate the reader's perspective and to signal the configuration between Bond and African-American culture. The reference to Voodoo, here, further emphasizes a sense of marginalization, as the narrative 'invokes a Caribbean, rather than an American, context for Bond's self identification as a "negro"' (Halloran 2005: 164). In other words, the concept of 'Blackness' is itself considered from a marginalized perspective. Bond's imagined assumption of a Black racial identity in a *Caribbean* rather than a *North American* context suggests that Bond's is not a simple 'declaration of *a* black identity' (ibid., my italics) within North American culture, but one that is more nuanced and attuned to racial and cultural diversity. Fleming's conceptual alignment of Bond with African-American culture in this moment, then, is not appropriative but sympathetic, not invidious but relational. As Halloran notes, 'Bond does not feel envy but rather sympathy' with African-American culture within the novel (ibid.). Lisa M. Dresner has argued that the frogman's suit which Bond later dons in his underwater swim from Beau Desert to the Isle of Surprise – which he refers to as his 'black skin' – represents Fleming's 'fear of racial fluidity' (2011: 284). However, I suggest that Dresner has, in her reading, overlooked the contextual usage of this term within Fleming's overarching narrative commentary, particularly during the airport scene in which the character imagines himself to be 'like a negro'. Fleming uses the term 'the debris of his black skin' precisely twice in the novel, both times in the chapter 'Bloody Morgan's Cave', and both times to describe Bond himself (Fleming [1954] 2012b: 267, 271). The term 'debris' is, in these instances, not derogative but descriptive: Big's associates have cut Bond out of his black wet suit, which now lies in sliced tatters around his feet. In this context, the forced removal of his 'black skin' suggests not Bond's fear of inhabiting such an identity but an end to the period of imagined racial liminality in which he can successfully 'negotiate the blurry space of the American colour line', which he has occupied for most of the novel (Halloran 2005: 165). In *Live and Let Die*, Fleming cultivates not a fear of racial fluidity as much as he offers a contemplation of Bond's potential to pass as mixed race: the narrator notes, for instance, that the frogman's suit 'fitted [him] like a glove' (Fleming [1954] 2012b: 242), suggesting within this narrative's metaphoric economy that such an imagined racial identity is not as unimaginable to Bond (indeed, to Fleming) as we might otherwise think. Gazing into a hotel mirror at an earlier point in the novel, Bond reflects on his own physical features and on his capacity to blend in within/amongst hybrid America: 'Nothing could be done about the thin vertical scar down his right cheek, although the FBI has experimented with Cover-Mark, or about the coldness and hint of anger in his grey-blue eyes, but there was the *mixed blood* of America in the black hair and high cheekbones and Bond thought he might get by' (30–1, my italics). Thus, it is not simply the case that Bond and Big are presented as racially diametric to one another: in the imagined racial economy of Fleming's text, and through Bond's imagined (albeit problematic) assimilation of a Black racial identity, both Bond and Big are, together, presented in some ways as mixed race.

Moreover, the narrative cements a kind of mutual recognition between Bond and Big that is predicated on race. No sooner has Bond arrived at his hotel in downtown New York than Mr Big makes his first appearance. Standing outside the hotel unloading his luggage,

> Bond looked past [Halloran, his American escort from the Department of Justice] across 55th Street. His eyes narrowed. A black sedan, a Chevrolet, was pulling sharply out into the thick traffic … and through the rear window he had caught a glimpse of the single passenger – a huge grey-black face which had turned slowly towards him and looked directly back at him, Bond was sure of it … the giant shape in the back seat? That grey-black face? Mister Big? (Fleming [1954] 2012b: 7–8)

There are a number of points of note in this scene, the most important of which, perhaps, is not what is said, here, exactly, but rather where this scene sits within the narrative chronology. This scene appears midway through the novel's first chapter; it is not until chapter two, which features in retrospection Bond's mission briefing from M, that the reader understands the context for the above exchange. In other words, the narrative is presented out of sequence: chapter one commences in medias res with Bond's arrival to New York, while, in chapter two, the narrative performs an analeptic shift, taking the reader 'back two weeks to the bitter raw day' Bond first receives his mission (ibid.: 12). The effect of this achronological arrangement is to limit the reader's understanding of the significant exchange between Bond and the passenger in the back seat of the sedan. Had the novel opened with the scene of M's briefing, then the significance of Bond's observations on the mysterious passenger would resonate with the reader; however, as it is, the reader is left somewhat in the dark, at first, about the passenger's identity. It is clear from this sequence that Bond is meant to already know who Mr Big is, but that the reader is not. This brief moment of recognition between the two characters, from which the reader is partially excluded, underlines the point that both Bond and Mr Big are equally knowable to one another and that one can recognize the other (or make a guess as to the other's identity) merely by *looking* at them. Their act of mutual recognition further reinforces the threat of surveillance by and through which both men are partially bound together. Mr Big foolishly exposes himself by coming out of hiding and performing in front of Bond and the American authorities an audacious reconnaissance of his opposite number; Bond, in his small but nevertheless conspicuous diplomatic cavalcade from the airport, marks himself as someone of significance brought in under the auspices of the US government. Both men's covers last but a handful of pages. Ironically, in this moment, Bond's paranoia about his anonymity while on the United States' territory is proven to be well judged, for in arranging so official an escort for him, the American agent inadvertently exposes Bond and puts him at risk by identifying him in front of Mr Big. It is not made clear at first how Big knows of Bond's imminent arrival, but the exchange of knowingness which occurs between the two characters in this scene is implicitly couched in the politics of race. In his discomfort at being in the United States, and in his jealous concern for personal anonymity within that cultural context, Bond has already acknowledged that '[here] in America ... he felt like a negro' (ibid.: 2). In his use of simile, Fleming draws a particular equivalence between the ever-present threat of racial violence towards African Americans by white Americans and the deathly consequences of Bond being *seen* by Mr Big and his associates – not as the white American businessman he purports to be, but as the white British spy he is. In this context, Bond assimilates a shared African-American experience: fear of visibility within a culture of (white) hyper-surveillance. But by framing Bond's fear of US culture specifically in racial terms (he is 'like a negro'), the novel succeeds (questionably, for sure) in displacing narratives of Black disempowerment onto Bond himself. Both Bond and Mr Big share a desire for anonymity (to avoid being surveilled). But whereas Bond's desire for anonymity is characterized by fearful self-preservation within the political context of Harlem's charged racial ethnoscape, Big's is characterized by a flagrant disregard for the apparatuses of white authority – hence the ostentation of his first appearance to Bond in the sedan, which can be said to have purposefully attracted Bond's attention rather than dissimulating Big's presence. Like 'one of those great Egyptian fresco painters who devoted their lives to producing masterpieces in the tombs of kings', Big attempts to fashion for himself a vacuum where 'no living eye would ever see [him]' (ibid.: 94), but from whence he may retain what Joyce Goggin refers to as a 'panoptic all-knowingness' (2018: 148). It is no coincidence that Big's expansive network of spies dotted throughout the United States is known as 'The Eyes', an epithet which emphasizes ocular surveillance and which underlines the text's motifs of visuality and racial (in)visibility. As Solitaire later remarks to Bond, '[Big's] got a whole team of spies called "The Eyes" and when they're put out on the job it's almost impossible to get by them' (Fleming [1954] 2012b: 133). In other words, Bond simply cannot avoid being seen. In the charged racial context of mid-twentieth-century New York, Bond is hyper-visible – a point which the text is at pains to stress in the character's imagined assimilation of a Black racial identity. That Bond should feel 'like a negro' within an American context suggests that the economics of racial surveillance within the text have been somewhat upended. Instead of the white imperial British agent asserting mastery over the Black body (see, again, G. G. Sumatra's resistance to and total lack of awareness of Bond's imperializing gaze), it is the 'all-knowingness' of Mr Big's surveillance enterprise which maintains visual supremacy of and mastery over Bond throughout the narrative, as Bond is caught within the 'immense and utterly ubiquitous network of faceless black service industry workers throughout the USA' (Goggin 2018: 149), all of whom report back to Big. Thus, the novel actively subverts narratives of racial surveillance and policing. Big, the Black criminal, is configured in terms of his power of visual mastery (as one who can *see*), while Bond, the white spy who engages in a complex, imaginary process of African-American racial assimilation – he thinks of himself as being 'like a negro' in this context – is configured in terms of his powerlessness to that mastery (as one who is *seen*). Thus, Fleming can be said to engage in *Live and Let Die* a much more complex discourse surrounding race, power and surveillance than has previously been considered, one that is predicated on a shared, mutual desire between the white British Bond and the Black criminal Mr Big to avoid being seen or surveilled, and one which knowingly subverts traditional racial and visual paradigms.

Black power, resurrection and the figure of the zombie

Fleming's ambivalent politics with regards to issues of race coalesce much more clearly (and in far more interesting ways) in his presentation of Mr Big.[4] As with most aspects of *Live and Let Die*, critical opinion on Fleming's portrayal of Mr Big is also divided. Margaret Marshment, for one, considers Fleming's presentation of Big to be both suprahuman and subhuman at the same time: on the one hand, she argues, Big possesses 'the cunning of the devil'; on the other hand, he possesses 'the primitive violence of an animal' (1978: 336). Jeremy Black further contends that Fleming's portrayal of Big as 'an intimidatingly large Negro' focuses certain North American anxieties concerning the animalism of the powerful Black body, a fear which is as much geopolitical as it is racial (2005: 11). The novel configures the British Bond as being more ably positioned than his American counterparts in the CIA to manage and control America's racial anxieties by subduing the threat of the villainous Black body. Big's moniker is also suggestive of the extent to which the geopolitically weakened Britain, in the form of Bond, is punching above its weight in terms of its management of America's racial issues. Black argues that the novel authorizes a particular 'ethnicity of crime' which aligns the African-American male with criminality and which suggests that this figure poses a threat to the wealth economy of New York ex Harlem; Black also argues that this is part of Fleming's 'inherited racialist prejudices of [the] London clubland' (ibid.).

Fleming's portrayal of Mr Big, then, presents to certain critics a complex and negotiable racial politics which comes up against the enduring view of Fleming within the cultural imagination. Rather than a creation of out-and-out racism, it can be said that Mr Big evidences Fleming's ambivalent racial politics and his concession to the shifting geopolitics of an increasingly multicultural Anglo-American body politic. Raymond Benson, for one, has noted Fleming's ambivalent portrayal of African-American culture, generally, and Mr Big, more specifically. While he acknowledges that the representation of the African-American gangsters in *Live and Let Die* is replete with stereotypes – 'their speech is overwritten, with exaggerated colloquialism, and none of the minor characters seem very bright' – he also recognizes that Mr Big himself is 'quite brilliant', a 'meticulous' man who 'knows exactly what he wants' (Benson 1984: 97). Benson asserts that, in his choice of a mixed-race Black man for the novel's central villain, it is not necessarily the case that Fleming intended to disparage the African race. Gerald Early concurs, noting that, within Fleming's literary ethnoscape, 'the creation of a black criminal might be seen ... as something of an anti-racist stroke' (1999: 153). Early implies, here, that for Fleming to discount from his rogue's gallery a mixed-race Black villain would, in itself, amount to racism, given that, across the Bond canon, Fleming's villains all tend to be foreigners of racially ambiguous origins. Mr Big is no exception in this regard, and nor is he presented as any less successful in his criminal enterprises than his counterparts in Fleming's other novels. Indeed, Early proffers that Mr Big is 'the first great megalomaniac Negro character of English-language literature,[5] and that, however dubious, the character is representative of 'the progress of his race' which is 'throwing up geniuses left and right' (ibid.). Moreover, Early argues that the repeated emphasis which Fleming places upon the size of Mr Big's head – 'it was a great football of a head, twice the normal size and very nearly round' (Fleming [1954] 2012b: 78) – and on the character's fierce intellect – 'plenty of brains and ability and guts' (ibid.: 22) – 'works against the standard racist interpretation of the character' (Early 1999: 157).

However, it should be noted that, while Mr Big's race is almost always considered within traditional criticism as a correlative to his villainy, far more important within Fleming's geopolitical imagination is Big's connection to Soviet Russia, and his political leanings. As Lars Ole Sauerberg points out, it is Mr Big's connection to the Soviet Union – and not his racial identity – that precipitates Britain's involvement in the narrative (1984: 163). Similarly, Martha Mary Daas notes, 'although American, Mr. Big was trained in Russia, and his association with SMERSH proves that his loyalties do not lie with his country, which is anathema to James Bond' (2011: 166). Thus, the issue of Mr Big's race (while nevertheless a political one in itself, and not entirely irrelevant to the concerns of the narrative) does not actually underpin the politics of Bond's enmity towards Big; it is not Big's racial make-up that Bond objects to but his profound lack of nationalism. *Live and Let Die* is not a narrative of racial essentialism as much as it is a narrative of political or ideological essentialism: Mr Big is objectionable to Bond (and to Britain) on the grounds of his politics rather than his race. As an ally of communist Russia, Big stands in contravention to the political system which Bond authorizes and protects: that is, democratic commercialism. That Big intends to use plundered British gold supplies recovered from Henry Morgan's pirate hoard in Jamaica to finance Soviet espionage activity in the United States suggests that Bond's involvement is an issue of (inter)national commerce. Britain's fearful jealousy for its own capital, as well as the threat which Mr Big's criminal enterprises pose to that capital, suggests that Big represents not the white man's fear of the Black man, but the white man's fear of the '*emergent* black man', the moneyed Black man whose finance will liberate him from the racial 'hegemony of white capitalism' (Marshment 1978: 336, italics in original).

Indeed, much of the language Fleming uses to describe Mr Big orients the reader's attention towards the (re)emergent power of the character. On the one hand, the narrative stresses the similarities between Big's appearance and that of 'a week-old corpse': his skin is described as 'grey-black' due to chronic heart disease; the hair on his skin has all fallen out (he has no eyebrows and no eyelashes, and a 'hairless crown'); and his forehead bulges protuberantly as though posthumously swollen (Fleming [1954] 2012b: 78–9). To all intents and purposes, Mr Big resembles death.[6] Conversely, the narrative also stresses Big's vivacity and his liveliness of character. His eyes, we are told, 'seemed to fire', an image which, in its focus on an elemental, life-sustaining force, suggests a passionately vital personage. The narrator further notes of Big's eyes that 'when they rested on something, they seemed to devour it, to encompass the whole of it' (79), a comment which, at once, calls to mind the white man's historic fears of being cannibalized (or devoured) by the Black man,[7] and which also connotes life and nourishment through its imagery of ingestion, consumption and sustenance. Finally, the reader is told that 'there were few wrinkles or creases on [Big's] face' and that his skin was 'taut and shining' – a comment which, in contrast to the narrative's death imagery, further underlines Big's youthful vigour (78–9). As such, in addition to his racial hybridity (his Afro-Caribbean and French origins) and his 'double identity', as both American crime lord Mr Big and Caribbean Voodoo spirit Baron Samedi (Dresner 2011: 272), Big is also configured within the narrative as a liminal entity poised in stasis between life and death, an entity for whom 'the barrier between life and death has been overcome' (Black 2005: 13; see also Eco 1979: 38). Mr Big's process of bodily revivification, then, is a never-ending one, a continual rebirthing. In this sense, Big represents not simply the white man's fear of the economically emergent Black man, as Marshment argues, but of a *literal* return (from death) or re-emergence into white political consciousness of a subjugated Black body politic. If, according to Early, Big is representative of 'the progress of his race' (that is, of mixed-race Caribbeans), then it can be argued, within the context of Fleming's ambivalent narrative, that Big's continuously deferred process of revivification is representative of the political struggles of Afro-Caribbean communities – both in the race economy of the United States and in the colonial economy of the Caribbean – for political autonomy. As the 'corpse' of Mr Big exists in a state of perpetual (that is, figurative) return to life, so might it be argued that the island colonies of the Caribbean long subjugated to British and French governance (such as Jamaica and Big's native Haiti) exist in a state of perpetual rebirthing or in a state of deferred independent self-governance. Like Big, whose body metaphorically resists its own deathliness, the cultural identities of Britain and France's Caribbean colonies occupy a state of 'living death' between political subjugation and national independence.

This metaphor is given all the more credence by the fact that Mr Big purports to be 'the Zombie or living corpse of Baron Samedi himself, the dreaded Prince of Darkness' (Fleming [1954] 2012b: 26).[8] As Solitaire tells Bond on their escape to Florida aboard the Silver Phantom train, zombies are 'animated corpses that have been made to rise from the dead and obey the commands of the person who controls them', and 'Baron Samedi is the most dreadful spirit in the whole of Voodooism ... the spirit of darkness and death' (135–6). Lola Young argues that the figure of the zombie is a 'useful metaphor for colonial exploitation' precisely because it manifests the practice of colonizer–colonized relationships (1986:74). Much like the zombie's relationship to its master, the peoples of colonized cultures are forcibly subjugated by, and often put to work for the benefit of, the colonizer. As Mimi Sheller notes, the figure of the zombie 'literally spells out the suppressed relation of European colonisers to indigenous others' (2003: 148). In Haitian cultural lore and within certain Caribbean religious beliefs more generally, the figure of the zombie is 'the ultimate sign of loss and dispossession' (Dayan 1998: 37). In Mr Big's native Haiti, as Joan Dayan observes, 'memories of [colonial] servitude are transposed into a new idiom [the popular figure of the zombie] that both reproduces and dismantles a twentieth-century history of forced labor and denigration' on the island (ibid.). That Mr Big *purports* to be the 'living corpse' of the fearful Voodoo Baron Samedi himself suggests, then, that Big represents within the political economy of Fleming's text a powerful contrapuntal resistance to narratives of colonial subjugation. Of course, Big is not really the revivified zombie of Baron Samedi (Bond discovers, later in the narrative, that the sounds of the Voodoo drums which Big uses to stoke the fearful superstitions of local Jamaicans are nothing but an audio recording played through large speakers). Rather, Big's appropriation of this guise, and his manipulation of his followers' superstitions through the use of *obeah* iconography, suggests that he is not restrained by or bound within the traditional 'suppressed relation of European colonisers to indigenous others' which Sheller points out. Moreover, Big can be said to subvert the usual practice of colonizer–colonized relationships precisely because, as his own supposed zombie, he is not subject to anyone's will but his own. Thus, we may read Mr Big not just as a symbol for the revivification of a Caribbean Black body politic, but as a potent symbol of Caribbean resistance to Britain's colonial economy. Bond's assessment of Big's operations in The Boneyard nightclub – 'it was a close-up of the raw material on which The Big Man worked, the clay in his hands. The evening was gradually putting flesh on the dossiers he had read in London and New York' (Fleming [1954] 2012b: 69) – further emphasizes the fact that Big is not simply the object upon which Bond's (or the narrative's) orientalist practice operates, but that he is himself a powerful creator ('The Big Man worked ... the clay in his hands').

Moreover, Bond's observation ('the evening was gradually putting flesh on the dossiers') underlines the point that the object of Big's 'artistry' is the Black body itself: like a potter gradually moulding his clay, Big can be said to 'put flesh' upon the revivified and politically reanimated Black Caribbean body.

Within the structural economy of the text, then, Mr Big is fundamental to the politics of ambivalence which underpins Fleming's writings. On the one hand, Big may be read traditionally, as yet another incarnation of Fleming's highly racialized villains; on the other hand, Big can be read as a symbol of contrapuntal resistance to such narratives. When Solitaire tells Bond that 'you can't kill him' (ibid.: 137), it may be argued that she is referring both to the fearful belief, on the level of narrative, that Big is a zombie (one who is, in folkloric terms, already dead) and, metaphorically, to the unabated political nationalism of the Caribbean body politic which has sustained itself in spite of the figurative cultural 'death' brought about by European occupation of the region. Fleming's vision of Mr Big, then, certainly illustrates a political ambivalence regarding the subjugated and racialized Black Caribbean body as vengefully and powerfully revivified.

Revivification and reparation: remythologizing Fleming's Jamaica

The motif of resurrection that underpins much of the narrative of *Live and Let Die*, and which is illustrated most clearly in Fleming's presentation of Mr Big, is also an essential structuring principle of the novel's topopolitics and of Fleming's representational discourse. Although Bond does not arrive at Jamaica until the final third of the novel, Fleming's ambivalent representation of spatial and racial otherness in the Harlem sequence, and in the character of Mr Big, in particular, largely preconditions the ambivalence of the novel's Jamaican topopolitics. Within the narrative, the figurative topography of Jamaica extends the novel's metaphor of revivification: as Bond moves from Florida to Jamaica, he can be seen to transition from a space of death to one of revivification. Florida (Bond's final stop in the United States before the narrative shifts to the Caribbean) is portrayed in much the same way as Mr Big; Fleming uses the same imagery of death. Like Big's appearance, Bond notes that there is a 'dead, spectral feeling to the landscape' of the Everglades; that it has a 'grey skeletal' and 'dried-up' quality to it; and that everything there is 'baked and desiccated with the heat'. He muses to himself that 'nothing could be living … except bats and scorpions, horned toads and black widow spiders' (Fleming [1954] 2012b: 152–3). It is also not insignificant that Solitaire is wearing a black hat and veil on the journey aboard the Silver Meteor train.[9] Though she is wearing these clothes to disguise her appearance and to avoid detection by any number of Mr Big's spies, that she purports to be a figure in mourning, specifically, only further underlines the connection to death between Mr Big (from whom she's been secreted away) and the Florida location (itself a landscape of death to which she has been escorted by Bond). Death imagery is pervasive in this sequence. Of St Petersburg, the port of operations for Mr Big's criminal enterprise, Bond quips that 'everybody's nearly dead … It's the Great American Graveyard', a place one goes to 'to get a few years' sunshine before [one] dies' (ibid.: 148). Felix Leiter, who meets Bond and Solitaire in St Petersburg, also notes that the 'place is full of undertakers' (ibid.: 169), emphasizing once again the deathliness of the landscape. When Bond encounters 'The Robber', who operates the Ouroboros Worm and Bait Shippers Inc., the shell company of Mr Big's smuggling enterprise, the narrator notes that he has a 'thin, hatchet face' and that his 'lips were thin too, and bloodless' (ibid.: 170).[10] Bloodless and carrion-like, The Robber's violent nature is physiognomically inscribed upon his features (his face resembles a deadly weapon, as it were); his wanton murder of an innocuous great pelican on the docks signals to the reader the deleterious relationship between human and environmental geographies within the text, as Mr Big's deathliness subsumes Florida's organic biota.[11] If Mr Big/Baron Samedi is the text's figurative Hades, a Voodoo iteration of the Greek mythological God of the Underworld, then The Robber, sitting at the edge of the docks, overlooking the waters of the Gulf of Mexico, is Charon the ferryman. As the front man for Big's smuggling operation, it is The Robber who navigates the *Secatur*, the boat upon which the smuggled gold is transported from Jamaica to the United States (disguised as cargoes of conch shells and tropical fish) before it is disseminated through Mr Big's network. Indeed, David Ormerod and David Ward identify a number of crossovers between *Live and Let Die* and classical mythology. The Ouroboros (after which Mr Big's shell company in St Petersburg is named) is the name of the great worm of ancient mythology. Ormerod and Ward note that, while there are many variants of this myth, 'the one that is alluded to here is that of the gigantic serpent who encircles the globe and holds the world together. If the serpent is cut, chaos and universal dissolution follow' (1965: 44). They also argue that Fleming's 'Harlem is an underworld, whose name stands in antithesis (happy – more light) to the terror and darkness which Harlem typifies', and that the connection between Fleming's novel and mythology is further reinforced in the naming of the nightclub 'The Boneyard', into which Bond and Leiter descend, 'a netherworld presided over by ... the Negro gangster who identifies himself with the Voodoo cult deity Baron Samedi, the lord of the dead' (ibid.).

In contrast to the imagery of death which characterizes those scenes set in Harlem and Florida, Fleming presents Jamaica as a site of resurrection, a place of respite and healing upon which Bond recovers and revives himself. As Bond flies out of Florida, the narrative emphasizes his movement away from the quiet decrepitude of America's 'acres of jungle and swamp without sign of human habitation' (Fleming [1954] 2012b: 211) and towards the sensuous clamour of the Caribbean. Upon his arrival to Jamaica, the reader is told that 'Bond gratefully drank in the sound and smells of the tropics' (215), a point which underlines the revitalizing and nourishing properties of the island to Bond's parched and faded spirit. Having done battle with the deathly machine of Mr Big's enterprise in the United States, Jamaica is configured as an elementary, life-giving force (he 'drank in' the island) that reawakens Bond's senses and figuratively revivifies him following his symbolic death and descent into the 'underworlds' of Harlem and Florida. Whereas both Mr Big and the dried-up landscape of the American south-east are described as 'spectral' and 'grey', to Bond's eyes the foothills of Jamaica's Blue Mountains are 'gleaming' in contrast (ibid.), and the cacophony of 'the shrill sound of crickets' in the roadside flora further contributes to Bond's (and the reader's) heightened multisensory impression of the island (ibid.: 214). In a few short sentences, Fleming gives us images of sound, smell, taste and sight; though undoubtedly orientalist in its descriptive economy, Fleming's literary Jamaica is a space that is portrayed, here, as vital, lively and sensuously rich. Note the detail with which Fleming infuses his description of Bond's first breakfast on the island: 'Paw-paw with a slice of green lime, a dish piled with red bananas, purple star-apples, and tangerines, scrambled eggs and bacon. Blue Mountain coffee – the most delicious in the world – Jamaican marmalade, almost black, and guava jelly' (ibid.: 224). As Sam Goodman notes, Fleming's literary spaces are 'primarily those of privilege and recreation', and, on Jamaica especially, 'Bond assimilates immediately into a culture of privilege and material comfort' (2016: 148).[12] Moreover, the island is shown to be a place for Bond's physical recuperation, and a place to which Bond is most certainly 'glad to be back and to have a whole week of respite before the grim work began again' (Fleming [1954] 2012b: 224–5). In one of Fleming's more tellingly ambivalent moments in the novel, Quarrel's treatment of Bond's bodily wounds – 'Quarrel produced an old medicine bottle and swabbed the bite with a brown liquid that smelled of creosite' (230; see also 233) – suggests something of a symbolic expiation or cleansing of Bond's colonial guilt. In submitting himself to Quarrel's tender care, the white imperial Britisher is shown to be (re)assured of his physical supremacy; but the mastery of his own body is secured, firstly, through Quarrel's medicinal care and, later, through the training routine Quarrel has devised for him. Martin Sterling and Gary Morecambe have argued that Mr Big represents the 'all-powerful father figure to Bond's helpless little boy' (2002: 39), but it is actually far more accurate to think of Quarrel as Bond's symbolic *paterfamilias*. Quarrel's tutelage of Bond can very much be read as a father taking his son's physical education in hand: under Quarrel's 'critical, appraising eyes' (Fleming [1954] 2012b: 233) Bond regains his bodily strength through various physical exertions (swimming, running, rowing, spear-fishing). After each day's workout, Quarrel massages Bond's body with palm oil and recounts to him his knowledge of the feeding habits and camouflage patterns of the local sea life. Indeed, Bond himself likens his week of training to 'paddling with his nanny beside him in the sunshine' (247), thus further underlining the analogy that Quarrel is his paternal protector and that he (Bond) is an infant in the process of maturation. By the end of the week's training, the narrator notes that 'Bond was sunburned and hard. He had cut his cigarettes down to ten a day and had not had a single drink. He could swim two miles without tiring, his hand was completely healed and all the scales of big city life had fallen from him' (235–6). Here, Bond's body has metamorphosed; his physical (re)development is complete. Like a (figurative) father who finds himself redundant as his son matures to adulthood, Quarrel can but watch in hope as Bond commences his underwater passage from Beau Desert to the Isle of Surprise.[13]

In contrast to the deathliness of Harlem and Florida, when Bond observes of Manatee Bay that 'there was no sign of life' (228), it is clear that this imperialist appraisal of the island's remoteness is 'illustrative of an establishment view of colonial space' (Goodman 2016: 149). This is not the same 'lifelessness' which Bond and Leiter observe of the 'Great American Graveyard' of St Petersburg, Florida; rather, Jamaica is portrayed, here, as a site of suspended animation, a place affected by the vicissitudes of neither life nor death. Indeed, the narrator notes that 'nothing has happened [there] since Columbus used Manatee Bay as a casual anchorage' and that 'Jamaican fishermen have taken the place of the Arawak Indians', all of which, to Bond's mind, gives 'the impression that time has stood still' there (Fleming [1954] 2012b: 229).[14] Whereas the landscape of southern Florida within the text can be seen to replicate (indeed, is metaphorically infected by) the decaying, grey deathliness of Mr Big, Jamaica's flora and biotic life remain seemingly uncontaminated from or free of symbolic decay, preserved in an originary or 'timeless' state. Goodman argues that the link made, here, to Columbus 'suggests Fleming's assessment of how Jamaica should remain: a colonial space ruled from afar, and subordinate to the Imperial centre' (2016: 149). Much of Jamaica's 'timelessness', I argue, is to be attributed to the moral economy of the narrative, and the ways in which landscape and environmental spaces are configured within the text as ideological psychogeographies. Consider, for instance, the metaphor Quarrel uses to conceptualize Bond's mission: he compares Bond to 'The Undertaker's Wind',[15] a colloquial name among local Jamaicans for one of the island's two prevalent winds. Quarrel notes that 'de Undertaker blow de bad air out of de Island night-times from six till six. Then every morning de "Doctor's Wind" come and blow the sweet air in from the de sea. … Guess you and de Undertaker's Wind got much de same job, Cap'n' (Fleming [1954] 2012b: 231). Here, Bond is configured as elemental (the wind), an environmental force whose presence not only sanctions and preserves Britain's colonial administration of the island but also cleanses and 'airs' Jamaica of its perceived malodours: that is, of the threatening influence of communism represented by Mr Big. The narrative thus endorses the view that Bond's (and Britain's) presence in Jamaica is not simply political but a matter of environmental determination. Within the framework of this environmental metaphor, Bond's presence is very much configured as a condition of the island's diurnal weather pattern. Whereas Florida's natural environment is shown to be determined by and symbolic of Mr Big's rotten, infecting presence, Jamaica is configured in the text as a space activated or revivified by the elemental Bond, whose presence can be said to metaphorically cleanse the island of Mr Big's putrefying essence. Indeed, Raymond Benson has noted that this environmental metaphor 'leads directly to Fleming's major theme, which fulfils the prediction Mathis made toward the end of *Casino Royale*: that Bond would surely seek out the bad men of the world and terminate their existence' (1984: 96). Furthermore, Bond's training off the coast of Beau Desert, and his tutelage at the hands of Quarrel, who is reputedly 'the best swimmer … in the Caribbean' (Fleming [1954] 2012b: 222), associates him still with yet another element: water. It is clear that Bond himself is also quite knowledgeable about the patterns of Jamaican sea life: in his interview with Strangways, Bond's Secret Service contact in Jamaica, he is shown to know enough about the feeding habits of shark and barracuda (220–1). Bond's mastery of the ocean (in his submerged passage from Beau Desert to the Isle of Surprise) as well as the narrative's figurative alignment of Bond and 'The Undertaker's Wind' suggest that, in environmental terms, Bond is an elementally greater force than Mr Big, who is, throughout the narrative, often associated with fire and fire imagery (78–9).[16]

However, in spite of the analogous environmental topography of Fleming's Jamaica, in which Britain's presence is seemingly made determinate by the narrative's alignment of James Bond and the elemental forces of nature, it is not simply the case, as Matthew Parker insists, that Fleming unquestioningly presents Jamaica as Bond's (and Britain's) tropical enclave (2014: 100). Rather, there is actually a good deal of implicit debate within the novel over Jamaican territory and the issue of rights of inheritance. On the level of bureaucracy, there are a number of exchanges between various national intelligence organizations concerning the precise jurisdictional nature of the Jamaican operation. As a colonial outcrop of Britain's (nevertheless fading) global empire, Jamaica comes under Bond's and Britain's jurisdiction; but given that Mr Big is using gold recovered from Morgan's treasure hoard in Jamaica to destabilize North American markets and to finance Soviet operations on US territory, Bond is also seconded to the US government for much of the mission. Within US intelligence, jurisdiction for the mission is further subdivided between the FBI and the CIA, the former of whom control the investigation on American soil, while the latter is concerned with the mission's overseas implications. Like Bond, Felix Leiter (who works for the CIA) is seconded to the FBI as a liaison of sorts between the various American organizations. Thus, from the off, there is much confusion as to the political responsibilities of the Jamaican case.[17] Beyond the question of official jurisdiction, though, *Live and Let Die* can be seen to negotiate a number of Fleming's fears concerning not only communist infiltration of Jamaica but also his increasing ambivalence over US interference on the island. In many ways, the novel stages a geopolitical battle between Britain, the United States and Russia for control of Jamaican territory. Indeed, much of the novel's action is set against the backdrop of Western '[fears] of communist infiltration in the Caribbean' (Parker 2014: 149), a landscape which is configured as a site of strategic geographic importance between the United States and Britain, potentially vulnerable to penetration by Russia. As such, Joyce Goggin misses the mark somewhat in her assessment of the novel: she notes that *Live and Let Die* focuses 'more concertedly on the internal conflict of the West, rather than embracing global struggles such as communism versus capitalism, or West versus East' (2018: 146). She adds, 'Instead of sketching out the customary geography of larger global conflicts and information wars between the Soviet Union and the free world, as is Fleming's usual practice, he focuses here on the internal politics of race and economy in the USA' (147). However, Fleming's focus on race and race politics in *Live and Let Die* is not, as Goggin attests, at the expense of global political conflicts; indeed, race is very much the vehicle through which the text's overarching concerns – the politics of democracy versus communism – are carried. Mr Big's villainy is more political than it is racial; as I have said, Fleming presents him as objectionable not on the grounds of race but on those of political ideology. Big is trained and employed by the Soviets; his race has nothing whatsoever to do with his particular politics. Parker argues that, with the more fantastical, orientalized aspects of the story stripped back, 'Bond's mission is to defeat a communist agent established in Jamaica' (2014: 149). That the communist threat operates out of Harlem and Florida rather than Russia, Parker adds, suggests that 'the greatest threat to [Fleming's] Jamaica was not the Soviet Union, but Uncle Sam' (ibid.). Mr Big is an *American* citizen, after all. *Live and Let Die*, then, might more accurately be thought of as an expression of Fleming's fears over modern American politics: as Parker notes, 'sometimes Fleming's anti-Americanism trumps even his anti-communism' (ibid.). We might also say that his anti-Americanism trumps his considerations of race, too.

Fleming's Jamaican psychogeography is presented as the site for a number of negotiable political issues over which Fleming himself entertained a great deal of ambivalence. Paul Anthony and Jacqueline Friedman have argued that 'because of its hostile marine life, Jamaica is often chosen as the setting for the showdown [between Bond and his opponent]' (1965: 111), a comment which, in its reductionism, overlooks the nuances of Fleming's Jamaican topopolitics. They are somewhat closer to the mark in noting that, 'in moving Mr. Big out of Harlem' – in other words, in relocating Bond's final encounter with Big to Jamaica – 'Fleming removes the justification which would belong to a Negro killing a white man there'. Were Bond to openly attack Big in Harlem, they suggest, 'we would have had a feeling that Mr. Big was merely defending his own territory' (ibid.). But this is not quite accurate, either; in relocating the action to the Isle of Surprise, a small island off the coast of the main island of Jamaica, Fleming engenders within the narrative a further topopolitical conflict. While Jamaica itself is part of the British Commonwealth, the Isle of Surprise is owned by 'an anonymous New York syndicate' who 'purchased the island for a thousand pounds from the present owner of the Llanrumney Estate' (Fleming [1954] 2012b: 217). It is strongly implied that the syndicate is a cover for Mr Big's organization, and that Big himself is the head of it. More significantly, this point undermines the credibility of Anthony and Friedman's argument, which asserts that 'James Bond has every right to try to defend this last bit of Empire' (1965: 111). The Isle of Surprise is an American-owned property; it is entirely

Mr Big's territory, over which the British cannot be said to have right of possession. Within the narrative, Harlem and the Isle of Surprise function as topopolitical correlatives to one another: through Mr Big's mastery and control, Black Harlem, islanded within the vast metropolis of white Manhattan, is made analogous to the Isle of Surprise in Jamaica. Whereas Jamaica is annexed to Britain as part of the Commonwealth, the Isle of Surprise is annexed to America through Big's commercial ownership. That Big has purchased the Isle of Surprise from 'the present owner of the Llanrumney estate' is also telling in terms of the text's ambivalence concerning the rights of political ownership and racial inheritance. Llanrumney, originally a suburban district of Cardiff in Wales, was also the name given to an area in the Saint Mary region of Jamaica, on the north of the island. Keith Phillip Jones has noted that 'the most well known of the Llanrumney Morgans was Sir Henry Morgan', who was born on the Llanrumney Estate in Wales and who was later made deputy governor of Jamaica, where he 'left one of his properties to his wife and named it Llanrumney' (2010: n.p.). Fleming, of course, was much intrigued by the romantic figure of Henry Morgan, and by the sunken treasure that was reputed to exist in the scuppered wreckage of Morgan's ship in Shark Bay, where the Isle of Surprise is situated. Through his mouthpiece, Strangways, Fleming recounts in brief Morgan's history on the island and the dubious privileges which were afforded the pirate by the British government. He notes that 'the Crown wished a blind eye to be turned on Morgan's piracy until the Spaniards had been cleared out of the Caribbean', and that, officially, 'his actions had to be disavowed to avoid a European war with Spain'. When he successfully cleared the region of Spanish forces, Morgan was given a knighthood and the governorship of Jamaica (Fleming [1954] 2012b: 216). Mr Big's purchase of the Isle of Surprise from the owner of the Llanrumney Estate is, on the level of narrative, ostensibly about positioning himself closer to Morgan's sunken treasure trove so as to carry out his operation – destabilizing the US financial economy and funding Soviet activity on American territory. On an ideological level, though, Big's appropriation of the Llanrumney property, and his redistribution of Morgan's salvaged treasure among America's Black communities, can be read as a complex facet of the novel's political ambivalence and resistance to more traditional (and far more simple) imperialist readings of Fleming's work, and of his racial politics. For Mr Big's dissemination of Morgan's gold – which was, it should be underlined, itself pilfered from native Caribbean island nations by Morgan, an unofficial emissary of the British government – can be read as an act of financial reparation or redistribution of reappropriated imperial gold among its rightful, disenfranchised Black inheritors.[18] Bond's defeat of the villain – while often seen as the fait accompli of each of Fleming's novels, and as a moment of narrative jouissance – problematizes in conspicuous fashion *Live and Let Die*'s neatly paradigmatic moral vision of 'good versus evil'. In scripting Bond's defeat of Mr Big's scheme, Fleming's text calls to mind Britain's ethical responsibility to apportion reparation finances whilst nevertheless advocating a moral vision in which the novel's white saviour is shown to perpetuate (through murder) a systemic denial of the inherited rights of Black communities. Big's adoption of the myth of Baron Samedi – the novel's vision of an indefatigable Black body politic – is thus a highly politicized and radicalized embodiment of Black resistance within the text. The motifs of rebirth and resurrection that Fleming employs through his use of the zombie are very much tied to a contrapuntal racial politics of Black empowerment. Indeed, Big fashions himself as a great hero of 'negro emancipation' (Fleming [1954] 2012b: 279), thereby underlining the political connection between Big's figurative reparation of reappropriated imperial gold and Black identity politics. In this context, Big's reference to Henry Morgan as a 'kind patron' (280) – as well as his imploration to Morgan to 'give us a fair wind' (289), in order that the *Secatur* might make a quick escape – can be read ironically, as a wry acknowledgement of his reappropriation of the Caribbean gold initially pilfered by Morgan. Moreover, it can be said that Mr Big's financial reparation scheme is never expressly vilified within the narrative. Ideologically, Bond's political motivation, and his objection to Big, is contingent upon Big's affiliation with Soviet Russia; the gold is merely the precondition of Britain's involvement in the plot and a predicate to the narrative's primary ideological concern: the suppression of communism (and not the suppression of race). I am not suggesting that Fleming's approach to the imperial politics of his James Bond novels was radical or revisionist; however, I do contend that *Live and Let Die* entertains something of a political ambivalence towards the idea of racial reparations. Indeed, when Bond passes through the concealed underwater entrance to the Isle of Surprise, he contemplatively evokes the history of the Caribbean slaves who, under Henry Morgan's command, were the first to have broken through the rock face of the island to the cave within: ' "at least another twenty yards to go, men," Bloody Morgan must have said to the slave overseers. And then the picks would have burst suddenly through to the sea and a welter of arms and legs and screaming mouths, gagged for ever with water, would have hurtled back into the rock to join the bodies of other witnesses' (Fleming [1954] 2012b: 263). Here, Bond's reimagining of the fateful plight of the indentured Caribbean labourers is framed in sympathetic terms. This reimagining is not presented as an act of narrative expropriation; rather, Bond's own experience of trauma in passing through the cave's entrance invokes the violent racial history of Jamaica not as a point of comparison – Fleming is not attempting to forge an equivalence between Bond and the Caribbean labourers he imagines – but as a point of sombre memorialization.

Fleming is his most political, though, in the sequence which shortly follows this one, in which Bond further reimagines the fate of the local Jamaican fisherman who rediscovers Morgan's hidden treasure, and who seeks out Mr Big's assistance to salvage the gold. Bond imagines that this fisherman would have 'known he would need help to dispose of [the treasure]. A white man would cheat him. Better go to the great negro gangster in Harlem and make the best terms he could. The gold belonged to the black men who had died to hide it. It should go back to the black men' (ibid.: 264). Here, Fleming makes explicit the political and moral ambiguity of Mr Big's scheme: Big intends to use the gold to finance Soviet espionage and to precipitate the expansion of communism in the United States, but the narrative also makes it clear that this enterprise is implicitly predicated on the financial remuneration of disenfranchised Black communities. Big's actions cannot simply be said to represent a form of reverse colonization, in which the appropriated gold and antiquities of Caribbean cultures are reappropriated and disseminated amongst their rightful inheritors; within the moral economy of the text, his political allegiance is a stain. Nevertheless, the narrative engages in a complex negotiation of ambivalence in which Bond's Manichean politics are complicated by the counter-colonial ethics of Big's reparation scheme. Within the moral economy of the text, Mr Big can be read as an efficient and powerful Black leader who attempts to harness a 'diasporic network of peoples of African descent' and to 'fund communist revolutions' with a treasure that has been reappropriated from colonial Britain (Halloran 2005: 170). He is a 'racial rebel', a political figurehead for an alternate, Black power within the text (Landa 2006: 87). Indeed, Gerald Early notes the equivalence that Fleming draws between Mr Big's power and the power of the British Secret Service through the narrative's visual imagery. When Bond encounters Big in the treasure cave, he observes that Big is seated behind a 'green baize card-table, littered with papers' (Fleming [1954] 2012b: 267). Early suggests that Big's 'underground world of organized plunder is an extraordinary inversion of [Bond's] own world of intelligence, which, too, is an underground world ... a world of secret operatives, and headlined ... by the mysterious M at his green baize desk' (1999: 158). Fleming's narrative, then, far from simply polarizing Bond and the racially and politically otherized villain Mr Big, can be said to draw further equivalences between their worlds. Early summarizes this point rather conclusively when he queries the following: 'Are the blacks [in *Live and Let Die*] the moral opposite of the whites, and thus the villains, or are the whites and the blacks morally equivalent in a world where the blacks themselves were at one time plunder for the white?' (58–9). The nature of Fleming's political ambivalence throughout the novel is such that this question cannot be answered in a meaningfully conclusive way; there is, of course, much evidence to support both sides.

One final point that, I suggest, might advocate for the latter view is Bond's reaction to the signal he receives from M in London concerning the recovery of Morgan's gold supply for Her Majesty's government. Bond muses out loud to Strangways, 'It's so like the old devil to think of the gold first … Suppose he thinks he can get away with it and somehow dodge a reduction in the Secret Fund when the next parliamentary estimates come round' (Fleming [1954] 2012b: 306). Bond's admission is telling. Given the narrative's sometimes confused political and racial ideologies (Bond's mission is concerned overtly with the suppression of Soviet communism but, more covertly, it is about the suppression of Mr Big's programme of Black reparations), that Bond is shown to imagine M's financial manoeuvring introduces to the final pages of the narrative a questionable note regarding the legality of the British financial authorities' reclamation of the treasure – and a further point of moral equivalence between the conduct of the British government and the machinations of Mr Big.[19] Such a note of doubtful legitimacy would sound much louder in Fleming's subsequent Jamaica-set James Bond novel, *Dr. No*, published in 1958 during a period of more heightened British-Jamaican political agitations, in which questions of legitimacy, rightful inheritance and jurisprudence were to become much more pressing, as Jamaica moved ever closer to attaining its independence.

2

Invasion, animality and bodily transgressions in *Dr. No*

Originally titled 'The Wound Man'[1] – so called because of Dr No's scientific curiosity about 'the anatomy of courage' and 'the power of the human body to endure' the infliction of physical pain (Fleming [1958] 2012f: 257; see also Chancellor 2005: 110) – *Dr. No*, published in 1958, returns James Bond to Jamaica for the second time in the series to investigate the disappearance of Strangways, the section chief with whom Bond worked in *Live and Let Die*. His investigation leads him in earnest to Crab Key, the island hideaway of the titular Dr No, whose presence in Jamaica has aroused the suspicion of the Audubon Society, a not-for-profit US environmental organization who are concerned after two of their members die in an apparent plane crash on the island. As Sam Goodman notes, Fleming's plot reveals the intricacies of contemporary Anglo-American geopolitical relations. That British Intelligence releases one of its own agents at the behest of the American bird lobby suggests within the political economy of the text that the 'defence of the colonies is paramount because it facilitates the security of the home isles via the UK-US alliance' (Goodman 2016: 147). Indeed, the novel illustrates Fleming's growing ambivalence regarding the United States' presence in geopolitical world affairs. If *Live and Let Die* belies Fleming's anti-Americanism and his fears of US interference in the Caribbean (Parker 2014: 149), *Dr. No* suggests that, in the power base of the novel's wildlife conservation lobby ('these bird people are pretty powerful in America' (Fleming [1958] 2012f: 37)), the United States asserts considerable influence over, and effects great change upon, global affairs. The novel is torn begrudgingly between mockery (i.e. M's disdain for what he sees as the absurd causes of 'old women's societies' (41)) and a healthy respect (i.e. the chief of staff's pragmatic approach) for America's political clout. But as much as *Dr. No* reflects a shift in Fleming's ambivalence towards the global geopolitical landscape,[2] so too did the cultural landscape of Britain seemingly undergo a cultural shift in response to the publication of *Dr. No*. Even though James Bond had been a recognizable literary figure for the five years preceding the publication of *Dr. No*, it was with Fleming's sixth novel, according to Laura Lilli, that public discourse surrounding Bond's social function was ignited (1966: 148). As Ann S. Boyd notes, 'the great critical hoopla about all of the Bond books began to snowball after the publication of *Doctor No* ... Although the first five adventures had met with only routine responses from newspaper and magazine critics ... *Doctor No* provoked explosive reactions when it was published' (1967: 37). Part of this was because of the timing of the publication. As G. B. Zorzoli notes, the novel mapped perfectly onto the 'period of great panic in the West [in the late 1950s] at the revelation of the technical-military capacity of the Soviet Union', who had 'successfully launched the first intercontinental missile and put the Sputnik into space, while corresponding American programmes complained of notable setbacks and ran into a rather numerous series of failings' (1966: 124). Fleming's fictional plot had hit almost exactly upon the zeitgeist. Public reaction to the novel was also, in part, ignited by the increasingly vociferous reaction of literary critics to the perceived immorality of the Bond books.[3] Most famously, Paul Johnson derided *Dr. No* as 'the nastiest book I have ever read', replete with 'the sadism of a schoolboy bully, the mechanical, two-dimensional sex-longings of a frustrated adolescent, and the crude, snob-cravings of a suburban adult' (1958: n.p.). Such views only succeeded in whetting the public's appetite for Bond.

Though British-Jamaican race relations were certainly a concern in *Live and Let Die*, they became much more pressing in *Dr. No*. The intervening four years saw an increase in nationalist agitation in Jamaica, and British fears of racial and political uprising in the soon-to-be-independent Caribbean colonies were given credence in Fleming's novel, the 'ideological framework' of which, according to Charles W. Mills – 'explicitly racist, fusing the communist threat, racial upheaval, and the terror of black-on-white "miscegenation"' (2010: 109)[4] – succeeded in augmenting Britain's historical prejudices and beliefs in racial classification. Certainly, M's dismissive claim that 'sex and machete fights are about all [the Jamaicans] understand' is spitefully reductive (Fleming [1958] 2012f: 35). Sam Bourne, the nom de plume of Jonathan Freedland, acknowledges that Fleming's use of certain racial epithets and vocabulary 'comes with the territory of a book first published in 1958' (2012: xi). Such a defence is frequently employed in excuse of particular social anachronisms (problematic views on race, most prominently), and it is difficult for the modern conscience to concede to the view that 'Fleming was writing in, and therefore about, a very specific time period' (ibid.: x–xi). To concede to the view that Fleming's writings are products of a specific historical context – and therefore temporally distanced from the political sensibilities of the modern reader – may represent all too easy an expiatory fix, both pardoning Fleming's rhetorical missteps as well as making excuses for the contemporary reader's enjoyment of the novels' retroactive politics. But to condemn Fleming outright as an ex post facto racist is to deny the powerful historicizing magnitude of those imperial and racial discourses that have defined British consciousness for much of the preceding several centuries – which are, of course, localized within individuals but which are also endemic to the historical and cultural imagination of Britain's national consciousness at large.[5] Fleming's fictive universe is one that is 'caught between the dusk of empire and the dawn of decline'. As Bond 'sits intriguingly on that cusp' (ibid.: xi), so too must critical reconsiderations of Fleming's work necessarily incorporate a regard for those discourses of political and racial ambivalence which are conditioned by the juxtaposition of those historical discourses of empire and Fleming's own individualizing world view. Bourne implicitly acknowledges such an ambivalence: he believes that 'Fleming is doubtless acting as a reporter, accurately passing on the prejudices of his age', whilst also conceding that these are prejudices 'he *might* well have shared' (ibid., my italics). Though Bourne certainly marshals from within *Dr. No* evidence of the narrative's endorsement of certain political and racialist attitudes and beliefs, he nevertheless remains ambivalent in his rhetoric about the issue of Fleming's actual racism; Fleming *might* be a racist, he suggests, though not an irrefutable one, and certainly not a proven one. 'Some staples of our common culture are so established,' Bourne contends, 'so embedded in the collective consciousness, that we think we know them even if we don't' (ibid.: ix). He is speaking, here, of the ubiquity of the Bond phenomenon in general, but it is equally likely that these words could be offered in survey of Britain's cultural opinion of Fleming's perceived racism. That is to say, Fleming's perceived racism has become so essential to contemporary considerations of his work, so embedded within the collective critical consciousness of the James Bond universe, that it is virtually impossible to approach the Bond novels without an awareness of Fleming's supposed attitudes and beliefs with regard to such issues.

But if the James Bond universe is, indeed, hermetically sealed within Fleming's racism, how, then, does one account for Britain's fervent patriotism and the aggrandizing national hysteria which accompanies the release of each subsequent film in the series – not to mention the steady readership and healthy profit which the novels continue to enjoy? If it is truly the case that modern appreciation of the James Bond novels and films is inextricable from Fleming's (perceived) questionable and troubling politics of race, then this suggests a number of points of significance. Either British consumers of such fictions are wilfully racist (or wilfully ignorant of their own racism – which seems far more likely) and/or such consumers have found points of ingress to Fleming's fictional universe that are not contingent on the politics of race. On the one hand, we might forgive Fleming's writings as anachronistic products of a specific period of history, outmoded in their startlingly casual racialism; on the other hand, though, and as Bourne himself makes clear, the Bond novels 'yield an unexpectedly rich insight into an era now long gone' (ibid.: x). Fleming is derided in a modern context because his works are seen as effigies of political incorrectness, yet he is praised in exactly the same breath for his skilful power to transport the reader back to this outmoded period. To the contemporary reader, his novels evoke a 'surprise and shock' which 'would have been uncontroversial at the time' (ibid.: xi). In a modern context, Fleming cannot win. Contemporary critical considerations of his novels are, by nature, ambivalent. Bourne acknowledges wryly that the pleasure of reading Fleming derives from 'the opportunity to glimpse, even to revel in, how things used to be before progress and equality spoiled all the fun' (ibid.: xiv). To read Fleming at all in the modern context, then, one must necessarily embrace an ambivalent regard for the politically (in)correct matters that he writes about. Indeed, one's pleasure in reading Fleming's work is precisely conditioned by such ambivalence. Fleming's supposed racism has become so established within contemporary critical considerations of his work that little space has been afforded to interrogate the veracity of his racial politics within the writing itself. Jeremy Black, for one, is somewhat more concessionary than Bourne in his appraisal of Fleming's racial politics, demonstrating a historical and cultural (as well as temporal) relativism with regard to his reading of the novels. He says, 'Today, [Fleming's] presentation of alleged national characteristics and conduct … would lead to criticism on the grounds, at the very least, of insensitivity, if not racism, while his belief in racial characteristics might also lead to charges of naivety or worse' (2005: 81). Here, Black accuses Fleming of insensitivity ('at the very least'), but he does not denounce Fleming as an avowed racist – the firm 'today' with which he begins suggestive of the dispensation he affords the historical context of Fleming's writings. Indeed, Black seems less concerned with Fleming's reputed racism than he is in pointing out Fleming's transgression of boundaries: 'Fleming was criticized frequently for crossing, if not ignoring, boundaries … of judgement, taste and sensitivity' (ibid.). With all awareness of the 'charges of naivety or worse' that may be levelled against my own writing, I argue that Fleming's supposed racism, then, is not isolated bigotry; he is not simply a racist, if he is to be truly considered one at all, but someone who can be seen to transgress in egregious fashion the customary social and political limits of contemporary cultural, racial and gender politics. But he is a transgressor only in so far as the modern-day reader is cognizant of, and learned in, those limits; to his literate contemporaries, he was simply tasteless, a pulpy purveyor of mainstream views on race and gender. It is our reading of the Bond novels from a contemporary perspective that marks Fleming's work as particularly engaging; Fleming's writings are not interesting (or perhaps less interesting) in the historical context of their production precisely because, during this period, there were relatively less objections within Britain to the views posited within the Bond novels. Until *Dr. No*, it seems.

Jeremy Black has argued that 'the Bond persona, from start to finish, is all about limits' (2005: 82). But this is not quite right. Fleming has already demonstrated in *Live and Let Die* a propensity for tasteless transgression, while the Voodoo Baron Samedi's apparent ministry of the borders between life and death suggests a further transgression of magic realist proportion. Black himself acknowledges that, in that novel, Bond's search for Mr Big 'leads him to cross boundaries' (13). Bond's passage into the 'underworlds' of Harlem and Florida, if anything, suggests precisely that he is *un*limited in his mobility. It is for similar reasons that I dismiss Daniel Ferreras Savoye's claim that Bond's name is suggestive of his function within Fleming's narrative structure: 'he is literally the *bonding agent* of a social and political order that threatens to become *un-bonded*' (2013: 34, italics in original). While it may be the case that Bond functions as a representative of Her Majesty's government whose job it is to maintain the political status quo within Britain's colonies, in his transgression of limits, and his passage through and within various cultural, racial, national and political geographies, Bond himself remains unbound by limits or borders. The hints of transgression which are to be found in *Live and Let Die* (such as Baron Samedi's magic realist pose between life and death) are matured in *Dr. No*, a novel almost entirely concerned with the incursion of physical boundaries. As I will argue below, *Dr. No* establishes the fluid and ambiguously mobile nature of physical, temporal, bodily and material limits within Fleming's Jamaican psychogeography. Such fluidity, I contend, further metaphorizes Fleming's ambivalent concern towards British-Jamaican sociopolitical relations.

Approaching the limits of colonialism: Fleming's shifting prejudices

By the time *Dr. No* was published, colonial unrest was endemic within British and French colonies in the Caribbean. Elsewhere in the world, Britain had already taken steps to neutralize a Mau Mau uprising in Kenya, while both Malaya and Singapore had been granted self-rule (Goodman 2016: 150). India, too, had been granted independence and Britain had seen almost a decade of new arrivals to its shores of immigrants from former colonies. John Griswold has argued that 'the general policy of the British Government toward the colonies was to encourage progress towards self-government' (2006: 218–19). However, Sam Goodman asserts that, in an effort to consolidate its control in the Caribbean, Britain actually doubled down on its commitment to its colonies there. Investment had been poured into the colonies in 1940 and 1945, as the intention was to strengthen Britain's political position as essential and benevolent colonial administrators (147). Goodman further notes that Britain's consolidation of its Caribbean colonies was part of a commitment to the NATO alliance at the time to curtail communist insurgency in the democratic West (ibid.). Less than a decade prior, China had become a communist country; the Korean War was fought between North Korea (allied with China and the USSR) and South Korea (with the support of the United Nations, and the United States in particular); and French and Japanese forces had suffered defeat by the Viet Minh over control of Vietnam in the First French–Indochina War, in 1954 (Early 1999: 160). In 1952, the governor of Jamaica, Sir Hugh Foot, had denounced the communist movement in Jamaica; he viewed the Chinese community on the island as 'a Maoist vanguard' and 'ordered that all Chinese incomers be fingerprinted and photographed' (Parker 2014: 147). Foot also suggested that the Jamaican nationality of all previously naturalized Chinese citizens on the island be revoked.[6] As Gerald Early notes, for most of the Cold War period preceding the release of *Dr. No*, 'Asian Communism, Asian technological advances ... and formidable Asian military resistance to the west' posed a considerable threat to British and American political interests (1999: 160). Fleming's racialized profile of a Jamaica in peril in *Dr. No*, though certainly informed by the contextual anxieties of the West's fearful regard for Asian military and technological supremacy, nevertheless belies a deep personal and political tension that, much like Mr Big's communist allegiance in *Live and Let Die*, is focalized through and framed by discourses of British-Jamaican relations.

As with *Live and Let Die*, there is much evidence in *Dr. No* to suggest that Fleming's treatment of race is simply problematic.[7] Equally, however, the novel's treatment of race can be read not simply as a prejudicial marker against Fleming in particular but as part of a historically discursive framework for engaging with the conditional category of 'Other'.[8] Certainly, we saw this with Mr Big in *Live and Let Die*, whose villainy is less racial than it is political and ideological: he is Black, but he is also a career-criminal communist, Bond's moral and ideological other. I am in agreement with Cynthia Baron's assertion that the narrative of *Dr. No* remains 'steeped in the discourse of "Orientalism" which [positions] the East as mysterious, incomprehensible, and pathologised in order to justify Western imperialism', as well as her acknowledgement of Fleming's self-reflective employment of this discourse ([2003] 2009: 153). It is not simply the case that Fleming's racial classification is unidirectional; rather, as Baron makes clear, Bond's relationship to race and to otherness in the text also invites the reader to 're-examine British strategies of self-definition in the post-colonial era' (ibid.). In *Live and Let Die*, the structural relationship between Bond and Mr Big shores up those delineations between Bond's Anglo-Saxon 'purity' and his own perceptions of racial otherness; Bond's racial identity is never actually threatened within the course of the novel. Indeed, Bond's imagined assimilation of a Black racial identity, though certainly questionable, suggests that his figurative racial fluidity is predicated upon a comfortable assurance in the actual indissolubility of his own Anglo-Saxon heritage. Bond's assurance is, perhaps, conditioned by Fleming's political certainty, at the time, of Britain's positional superiority over the non-anglophone and non-Anglo-Saxon world, and by the subservience of Britain's many colonies to the empire. As the ideological emissary for Britain's powerful global empire, it is presumed that Bond need not entertain doubts in either his righteousness or his own national, racial or cultural identities.

However, by the time *Dr. No* is published, Fleming's considerations of the supposed indissolubility of Anglo-Saxon racial and national identity are not without concession to the political and sociocultural realities of Jamaican independence, British immigration from the Caribbean and the burgeoning multicultural landscape of modern-day Britain. In other words, having borne witness to momentous social, cultural and racial changes on the landscape of Britain, Fleming can no longer deny in his writings Britain's own 'otherness' to itself. *Dr. No* evidences not just Fleming's ambivalent concern with otherness as it is configured through discourses of race in the Caribbean; the narrative also forcibly contends with Britain's renegotiation of its own colonial administration of Jamaica, as well as the renegotiation of the jurisdictional boundaries of Britain itself. There has been some contention over the degree to which Fleming himself can be said to be conscious of this in his work, and, indeed, of the extent to which his political intentions are brought to bear (or matter at all) within the text. Christine Berberich argues that 'Fleming seems to have closed his eyes to [the] fact' that Britain had become a multicultural society (2012: 25). His yearly sojourns to Jamaica, from the mid-1940s onwards, happened to coincide with the first decade or so of the Windrush migration. As Lisa M. Dresner notes, 'just as the wave of Caribbean immigration was coming to England, Fleming himself was doing a "reverse immigration" to Jamaica' (2011: 282–3). Fleming's seemingly wilful disregard for racial integration in Britain and for progressive British-Jamaican relations in the Caribbean – which corresponded to the precise period in time when he was establishing his own veritable planter economy in Oracabessa, Jamaica – would seem to support Sam Goodman's view that, 'for Fleming, continued British governance of the West Indies appeared a given' (2016: 146). At the same time, Goodman concedes, 'despite the seemingly backward-looking character of *Dr. No*, with its colonial governors and mansion houses, contemporary events were not lost on Fleming' (ibid.: 150). Goodman believes that Fleming uses *Dr. No* to 'warn against the danger of colonial emancipation by amplifying the scale, prevalence, and grisliness of the potential violence that the native might inflict on the white body' (ibid.). While *Dr. No* is certainly a novel of violence, it would be more accurate to claim that such violence is directed against the infrastructural apparatus of the colonial administration rather than against the white body, specifically. The murder of Strangways and his assistant, Mary Trueblood, in the novel's opening chapter is – aside from a precondition of Bond's involvement in the plot – no more or less violent an affair than any of Fleming's other scenes of murder throughout the series, which are unhampered by concerns of race and racial prejudice.[9] On the one hand, the novel seems to endorse a scornful view of Jamaican national self-determination: the colonial secretary's derisive claim to Bond that Jamaican people 'can't even run a bus service' (Fleming [1958] 2012f: 71) is augmented within the narrative by moments of racialized violence which are meant to be suggestive, it would seem, of the Jamaicans' intemperance – and, ultimately, of the ineffectiveness of their self-governance.

Conversely, Fleming's narrative is also highly critical of Britain's colonial administration of Jamaica. As Jeremy Black notes, the principal threat within the novel is posed neither by Soviet Russia nor by SPECTRE, the organization for whom, it is later shown in the film version, Dr No works, but by the inability of the British administration to govern effectively upon the island (2017: 24). The colonial secretary's imploration to Bond to 'start another bonfire ... here. Stir the place up a bit' (Fleming [1958] 2012f: 71) at once calls to mind the imperial dimension of Bond's last outing to Jamaica, in the novel *Live and Let Die*, during which he vanquished the threat of communist insurrection on the island (in the form of Mr Big), effectively reinstating British colonial leadership. This invocation – what Black refers to as 'a call for distraction from the pressures and frustrations of a weakening imperial grasp' (2005: 34) – also serves to underline the administration's incapacity to manage without Bond. The implication seems to be that, without Bond's micromanagement of the Colonial Office's affairs, Jamaican independence is a loss that Britain has brought upon itself entirely through its own mismanagement. Cynthia Baron argues as much, citing as the cause the inveterate liberalism of modern British politics. She notes that neither Fleming nor Bond 'critique[d] Britain's welfare state or class system, but instead implicitly attacked the older generation's "liberal" complacency and inveterate mismanagement (the charge of mismanagement being tantamount to that of failing to be British)' (Baron [2003] 2009: 154). Indeed, many of the novel's more objectionable opinions on racial issues and on the perceived problems of race are propounded by the administrative figureheads of the Jamaican Colonial Office, the Acting Governor and Mr Pleydell-Smith, the colonial secretary.[10] Like *Live and Let Die*, in which Fleming can be seen to partially inoculate Bond from the text's more controversial rhetoric by placing the most nefarious racial discourse in the mouth of his American counterpart, Felix Leiter, *Dr. No* continues this tradition. But whereas Leiter can be seen to forge some degree of racial *détente* with Blabbermouth, one of Mr Big's men, through their shared love of Dixieland jazz music, the uncurbed racial malice – not to mention the complete inactivity and disengagement from Bond's mission – of the Governor and the colonial secretary emphasizes their disconnection from both the country they ostensibly govern and the Jamaican people about whom, apparently, they know so much. If Fleming's narrative is, at times, seemingly uncomplimentary of the Black Jamaican, it is nothing less than scathing of Jamaica's white colonial administration.

Take, for instance, Fleming's presentation of the Acting Governor, in particular: Bond is positively hateful in his consideration of the man. The 'cream tussore suit' and 'inappropriate wing collar and spotted bow tie' with which he adorns himself suggests to Bond an insubstantiality and foppish affectation unbefitting the office of governor (Fleming [1958] 2012f: 68). That his desk is empty of everything but a copy of 'the *Daily Gleaner*, the *Times Weekly*, and a bowl of hibiscus blossoms' (ibid.) indicates a certain fecklessness, the ineffectual malaise of a man of far too much self-importance and far too little duties with which to occupy himself, other than consulting the stock exchange. And the disdainful satisfaction with which he delivers the epithet 'Young whippersnapper' to Bond's departing back hints at his own anachronism and misaligned self-regard (ibid.: 71). The Governor's ineptitude is evidenced by his cast-iron assurances to Bond that Strangways 'obviously did a bunk with [his secretary]' and by his misplaced confidence in the abilities of his own police force to locate the missing couple (ibid.: 69). Moreover, his efficacy as governor has already been called sharply into question in the narrative, when Bond recalls in an aside the words of a friend of his at the Colonial Office: '[the Acting Governor's] nearly at retiring age. Only an interim appointment. ... This man's not even trying ... He knows he's only got the job for a few months ... Now all he wants is to retire and get some directorships in the City' (ibid.: 68). For Sam Bourne, the Acting Governor is 'weak' and 'calculating', a man who 'embodies the twilight empire of the postwar period' (2012: xiii). Indeed, the veritable deathliness of this man is underlined with irony when Bond discovers that the fruit basket that has ostensibly been sent to his hotel suite 'with the Compliments of His Excellency the Governor' turns out to be riddled with cyanide as part of a trap laid for him by Dr No's emissaries (Fleming [1958] 2012f: 84).

Moreover, when full evidence of Dr No's crimes are presented to the Acting Governor at the novel's end, his incredulity over the fact that 'these things have been going on under his nose, in one of Jamaica's dependencies', is wryly mocked within the narrative (ibid.: 315). His subordinates demonstrate very little respect for him, their disregard evident in the narrative's subtle descriptive asides. The Brigadier in charge of the Caribbean Defence Force, and a friend of the murdered Strangways, who is described as a 'modern young soldier' and who refers to the old colonial brass as 'feather-hatted fuddy-duddies' (ibid.: 316), is very much the political opposite of the Governor. The unmissable sarcasm with which he urges the Governor to action ('if the programme of receptions and cocktail parties ... could possibly be deferred for forty-eight hours or so ...' (ibid.)) suggests that Bond's earlier assumptions about the Governor's pose and inefficacy are not misjudged. The Police Superintendent, sensing which way things are going, immediately offers to the Brigadier his concurrence. The Superintendent's narrative aside ('quick action might save him from a reprimand, but it would have to be quick' (ibid.)) further implies that the Governor is less adept at gauging the politics of the situation than those around him. Indeed, the Superintendent's demeanour is described as 'edgy' (ibid.), an adjective which conveys both his apprehension of the dangerous political fallout of the situation as well as his position of relative modernity in contrast to the anachronistic Governor. While his subordinates are presented as guileful, pragmatic and politically realist, the Governor is portrayed as self-concerned (he imagines himself as the 'island's strong man' whose decisive action is looked upon favourably by the press (ibid.: 319)), patronizingly familial (his voice is described as 'avuncular', as though 'telling the children that just this once … "I accept your verdict"' (ibid.: 320)) and as a man whose false deference to the opinions of others ('"what d you think, Colonial Secretary?" the Governor's voice was hustled' (ibid.: 317)) conceals his own inadequacies. On Bond's part, it is made explicit that he 'had no sympathy for the [Governor]' and that he 'hadn't liked the reception he had had on his last visit to King's House' (ibid.: 315). The Governor's 'regal' inclination of his head in patronage of Bond's service (ibid.: 320) is set pointedly in relief against the image of the portraits of King George VI and Queen Elizabeth II which adorn the walls of the conference room, and which look down upon the occupants 'with grace and good humour' (ibid.: 317). The Governor's appropriated regality, which the text implies is derisible, underlines the gradual dissolubility of the monarchy's power within its Caribbean colonies, as the good-humoured figures in the portraits can be seen to gaze in mockery not only at the Governor's laughable pretensions to power but also onto a world which signals their own redundancy.

Colonial Jamaica, the Governor's world of torpidity and corruption in the novel, is presented in the text as a world that is anathema to Bond. Not only does Fleming lay stress upon the Governor's political anachronism, but Bond's daydream during the debriefing – in which 'his mind drifted into a world of tennis courts and lily ponds and kings and queens, of London' (ibid.) – suggests a spatio-temporal remove from the landscape, as though Bond himself were a figure out of place and time in this colonial enclave. This spatio-temporal distance is emphasized through Bond's partial perception of the sounds through the windows of 'tennis balls being knocked about' and 'a young girl's voice', which are described as 'far away' and 'distant', respectively (ibid.), underlining once again his physical and mental remove from the Governor's world. But Bond does not stand in simple observation of colonial anachronism; he can no longer bear the colonial torpor of the tropics as he once did in *Live and Let Die*. While Bond's spatio-temporal relocation is configured through his daydream, during which he imagines himself back in England and surrounded by the vestiges of British culture, power and empire, his later desire 'to get the hell away from King's House, and the tennis, and the kings and queens' in his car (ibid.: 322) suggests that the fantasy of Britain's imperial pre-eminence in Jamaica, evidenced through the charlatan Acting Governor, is now a distasteful one to him. That Fleming should elect to use the same word-images (tennis, kings, queens) to characterize Bond's imagined spatio-temporal relocation to the Britain of his fantasy as well as his hasty physical and literal retreat from the Governor's residence following the debriefing also suggests that the historical reality of Britain's waning position in the Caribbean is not actually as powerful as national fantasy might suggest. The vestiges of Bond's England, as configured through these symbols, is, as Sam Goodman notes, 'constructed from the imagery of privilege and anonymity in urban space' which the British Empire's conquest of space has afforded itself (2016: 54). These images represent 'unformed and porous [ideas] of national identification … able to be shaped to any particular need and accept those who subscribe to its ideology' (ibid.). It is clear that in this, the novel's final moments, Fleming suggests Bond's figurative and literal disengagement from the vestiges of Britain's waning colonial administration. In his less than favourable presentation of British administration on the island, Fleming can be said, at the very least, to offer a check to colonial rule in Jamaica. This very much goes against a great deal of those critical readings of Fleming which argue that his fictional universe is one of simple, heavy-handed imperialism. Fleming's critical portrayal of Jamaica's colonial administration, then, necessitates a much more probing, revisionist stance on his view of British-Jamaican political relations during the lead-up to Jamaican independence. Contrary to the popular belief that James Bond is simply a colonial cipher, *Dr. No* presents a fraught, politically negotiable world in which British sovereignty is presented as 'graduated rather than absolute', and in which Britain is shown to be '[in]sufficiently adept at administering and monitoring the activities of others' (Funnell and Dodds 2017: 7).

Invasion and transgression: complicated border crossings

The graduated rather than absolute nature of Britain's colonial power that Fleming presents within the novel is configured largely through a number of interconnected metaphors of spatial invasion and temporal transgression. *Dr. No* is replete with scenes of complicated border crossings and transgressions of boundaries that are characterized by images of penetration and violent intrusion. Such imagery is undoubtedly drawn from Fleming's own vivid conception of the changing urban and political geographies of both Britain and Jamaica at the time, the respective social landscapes of which have undergone momentous change. In the case of the former, Fleming has, since the 1940s, borne witness to the hitherto single greatest period of immigration Britain has seen in its national history, with the influx of the Windrush generation not only from the Caribbean but also from Central and Eastern Asian countries such as Pakistan and India. In the case of the latter, 'Fleming's island' in the Caribbean has become a site of racial agitation and national resistance and a place in which Britain's colonial administration was seen to be increasingly out of touch with geopolitical reality. The once firm territorial lines which Britain maintained between itself and the non-anglophone world of its colonies were becoming dissoluble. Fleming's use of violent images of invasion, penetration and the transgression of established material and spatial boundaries, then, is part of his own ambivalent and reactionary response to the realpolitik of decolonization. The violent imagery of the novel's opening chapter, for instance, in which three of Dr No's Chinese-Jamaican employees (crudely referred to as 'Chigroes'[11]) assassinate Strangways, the regional control officer for the Caribbean, along with his secretary, Mary Trueblood, is suggestive of the potential for unchecked racial violence in the postcolonial period meted out by Black Jamaicans in recompense for Britain's maltreatment of the island and its people. Indeed, it has been argued that the name of Strangways' secretary ('True-blood') is connotative of the novel's underlining threat of miscegenation and of Fleming's fearful regard for the dissolution through racial mixing of Anglo-Saxon 'purity' (Parker 2014: 232; Baron 2009: 154).

However, contrary to the opinion of Tony Bennett and Janet Woollacott, who refer to the killing of Strangways and Trueblood as an 'enigma' for Bond to solve (1987: 103), the murders are not shown to be a mysterious or arbitrary act of violence committed by Black islanders against white colonizers. This violence is not conditioned by race but paid out for by Dr No against the interference of the British into his own private affairs. The Chinese-Jamaican assassins are but intermediaries in Dr No's long-range rebuff of the Colonial Office's meddling; as Matthew Parker notes, 'they are only operating on behalf of Dr No', which means that 'it is still the outside who represents the greatest threat to Jamaica in the novel' (2014: 234).[12] By 'the outside', Parker is referring, here, to the threat embodied not by the indigenous islanders but by the foreigner Dr No. The scenes of violence which open the novel are not simply reproductions of the essential, bestialized 'savagery' of the formulaic 'native' one might find in those novels of racial hysteria by Joseph Conrad or Rider Haggard, for example, in which violence is portrayed as cultural and racially endemic. Rather, the racial violence of these scenes is conditioned, firstly, by Dr No's external agitation and, secondly, as a consolidated form of resistance to a particular system of political, social and racial oppression that was, at the time Fleming was writing, at risk of dangerous implosion. Fleming, I would suggest, is all too aware of this. Indeed, his Jamaican writings are increasingly characterized by an ambivalent regard for both the ills and necessities of violence. Such violence can be said, by extension, to precipitate Bond's involvement in the narrative, whose presence brings about the eventual resolution of the narrative's central conflict, but it is also illustrative of Fleming's political ambivalence and his censorious consideration of the very system by and through which Bond himself is deployed. Indeed, the novel's opening paragraphs betray something of Fleming's restrained contempt for Jamaica's colonial culture. 'Rich Road', the avenue on which both the Governor's House and the Queen's Club are situated, and on which many of the island's wealthy (white) elites reside, is described as '[holding] nothing but the suspense of an empty stage and the heavy perfume of night-scented jasmine' (Fleming [1958] 2012f: 2). Through the image of a decadent theatre scene poised in readiness for its performers to arrive, this comment underlines the very artifice of the lifestyle enjoyed by the occupants of this avenue. That Fleming notes the impending arrival to the avenue of 'the cocktail traffic' (ibid.) further suggests the whimsy and capricious malaise of the avenue's society set (whom Fleming abhorred in real life[13]), a foreshadowing, perhaps, of the feckless Acting Governor whom Bond is soon to meet, who is similarly engaged in trivialized inactivity. And Fleming's contempt for the occupants of Rich Road is all but felt in his derision of 'the "best" people [who] live in its big old-fashioned houses' (ibid.: 2), the inverted commas around which is connotative of the narrative's ambivalent regard for this particular high society.

But amid the pedestrian descriptions of the white-wash mansions, verandas and tennis courts which line Rich Road, a certain threat intrudes upon the narrative. Without missing a beat or signalling, to any degree, a shift in register, the narrator suddenly notes the following:

> Such stubborn retreats will not long survive in modern Jamaica. One day Queen's Club will have its windows smashed and perhaps be burned to the ground, but for the time being it is a useful place to find in a sub-tropical island – well run, well staffed and with the finest cuisine and cellar in the Caribbean. (ibid.)

This moment is, as Parker notes, a 'shocking and fascinating aside, calling to mind ... the deep fear that haunted the white community from the first days of slavery' (2014: 231). Here, Parker is, of course, talking about the prospect of revolution, the overthrow of the white colonial overseers by their subjugated Black slaves. Placed in the context of the narrative's opening paragraphs, though, and in the context of contemporary nationalist movements in Jamaica, this brief paragraph represents an intrusion into the political economy of the Bond novels as a whole – which have been, up until the publication of *Dr. No*, unabashed in their avowed imperial ideology. Here, Fleming introduces to his fictive universe (hitherto ordered by the assurances of Britain's perceived racial and cultural supremacy) considerable doubt as to the longevity of the very political system James Bond is tasked with ordering – and by which he himself is ordered. This paragraph not only 'makes us look back on the preceding four paragraphs of the book' for signs of the potential for disorder which this aside prophesies, as Parker notes (ibid.), but it can also be said that the narrative intercedes upon itself and intrudes upon the listless reverie into which the reader has been lulled by the opening paragraphs. The point of Fleming's preceding four paragraphs in the opening chapter, then, is not so much to set the scene for the rest of the novel to come (as many of the Bond films' pre-title sequences successfully do), and nor do they serve to wholly venerate the world of colonial torpor which they depict (as I have said, Fleming is derisive in his appraisal of this world). Rather, Fleming's relatively expansive description of the colonial torpor of Rich Road conditions the very disruption of this world, as this, the fifth paragraph of the opening chapter, can be said to represent an almost violent incursion upon the narrative consciousness, and upon the consciousness of the reader. That Fleming describes the Queen's Club as a 'stubborn retreat' suggests a resistance of sorts, not just to the exoticist, tropical vision of Jamaica that characterized *Live and Let Die*, and which Fleming first lulls the reader into believing will characterize *Dr. No*,[14] but to an unwillingness to concede to the changing stimuli of Jamaica's fluctuating political and historical realities. Parker has argued that 'the Jamaica of *Dr No* is a similar "traditional" one – the Jamaica drawn in *Live and Let Die*, and written about by Fleming back in 1947 in his *Horizon* article' (ibid.: 229). But this is patently not the case. The casual violence contained within the above passage (smashed windows, the threat of arson) is almost disorientingly juxtaposed with the images of mundanity which flank it, suggestive of an impending cultural clash wherein tradition and progression are imagined to collide within this space.

Indeed, the appearance of the three 'Chigro' assassins disguised as blind beggars only a page or so later suggests that this collision is imminent. The narrator notes that the three men would be 'incongruous in Kingston', but that their presence in the socio-economically privileged area of Rich Road 'made an unpleasant impression' (Fleming [1958] 2012f: 4). In other words, after calling to mind the prospect of racialized violence, Fleming activates the very fears of incursion he prophesies. Though the three men do not actually proceed to attack the Queen's Club, neither smashing its windows nor setting it alight, the narrative does make it clear that they have broached an imperceptible cultural boundary ('the silence of Richmond Road was softly broken' (ibid.: 3)). Their passage from the streets of Kingston ('where there are many diseased people' (ibid.: 4)) to the clean and tidy neighbourhood of Rich Road connotes an equivalent transgression. In moving from their own sanctioned ethnoscape to the 'distinctly British zone of control', the narrative seems to imply that the three men 'breach what are considered fixed spatial and social boundaries' (Goodman 2016: 151). Goodman has argued that the 'ordered environment' of Rich Road, much like the British empire at large, becomes in the narrative 'haunted by the spectre of its own decline' (150). However, his further assertion – that 'Fleming's suggestion is that the native or the hybrid has no place in such an exclusive space' (151) – is not quite right. The appearance of the three 'Chigroes', who have seemingly strayed from one social sphere into another, is not arbitrary: their appearance is conditioned by the earlier aside and is presented as a narrative fait accompli, a moment of narrative jouissance, in which the prospective fears of racial violence that are raised by the imagined destruction of the Queen's Club are seemingly about to be actualized. In narrative terms, the implicit violence of the brief aside can be said to direct rather than merely reflect the incursion of Jamaica's ordered colonial routine. The narrative is not simply reflecting a particular (imagined) occurrence of violence; rather, the text itself is part of the mechanics by which that act of violence becomes mobilized and activated. In other words, the text itself calls forth that violence and signals the demise of the 'world of tennis courts and lily ponds and kings and queens' which Bond himself is later shown to reject (Fleming [1958] 2012f: 317). Indeed, the proleptic shift which Fleming employs ('such stubborn retreats will not long survive') suggests the narrator's omniscient prescience. It is significant, also, that at no point in the text does the narrator bemoan the prospect of Britain's diminishing colonial influence in Jamaica.

Moreover, the murder of both Strangways and Mary Trueblood is an act conditioned by (and framed within the racial context of) a violent resistance to British colonization.[15] While Goodman reads the extreme violence of the novel as an 'indication of how colonial space ... is perpetually on the brink of disorder', and as a justification for Britain's use of extreme force to maintain order (2016: 151),[16] I am more inclined to agree with Michael Denning, who argues that the violent opening to *Dr. No* should be read objectively as an act of decolonization or resistance to Britain's colonial mismanagement of Jamaica, characteristic of what Denning describes as 'the emergence of the character of the "Third World" [in the global economy of the period] as a result of protracted liberation struggles throughout Asia, Africa, and Latin America' (1987: 106). In much the same way that Mr Big and the undead Voodoo Baron Samedi can be read as a powerful conglomerate symbol of resistance to the economy of colonial subjugation in *Live and Let Die*, the racialized violence in *Dr. No*'s first chapter can be read as indicative of Fleming's regard for the shifting geopolitics of British decolonization in the Caribbean basin, which was to begin in earnest upon his beloved Jamaica only a handful of years after this novel was published. Parker notes that, 'having invoked the spectre of black revolution in Jamaica with his comments about Queen's Club being burnt to the ground and the murder of Mary Trueblood, Fleming backs away [from the issue]' (2014: 232). However, this is not quite accurate. That the remainder of *Dr. No* is replete with images of complex boundary crossings and various spatial, material and corporeal transgressions suggests that this conceit, embedded within the narrative, is essential to the interpretive framework of the novel as a whole and to comprehending Fleming's ambivalent responses to the remapping of various political, social and racial boundaries which characterized the move towards Jamaican self-governance.

Boundary crossings in *Dr. No* are not simply a racialized issue, though. Bond himself can be seen to undergo a complex process of spatial and temporal transgression of Jamaica's border space on his arrival to the island. Whereas in *Live and Let Die* Bond's arrival to Jamaica and his passage through Jamaican Customs is barely remarked upon ('Strangways, the Chief Secret Service Agent for the Caribbean, was at the airport to meet him and he was quickly through the Customs and Immigration and Finance Control' (Fleming [1958] 2012b: 214)) – then a condition of the white Briton's privileged status upon one of the empire's outlying colonies – in *Dr. No*, Bond's less mobile passage, characterized by his own complicated transgression of certain spatial and temporal borders, is representative of Fleming's concession to shifting British-Jamaican relations and to Britain's impending postcolonial relations with Jamaica. While Lisa Funnell and Klaus Dodds argue that '*Dr. No* establishes the social mobility … of Bond' (2017: 186), it would be more accurate to claim of this novel that boundaries and border crossings are presented in much more complex and nuanced terms than they were in Bond's earlier Jamaica-set adventure, and that Bond's mobility is actually relatively moderated, determined now by the narrative's concessionary approach to emerging postcolonial politics. Border crossings in *Dr. No* are complicated for Bond in a way they were not previously; unlike in *Live and Let Die*, Strangways is not on hand to usher him through the airport (because by this stage of the narrative, of course, Strangways is dead). The shifting realpolitik of British-Jamaican colonial relations, signalled in the novel by Strangways's assassination, is brought to bear upon Bond, firstly, in personal terms – through his body. The narrative emphasizes the physical effects upon Bond's body of his un-expedited entrance to Jamaica: 'He knew that by the time he had got through Customs he would be sweating' (Fleming [1958] 2012f: 45). In having to wait alongside every other passenger in the humid Customs hall, and afforded no favourable treatment by his government's local representative to speed up his passage through Immigration (a stark signifier of Britain's faded splendour on the island), Bond is shown to be very much the opposite of 'a man who might be thought of as "on the move"', and one whose mobility 'demarcate[s] access' to particular space (Funnell and Dodds 2017: 164). Indeed, the scene of Bond's border crossing is a slow, almost perfunctory one ('the Negro immigration officer handed Bond his passport with indifference' (Fleming [1958] 2012f: 46)), the recitation of which serves only to reinforce for Bond (and for the reader) the emerging power of Jamaican bureaucracy and its jurisdictional autonomy as a foil for Britain's crumbling administration of the island. However, the 'indifference' with which Bond's passport is returned to him by the immigration officer further suggests that this narrative sequence also functions to subtly undermine Jamaica's capacity to govern its own borders. The immigration officer's purported lack of concern as to Bond's purpose in the country belies, the narrative seems to imply, an inefficiency or political misrule of the affairs of state – and, it could be argued, a seeming disregard for the marshalling of Jamaica's border security. In this brief exchange, Fleming's political ambivalence is once again implicit: he concedes to the changing world order of Jamaica's imminent postcolonial ethnoscape while simultaneously insinuating that such changes are potentially problematic for the island's future security.

This moment is uncomfortably juxtaposed with the scene directly following it, in which Bond emerges from the Customs hall and is met by Quarrel, the Cayman Islander who assisted him in his assault on Mr Big's Isle of Surprise, in *Live and Let Die*. The narrator notes that '[Quarrel] was wearing the same old faded blue shirt and probably the same khaki twill trousers he had been wearing when Bond first met him five years before' (ibid.). Bond's (and the narrative's) appraisal of Quarrel's unaltered attire suggests that time has stood still on the island since the two men last met, and that Bond's appearance in Jamaica has seemingly 'reactivated' Quarrel, who is, it appears, simply mobilized and waiting in readiness to be told by Bond what to do. Through Quarrel's enduring physical appearance, the narrative attempts to reinscribe a certain timelessness onto the landscape itself (Bond first sees 'the tall brown-skinned man *against* the barrier' in the airport (ibid., my italics)), which enables Bond to decode as reassuringly accessible and traversable the cultural, social and racial geographies of a space that has been much altered since his last visit. It is with a restrained, almost overworked desperation that Bond notes, 'You haven't changed, Quarrel' (ibid.: 47), a statement which, in its implicit orientation of Quarrel's relationship to Bond, can be read as directive rather than reflective. It is not that Quarrel has changed, rather it is that Bond wants him, like the island of Jamaica itself, *not* to have changed. It is not insignificant, then, that when Bond goes to collect his luggage, the customs officer who, we are told, 'knew Quarrel' merely '[chalks] Bond's bag without opening it' (ibid.: 46). Thus, Fleming underlines the fact that the small privilege which Bond is afforded, here, as he is leaving the airport, is not on account of his own position as an envoy of Britain's government but on account of the esteem in which Quarrel is held by the local Jamaicans. It is Quarrel who provides Bond with the ability to re-enter old, colonial Jamaica, and it is Quarrel who affords Bond the fantasy of his own mastery of that space. Bond's mastery is ironic, of course, as Fleming makes abundantly clear: within the context of the novel's imminently postcolonial Jamaican ethnoscape, it is Quarrel and not Bond who is the unacknowledged master of the island. Indeed, Bond later refers to Quarrel as his own 'passport into the lower strata of coloured life which would otherwise be closed to [him]' (ibid.: 49). Though somewhat questionable, this comment simultaneously underlines Bond's jurisdictional powerlessness on the island while at the same time sanctioning Quarrel's relative ascendancy. Whereas Bond's actual passport is treated with 'indifference' by the immigration officer in the airport, Quarrel's power is embodied and inherent. Given the emphasis which the narrative of *Dr. No*, on the whole, places upon metaphors of bodily transgression (see the section below), it is somewhat telling that Fleming's ambivalent response to Jamaica's changing political ethnoscape is figuratively bifurcated between, and physically embodied within, images of both Bond's and Quarrel's bodies. Whereas Bond's sweating body in the customs hall connotes a cessation of the privileges afforded to an envoy of the British government by Jamaica's Colonial Office (i.e. Britain's diminishing hold on the island), Quarrel's body, in its timeless recognizability, reorients Bond within a familiar Jamaica, a fantastically reimagined Jamaica in which things are the same as they have always been under British colonial rule. In this sense, while Quarrel's body becomes metonymic of sustained, anachronistic British-Jamaican colonial relations (Fleming's anxiety for things to remain in Jamaica as they have always been), it is Bond's body upon and through which the effects of political and historical change are exhibited: having to wait in the customs hall, his body sweats profusely in a manner it is unaccustomed to.

This point is underlined by the appearance of the young Chinese photographer in the exit hall of the airport, who snaps a picture of Bond – ostensibly for the local newspaper, the *Daily Gleaner*, but who, in actuality, is in the employ of Dr No and has been sent to capture images of any significant personnel entering Jamaica. The narrator notes that 'Bond was vaguely worried' by this occurrence, and that 'there was no earthly reason why his picture should be wanted by the Press. It was five years since his last adventures on the island, and … his name had been kept out of the papers' (ibid.: 48). Here, Bond's recollection of his previous assignment to Jamaica (during the case outlined in *Live and Let Die*) is intended, once again, for comparative purposes, to draw the reader's attention to the momentous political changes that have taken place on the island (and in British-Jamaican relations, more generally) in the intervening period. By quite literally framing within a photographic image Bond's body as an object, his corpus itself becomes a historical artefact or marker of material and historical interest (the photographer tells Bond that 'you look very important' (ibid.)). While Bond's profuse sweating as he passes through the customs hall is indicative of an altered corporeal (and national) state, connotative of the unravelling of Britain's privilege on the island, the photograph that is taken of him, a static image which forever preserves his likeness within this particular chronotope, also implies an agedness (that is, Bond's agedness) between the events of *Live and Let Die* and the events of *Dr. No*. Like Bond's body, then, simultaneously aged and preserved in this moment vis-à-vis the photographic medium, Fleming's text identifies a Jamaica that is similarly caught in suspension, between an image of the island as it was (*Live and Let Die*) and an image of it as it currently is (*Dr. No*). But Bond's brief exchange with the photographer also marks Jamaica's border space as a site of surveillance and danger. Unlike Bond's totally unremarkable arrival to Jamaica in *Live and Let Die*, his reception by the photographer in *Dr. No* suggests that, where once Bond's mobility within and easy passage through foreign territories and jurisdictions was assured, now it is fraught. Whereas the narrative of *Live and Let Die* emphasized the potential threat of American and Soviet incursion into British territory in the Caribbean, in *Dr. No* the primary threat to Bond's mobile supremacy is no longer posed by external national governments or political ideologies but by the instigation of Jamaica's border politics and the spatio-temporal boundaries which Bond himself is now shown to be subject to. As such, Lisa Funnell and Klaus Dodds's assertion that, in *Dr. No*, Bond's 'ability to move is defined by physical and social rules' is much more accurate than their assumption that Bond represents a perennially mobile figure (2017: 164). As Bond's arrival to Jamaica in *Dr. No* illustrates, the island's emerging border politics pose a complex resistance to Bond's mobility. Thus, *Dr. No* makes clear that the spatial mobility afforded Bond by his role as an emissary of Jamaica's colonial administration is now in question, checked by the emerging postcolonial climate of politically nationalist Jamaica. Unlike in *Live and Let Die*, Bond's Jamaican border crossings are not without complication – indeed, they represent one of the novel's most pressing geopolitical concerns. Fleming's focus in *Dr. No* on the subtle politics of Bond's complex border crossings, though, suggests that the novel's motifs of transgression extend beyond social and racial boundaries and spatio-temporal geographies. As we will see in the next section, the narrative's concern with the incursion of spatial boundaries is also configured through metaphors of bodily transgression.

Bodily transgressions: animalism and trans-corporeality

In his study *Anatomy of the Spy Thriller*, Bruce Merry has argued that '*Dr No* and the other Ian Fleming novels make a strong emotional appeal against the "vices of the herd"' (1977: 44). By this, Merry suggests that the spy thriller is principally concerned with the border politics of the spy figure. He argues that the imaginary world of the thriller is usually 'populated by hard men who have chosen to live *outside normal boundaries*' – individuals who exist as 'separate and apart from the herd' (ibid., my italics). Merry ties together intimately the conventions of the spy genre and the notion that those characters who populate narratives of this genre are often shown to exist outside of traditional bounded norms.[17] But the transgression of 'normal boundaries' is not simply key to considerations of the spy genre as a whole. More specifically, this conceit can be seen to be fundamental to the politics of Fleming's writing in 1958. If *Live and Let Die* represented Fleming's experimental foray into magic realism, crossing the boundaries of the spy thriller's traditional conventions into a territory marked by a style of gothic tourism, then *Dr. No* represents Fleming's anxious experimentation not with the boundaries of form within the Bond genre (á la *From Russia with Love*) but with the limitations and boundedness of the body itself. Having (just) survived the poison violently administered to him by Rosa Klebb at the end of *From Russia with Love*, Bond's body is in a considerably weakened state at the beginning of *Dr. No* (no doubt, in part, a reflection of Fleming's own worsening physical health during this period of his life). Bond initially considers the assignment to

Jamaica as 'deferred punishment' from M for very nearly getting himself killed on his previous mission ('M couldn't bear his men to have an easy time. In a way Bond felt sure he was being sent on this cushy assignment to humiliate him' (Fleming [1958] 2012f: 43)). Dr No's obstacle course, then, an experiment in the *peine forte et dure* of the human body through which Bond is put, is a *rite de passage* which Fleming initiates as part of the novel's symbolic (re)assertion of Britain's endurance, its national-corporeal resilience to the seismic shifts in global geopolitics of the post-war period.[18] Fleming's ambivalent concern for the body politic of emergent Jamaican nationalism, as well as his corresponding ambivalence over the material limits of Britain's empire (Britain's weakened geopolitical position is metaphorized through Bond's previous near-death and his own bodily denudation), finds focus in his extensive interest within *Dr. No* in the many images of trans-corporeality and bodily transgression. Beyond Bond himself, the body becomes, in *Dr. No*, an experimental signifier through which Fleming can be said to come to terms with the impending fluctuation and disruption to traditionally bounded and spatially determined British-Jamaican relations (and to conventional political, social and racial boundaries which have existed between the two islands) which Jamaican independence will inevitably bring about. In *Dr. No*, the body becomes the vehicle through which newly emergent British-Jamaican border politics and spatial practice are negotiated, and Bond's torturous endurance of Dr No's experiments in physical pain is but one of the ways in which the novel's body politic is literalized throughout the narrative.

Fleming's focus on the body in *Dr. No* can be said to evidence a pressing contemporary concern: British fear of racial miscegenation and the 'despoliation' of Anglo-Saxon genetic 'purity'. This can be seen in the novel's questionable presentation of Jamaica's Black Chinese community. Much like the 'Irish Frankenstein', a parodic representation of Ireland's political agitation for home rule from Britain in the late nineteenth century,[19] the 'Chigro' is imbued in Fleming's writings with the qualities of a sort of Frankensteinian aberration. It is not simply the mixing of racial characteristics and the perceived dissolution of Anglo-Saxon genetic purity which the 'Chigro' embodies that frightens Fleming's contemporary reader, and nor is it the augmentation of one set of racial characteristics through their fusion with another. Rather, it is the broaching of physical, corporeal boundaries and the perceived limits and transgressions of the body-as-border which the 'Chigro' most fearfully symbolizes in the British imagination. Indeed, it is precisely the anticipation of a mobilized body politic among the 'Chigro' community which the colonial administration is shown most to fear. When Bond asks Pleydell-Smith whether the 'Chigro' people are 'organized', and whether or not their community has a leader, Pleydell-Smith responds, 'Not yet. But someone'll get hold of them one of these days. They'd be a useful little pressure group' (Fleming [1958] 2012f: 81). Like his superior, Jamaica's Acting Governor, Pleydell-Smith's information is shown to be out of date – for, of course, the de facto head of the 'Chigro' community in the novel is none other than Dr No himself, whose mobilization of this community demonstrates political cunning. In harnessing the threat of a potential race war in Jamaica, by ensuring that the foulest of his enterprise's deeds (e.g. the Strangways and Trueblood murders) are committed by 'Chigroes' and are made to resemble, in all respects, ostensibly unmotivated crimes of Black-on-white racial violence, Dr No is attempting to deflect attention away from his own political operations – which, in his efforts to destabilize American missile test launches from Cape Canaveral for the benefit of his Russian paymasters, have absolutely nothing whatsoever to do with the politics of race.[20] Dr No knowingly and actively manipulates those heightened racial tensions which characterize real-world British-Jamaican relations of the period by employing members of the Black Chinese community to carry out acts of murder. The 'Chigro' henchmen are shown to concern themselves with neither Dr No's political ideation nor his motivations: they benefit simply from being on his payroll. Dr No, too, is unconcerned with issues of race: his cover benefits from pre-existing racial tensions on the island, which dissimulates his own nefarious intentions to extort foreign governments. As Dr No is not particularly concerned with the politics of race, the narrative's tense navigation of racial politics is erroneously deflected onto the Black 'Chigro' body, which is made to shoulder the weight not only of Jamaica's colonial heritage but also of Dr No's crimes – to which, in actuality, it bears no connection or relation. Thus, the Black 'Chigro' body is the site upon which a particularly egregious narrative transgression takes place, for it is often made to stand in for, in metonymic displacement of, Dr No's own transgressions, and it is the object upon which much punishment within the narrative is wrought in recompense for No's crimes. The scene in which Bond murders a 'Chigro' guard in the swamp in Crab Key (by firing a bullet into him at point-blank range) is one key example not only of the text's excessive violence but also of the narrative's fixation on imagery of bodily transgression and viscera. The narrative certainly fetishizes the 'huge rent' of the gunshot wound in the side of the guard's body, as well as the 'Chinese Negroid head [which] broke the surface' with 'its eyes turned up and water pouring from its silently yelling mouth' (Fleming [1958] 2012f: 144–5). This sequence is replete with imagery of bodily inversion. The 'huge rent' suggests the man's loss of internal viscera (the pouring out as opposed to the containment within of his organs and blood) and the 'silently yelling mouth', *from* as opposed to *into* which the river water is pouring, connotes both a bodily and a biotic transgression, an inversion of the natural ecosystemic flow of the river and the human body alike. But it is also clear in the narrative that the Black 'Chigro' body is the part of the mechanics through which certain transgressions are effected within the text.

Much like the racial heritage of his 'Chigro' employees, Dr No himself represents a form of racial and cultural hybridity. As the 'only son of a German Methodist missionary and a Chinese girl of good family' (ibid.: 230), Dr No can be read, in the context of the novel's racial taxonomy, as genetically 'transgressive', a figure whose purpose it is to caution against the moral ills of miscegenation. Moreover, the text underlines the transgressive nature of Dr No's birth when No himself insists to Bond that he was born on 'the wrong side of the blanket' (ibid.), an expression which, in its discomfiting alignment of sordidness and childish comfort, suggests that his very existence is a violation or infraction of the natural order and that he has, in some way, breached a particular biological border. But whereas Fleming's narrative places a good deal of emphasis on the perceived racial transgressions of the 'Chigro' body and its infringement upon designated social and cultural boundaries within the text, it seems, conversely, to focus much less on racializing Dr No than it does on underscoring the character's inherent trans-corporeality. Dr No cannot be said to traverse from one social and racial terrain to another; his jealous concern and mania for his own privacy means that he is content to remain comfortably ensconced within the cavernous lair he has built for himself on Crab Key. However, irrespective of his racially hybrid makeup, Dr No's body itself is presented as a transhumanist aberration, a corporeal abomination that transcends the limits of biology and the bounds of natural physiognomy. While a good number of Fleming's villains are presented throughout the novels as physically abhorrent and repulsive (their physical appearance often preconditioned by and indicative of an equivalent moral and ethical deleteriousness), the overwhelming focus in *Dr. No* on the antagonist's body suggests Fleming's awareness of the growing threat to Britain's empire of the non-Anglo-Saxon body. If the 'Chigroes' represent within the British imagination the growing threat of Jamaica's Black body politic, then Dr No should be read not simply – or not *only* – as an embodiment of the *ideological* threat of the 'yellow peril' (the rise of Asian communism and the West's concurrent Sinophobia)[21] but as a *corporeal* threat, a threat to the very nature of humanity itself. Indeed, Dr No's trans-corporeality is Fleming at his most patently absurd and, equally, his most frighteningly prescient.²² Dr No informs Bond that he survived an assassination attempt against him by the Chinese Tongs, during which he was shot directly in the heart, only because he is 'the one man in a million who has his heart on the right side of his body' (ibid.: 232). Unlike his 'Chigro' workforce, who, as Vivian Halloran points out, are forcibly bred by Dr No (2005: 160), Dr No's physiognomic malformation and his moral disease are presented in the text as inherent and naturally occurring: his heart is literally not in the right place. But Dr No compounds his inherent physiognomic defects by undergoing intensive trans-corporeal surgery. In order to disguise himself from the Tongs, who have cut off his two hands in recompense for his having stolen a million pounds from their treasury, Dr No physically alters his appearance. He tells Bond that 'I had all my hair taken out by the roots, my thick nose made thin, my mouth widened, my lips sliced', and, in order to make himself appear taller, he 'had weeks of traction on [his] spine' to lengthen his body (Fleming [1958] 2012f: 233). Over his eyes, Dr No also wears contact lenses, which he proudly boasts of as 'one of the first pairs ever built' (ibid.). When he tells Bond that he has 'established a watch on the intelligence services in Jamaica and Cuba' (ibid.: 239), not only is the reader put in mind of Mr Big, whose network of spies in *Live and Let Die* is known as 'The Eyes', but it is also implied that Dr No's surveillance capacities are considerably enhanced by means of the 'artificial eyes' through which he views the world: 'These ... see everything,' he tells Bond as he taps the centre of each of his eyeballs (ibid.: 223). The 'dull ting' that is emitted in response is further suggestive of a sort of technocratic imperviousness. In place of hands, Dr No also wears, variously, mechanical pincers and hands carved from wax encased in gloves. Indeed, the description of his mechanical pincers – 'two pairs of steel pincers came out on their gleaming stalks and were held up for inspection like the hands of a praying mantis' (ibid.: 220) – further hints towards Dr No's trans-humanism. His hands are likened to the stems of herbaceous plants ('stalks') and to a Mantidae insect ('praying mantis'), both of which are biotic matter extraneous to the anthropoid.

Perhaps more than his 'Chigro' workforce, Dr No himself is the embodiment of Frankensteinian monstrosity, a medical miscellany of inorganic matter assembled around the ruined detritus of what once was human biota. Indeed, his body also becomes the site for self-administered experimentations on the ontological nature of humanity and technology's domination over biology. Thus, when Bond muses 'who *was* Doctor No?' (ibid.: 153), the answer has deeply philosophical implications. As Dr No continues his bodily experimentation into the transhumanist interstices between 'man' and 'machine', the more appropriate question to ask might well be '*what* was Doctor No?' Indeed, Ishay Landa levels against Dr No 'charges of lunacy with Nietzschean aloofness'; he reads him as a 'perverse and destructive *Übermensch*' whose immoral atheism, nihilism and sadism mark him as a transgressive overreacher (2006: 86–7). In Cynthia Baron's words, 'Dr No occupies the space of the threatening or boundary-crossing Other' ([2003] 2009: 159). Moreover, Dr No's express interest in 'the study of the human body' – his desire 'to know what this clay is capable of' (Fleming [1958] 2012f: 233) – not only reinforces the Frankensteinian overtones of the novel but also recalls the politics of Mr Big's operation in *Live and Let Die*. Of his reconnaissance of Mr Big's nightclub in Harlem, Bond notes that 'it was a close-up of the raw material on which The Big Man worked, the clay in his hands' (Fleming [1954] 2012b: 69). Thus, both Mr Big and Dr No are cast as perverse creators. But whereas Mr Big's 'artistry' is, as I have argued in the previous chapter, carried out upon the Black body, Dr No is the subject of his own trans-corporeal experimentations. Bond worries that Dr No, with his partially mechanized body, is 'impregnable' (Fleming [1958] 2012f: 240). However, much like the porosity of the 'Chigro' body, Dr No's body, too, is described in terms of its permeability. The narrative notes that Dr No's head is shaped like a 'reversed raindrop' and that his skin is 'of a deep almost translucent yellow' (ibid.: 219), images which suggest a thin and weak cellular poriferousness. Indeed, the manner of Dr No's eventual death (Bond buries him beneath a pile of guano) also suggests bodily permeability, as Dr No suffocates precisely as a result of ingesting the 'stinking dust' of the bird excrement (ibid.: 299). As part-man and part-machine, part-biotic and part-inorganic matter, Dr No is an inherently liminal entity.[23] It is Dr No's liminality that positions him as transgressive, as he extends and corrupts the borders of his own body.

But, as Fleming makes clear, it is not just the novel's villains that are presented in terms of transgressive, trans-corporeal imagery. If Dr No is to be read, in part, both as a transhumanist machine and as an amphibious sea creature, then Bond's trusty right-hand man, the Cayman Islander Quarrel, is shown throughout the narrative to straddle the boundaries between man and child, and man and animal. Charles W. Mills has argued that Quarrel is characterized in both *Live and Let Die* and *Dr. No* as 'kindly' and 'childlike' (2010: 107). This strategy is one that Fleming employs seemingly to ameliorate British fears of West Indians, who had been the subject of much scrutiny in Britain at the time, following the arrival to British shores of the first generation of Windrush immigrants from the Caribbean. Indeed, as Andrew Lycett has argued, Fleming's portrayal of Quarrel is sympathetic and loving ([1995] 2008: 309). It is with genuine fondness that, following Quarrel's death, Bond recalls 'the soft ways of the big body, the innocence in the grey, horizon-seeking eyes, the simple lust and desires, the reverence for superstitions and instincts, the childish faults, the loyalty and even love that Quarrel had given him' (Fleming [1958] 2012f: 318–19). The warmth and charm of the West Indian embodied in Quarrel is as much a part of the novel's racial and cultural politics as Dr No's personification of the abhorrence of Asian communism. But Bond's patronage of Quarrel also has the adverse effect of justifying Britain's imperial perceptions of its Caribbean colonies. If Quarrel is the impetuous, instinctive and 'savage' child of nature, then Bond can be read as the guiding and directive parent of British culture under whose tutelage Quarrel flourishes. However, this too must necessarily be tempered. As we have already discussed, Bond is shown to be much more reliant upon Quarrel's tutelage, training and local Jamaican knowledge than the other way round. Nevertheless, the character of Quarrel was objected to by some Jamaicans as 'holding Jamaica back'. Morris Cargill, Fleming's good friend in Jamaica, has denounced the representation of Quarrel, declaring that 'we have to stop being colonials and start being Jamaicans … The umbilicus which attached us so sadly to Mother England was as much a fantasy as a reality and had to be cut' (qtd in Parker 2014: 191, 193). Thus, Quarrel is a deeply ambivalent character, at once indicative of Fleming's abiding affection for the peoples of the Caribbean as well as an emblem of the need he perceived for Britain's continued governance of its colonies in the region.

Less ambivalent, however (though far more problematic), is the text's emphasis on Quarrel's animalism. While Quarrel's servitude to Bond is presented as an uncomfortable matter of course throughout the narrative (in one scene, Bond demands with casual peremptoriness that Quarrel fetch him his trousers (Fleming [1958] 2012f: 152)), it is also metaphorized through an insistence within the text on framing Bond's encounters with the Cayman Islander as that of a man and his pet. Bond's seemingly innocuous appraisal of Quarrel as the two men reconnect in the airport ('everybody loved him and he was a splendid companion' (ibid.: 49)) takes on, in the context of the narrative that follows, something of the patronage and unconditional love shared between human and domestic animal. Quarrel's voice is described in one scene as possessing a 'feline pleasure' (ibid.: 60), but, by and large, he is more commonly likened to a canine. During the scene in the airport, Quarrel's hand, which Bond shakes, is likened to a 'warm dry calloused paw' (ibid.: 46). On Crab Key, when Bond wishes to attract Quarrel's attention, we are told that he 'whistled softly and smiled as [the sleeping Quarrel's] eyes sprang wide open like an animals' (ibid.: 123).

Like a drowsy pup, Quarrel 'scrambled to his feet, almost guiltily' (ibid.). Later, when Quarrel first senses the sound of an approaching motorboat, we are told that 'his head swivelled round and pointed like a dog's' (ibid.: 124). His face is also described as 'pointing like a gun-dog's' when, even later, he notices the tracks of the dragon that purportedly roams Dr No's island (ibid: 148). Finally, Quarrel's natural instincts are even presented as animal-like. Recalling the life insurance policy which Quarrel took out before the two men commence their clandestine reconnaissance of Crab Key, Bond notes that 'Quarrel had smelled his death. Yet he followed Bond unquestioningly. His faith in Bond had been stronger than his fear' (ibid.: 184). Charles W. Mills has noted that Quarrel is, in all respects, a 'properly deferential' companion to Bond, precisely because he is 'not so much a man as he is a friendly animal' (2010: 107). Much like Dr No, who resembles in many respects an arthropod, Quarrel is presented in terms of bodily transgression as a hybrid species of sorts – not 'man' and 'machine', but 'man' and 'dog'.

An interesting complement to the narrative's representation of Quarrel-as-dog is also to be found in the maltreatment of the pack of Doberman Pinschers deployed by Dr No's 'Chigro' workers to hunt down Bond's party, who are concealed in Crab Key's mangrove swamp. While on the level of ideology, the text's configuration of the relationship between Bond and Quarrel is politically questionable, on the level of narrative alone Fleming attempts to make clear his protagonist's abiding (though, it must be said, somewhat patronizing) affection and love for the Cayman Islander. Perhaps deliberately, the fond relationship between colonial master (Bond) and his subordinate pet (Quarrel) is placed in relief alongside the abusive treatment by the 'Chigro' guards of their dogs, who are furiously whipped (one of the guards 'laid about him with the whip') and who are violently 'grasped ... by the collar and swung into the channel' (Fleming [1958] 2012f: 142). The juxtaposed placement of this particular scene within the framework of a narrative that repeatedly insists on underscoring Quarrel's affinity with canines implies something of an unsubtle point – that Bond himself has never abused Quarrel (his figurative dog) so. Moreover, that the 'Chigro' guards are shown to be impatient and to disregard their dogs' interest in the enclosed pool at the river channel's end (which is, unbeknownst to them, precisely the spot in which Bond, Quarrel and Honey have concealed themselves) is used to underline another unsubtle and contrasting point: unlike the 'Chigro' guards, Bond's benevolent treatment of Quarrel, and the trust he places in Quarrel's instincts, is repaid with valuable service, loyalty and friendship. Thus, Fleming's employment of dog imagery throughout *Dr. No* serves to draw an uncomfortable comparison between the 'Chigroes" mistreatment of their Dobermans and Bond's (it is implied 'superior') treatment of Quarrel. The distastefulness of this symbolic alignment is augmented (and made all the more uncomfortable for the modern reader) by the very thought that this comparison is expiatory in purpose. In the context of *Dr. No*'s fluctuating racial, cultural, social and political relations between a declining Britain and the emergent postcolonial ethnoscape of nationalist Jamaica, the significance of this comparison cannot be missed: this is the closest Fleming comes in the novel to a cautionary admonishment to the British reader about the 'proper' treatment of Britain's colonial 'subordinates' in a time of increased racial and national agitation.

The problematic racialism inherent in Fleming's use of dog imagery in his descriptions of Quarrel is, it must be said, diffused across his descriptions of the indeterminate animalism of the white British body, too. Both Bond and Dr No at times liken the 'Chigro' community to apes (Fleming [1958] 2012f: 186, 225), and Quarrel is, as I have said, metaphorically configured as Bond's obedient dog; but Bond himself is also frequently depicted within the narrative as a transgressor not simply of the human–animal binary but of the classificatory ordering of species categorization. Fleming never specifies what animal, exactly, Bond is meant to resemble. When Bond falls asleep on the sands of Crab Key, for instance, the narrator tells us that he did not care 'what *other* animals or insects might come to his smell and his warmth' (ibid.: 110, my italics). Here, the sentence construction is implicitly suggestive of Bond's own indiscriminate animalism; he is, himself, but an*other* animal on the island's shore. This view seems to be given credence in the narrative, when, as Bond and Honey physically consummate their relationship towards the end of the novel, they are described as 'two loving animals' whose intercourse, as animals who have come to one another, is considered perfectly 'natural' (ibid.: 327). When, in Dr No's elaborate torture chamber, Bond is electrocuted, we are told that he 'bent his head down and shook it slowly from side to side like a wounded animal' (ibid.: 263). Here, Bond's animalism is juxtaposed with the image of the electrified wire grille which shocks him and which Bond fears 'might strike at him again, like a snake' (ibid.). In a process of corporeal and material inversion, as Bond's body figuratively morphs within the narrative to resemble by greater and greater measure an animal's, it seems that the inanimate and inorganic matter of which the text's spatial environments are built seemingly take on the features of biotic fauna, too (in this case, a snake). Having sustained almost unendurable levels of pain during the obstacle course, we are told, 'Bond's lips drew back from his teeth and he snarled into the darkness', an 'animal sound' that derives from 'the end of [Bond's] human reactions to pain and adversity' (ibid.: 273). Here, Bond can be said to have reached and transgressed the very limits of humanity itself. In the seemingly limitless pain it continues to endure, Bond's body symbolically metamorphoses as he draws on his final 'animal reserves of desperation'. Once again, Bond likens himself to a 'strong animal' (ibid.), but which one, exactly, is never made explicit. For much of the narrative, therefore, Bond is presented as something of an animal in-becoming.

During one particular nocturnal scene, when Bond is asleep in his hotel, Fleming employs the following simile:'The moon coming in through the slats in the jalousies threw black and white bars across the corner of the room next to [Bond's] bed. It was as if he was lying in a cage' (ibid.: 89). The (symbolic) barred enclosure by which Bond is (figuratively) contained suggests a wildness, an indeterminate animalism which is, once again, offset by and juxtaposed with the 'hysterical chorus' of barking dogs Bond hears in the distance, as well as his instinctive perception of the centipede (the poisonous one sent by Dr No's emissaries to kill him) crawling up his body (ibid.: 90). Bond's sensory perception (both aural and physical) of the animal threat that assails him is framed within the context of his own symbolic animalism, and his wariness and alertness over the potential animal threat to his body indicates the splicing of his own human-animal instincts. His reactions are as instinctive as an animal's, but the rational analysis of his own fear ('Bond analysed the noise. It couldn't be! It simply couldn't! Yes, his hair was standing on end.' (ibid.)) is suggestive of the superiority of anthropoid logic. The 'animal Bond' is indeterminate, but Bond's mental operations during the scene underpin his reliable human instincts. In this instance, Bond can be read as a transgressive entity, both as wild animal and as rational human, neither wholly of one species nor the other. Indeed, the sentence configuration 'he stopped as dead as a live man can' is, in its evocation of Bond's fear, suggestive of a further transgression. In this moment of wild animal panic, Bond not only figuratively broaches the boundaries between one species and another (in 'becoming' a wild animal himself with a 'snarling mouth' (ibid.: 92)), but his body is also held in a Schrödingerean suspension of sorts between life and death ('Bond lay frozen'; 'Bond's whole consciousness had drained' (ibid.: 91)).

Animals and animal imagery are harnessed within the text as part of the narrative's transgressive economy, and Fleming's concern with the transgression of spatial boundaries, which is analogous to his ambivalent concern for the shifting bounds of British-Jamaica racial, social and cultural relations in the postcolonial period, is configured through the novel's trans-corporeal and transhumanist imagery. We see this most clearly in Fleming's presentation of Honey Rider, whose body is constructed throughout as an embodied space for the negotiation of fluctuated British-Jamaican cultural relations in the imminent postcolonial period. As the beneficiary of Bond's sexual and political desires, as well as the personification of Britain's supposedly benevolent relations with its Caribbean protectorates, Honey is, I contend, the material conduit through which much of the novel's ambivalent political ideation flows, and upon whom Bond's attempts at political reincorporation operates – and, I argue, can be read as an embodiment of Jamaica itself. Much like the figure of Solitaire in *Live and Let Die*, Honey is a Caribbean Creole, born to an established colonial planter family on the island. Honey's cultural and ancestral heritage is further complicated by the fact that, after her parents die in a house fire, she is raised by her Afro-Caribbean nanny in the ruins of their estate. Vivian Halloran has argued that Honey is already an 'inhabitant of a multicultural society'. As such, Honey 'does not find racial intermixing unusual or even remarkable' (2005: 169). Lisa M. Dresner reads Honey as a 'good example of the ethnically and geographically displaced Bond girl, a figure who *may reflect* the waning of the British and European colonial empires' (2011: 276, my italics). Dresner's conditional use of the word 'reflect', here, suggests a further positional ambivalence: it is unclear whether the reader is supposed to view Honey's embodied 'reflection' of those political events around which the novel is based as beneficial (the prospect of Jamaican autonomy from Britain) or detrimental (Britain's waning control of Jamaica). In other words, it is unclear whether the character's ethnic and geographic displacement is either an injurious condition of the colonial status quo or a welcome precondition of impending Jamaican independence. This point is seemingly emphasized by the fact that Honey's ancestors were anti-regents who were gifted the lands and the Great House of Beau Desert by Oliver Cromwell for having signed King Charles I's death warrant. Thus, Honey's patriotism for her ancestral homeland is also a questionable issue. Either way, the novel makes it clear that the effects of British (de)colonization are written onto and are reproduced upon her body. That Bond likens Honey to Botticelli's Venus, though, does suggest a particularly European (as opposed to Caribbean) frame of reference through which the reader is encouraged to interpret the character, which further suggests something of the narrative's underlying political purpose. Bond's protection of Honey parallels his attempts to reincorporate Dr No's island lair within the spatial territory of the British Empire; as a figurative embodiment of Britain's Jamaican colony, Bond's rescue of Honey from the threat of Chinese communism may be read as tantamount to the ideological reincorporation of the island under British rule.

Sam Bourne highlights another of Honey's positional ambiguities: she is depicted in the novel as 'part intuitive animal, part innocent child' (2012: xiii), as yet another example of the novel's insistence on transgressive hybridity. As Quarrel is the 'kindly' and 'childlike' Cayman Islander who is frequently likened to a dog (Mills 2010: 107), Honey is frequently presented as both animal and child-like. Bond compares her to 'an animal whose cubs are threatened' and to 'a dog that nobody wants to pet' (Fleming [1958] 2012f: 117). He finds 'sensually thrilling' her 'warm animal smell' (ibid.: 154), while he conceives of the misfortune of her involvement in Dr No's affairs in the following metaphoric terms: 'She doesn't know that she's been swept out of her rock pool into the dirty waters' (ibid.: 132), a comment which implies both bodily transmutation and spatial transgression. (In this analogy, Honey is a form of sea life that has transgressed the bounded safety of her rock pool.) Thus, as Tony Bennett and Janet Woollacott have argued, Honey is presented as 'a creature of nature with a curious affinity with animals' (1987: 121). Far more problematic than Honey's (comparatively permissive) transgression of the human–animal and culture–nature divide, though, is the narrative's configuration of that most intolerable of cultural transgressions: child sexuality. Throughout *Dr. No*, it is made clear that Honey is the innocent child to Bond's knowing adult – her innocence, as Bruce A. Rosenberg and Ann Harlemann Stewart acknowledge, 'an ideal target for Bond's admiring condescension' (1989: 100). When Bond and Honey are captured by Dr No's forces in the swamplands, Bond reinforces a particular parent–child dynamic when he tells Honey, 'Don't you say anything, I'll talk for both of us' (Fleming [1958] 2012f: 181). When, in their mink-lined prison within Dr No's cavernous lair, Honey wants to 'play at being married', Bond gently kisses the top of her head and hurries her along to eat her breakfast as though he were a father softly chiding his young daughter (ibid.: 204). And later, ahead of their dinner with Dr No, Bond selects Honey's food for her as though she were a dependent, unable to do so for herself (ibid.: 213) – although this may also be because Fleming wishes to lay stress upon Bond's culinary connoisseurship. Indeed, when Honey later faints at dinner, the reader is told that Dr No's henchmen 'plucked her bodily out of the chair as if she had been a child' (ibid.: 256). That the novel goes to some length to stress the childliness of its female protagonist is all the more disturbing when it is noted that these particular qualities are juxtaposed in the narrative with Bond's musings on his sexual attraction to Honey. It is as Honey's substitute father that Bond wishes to 'buy her dresses, have her hair done, get her started in the big world', but it is as her prospective lover that he muses on 'the other side [of their relationship]', 'the physical desire he felt for her' (ibid.: 171). What follows is an insight into Bond's internal narrative, in which he seems to offer an uncomfortable justification for his own rapacious interests: 'One could not make love to a child. But was she a child? There was nothing childish about her body or her personality' (ibid.). I am, of course, not suggesting that we are meant to consider Bond in paedophilic terms. While it is certainly a discomfiting part of the narrative's sexual economy, Honey's childliness is much more a part of the text's political economy and of its configuration of British-Jamaican relations at large than it is an implicit commentary on Bond's sexuality. If Bond is to be believed – if, indeed, there is nothing childish about Honey's body or personality – then whence does Honey's ostensible childliness come? The answer is from Fleming himself. Honey's childish qualities are not inherent or essential to her character; rather, they are purposefully ascribed to her in narration, through the authorizing voice of Fleming's narrator. Honey's childliness, then, is a fundamental component of *Dr. No*'s politics. As a Jamaican Creole, Honey's cultural hybridity suggests a resistance to Bond's efforts to imperialize her. As the descendant of British colonial landowners, Honey's ancestral Britishness indicates a certain historical affinity to Britain and its empire. As the 'adopted' child of her Afro-Caribbean nanny, raised in the ruins of a great plantation mansion, Honey's 'imperious attitude and her quality of attack', as well as her 'imperious glint' (ibid.: 117, 327), are indicative of her internalized resistance to the authoritative officiousness of colonial management which Bond represents. Whereas Quarrel is configured within the text as Bond's faithful guard dog (and as another of his symbolic children), Honey patently resists Bond's attempts to subordinate her. The authoritative command which she issues to Bond in the novel's final line ('Do as you're told' (ibid.: 329)) is, in its very finality, indicative of her dominant position within the couple's power dynamic, which is further endorsed by the fact that the narrative concludes then and there. Furthermore, her use of the idiomatic phrase 'slave-time' (ibid.: 172, 329) to describe fornication with Bond suggests a particular sexual dynamic which, in an uncomfortable irony, gestures towards Honey's liberation from her gendered sexual enslavement by Bond (i.e. *her* sexual domination of *him*).

If we read Honey as an embodiment of Jamaica, then *Dr. No* can be said to initiate a particular kind of political conflict. The clash within the narrative between Honey's subordinate childliness and her dominance and independence is metonymic of the novel's (and Fleming's) consideration of impending Jamaican independence from Britain. The novel's primary conflict is thus inherently ambivalent. On the one hand, Honey's resistance to Bond's (and to Britain's) authorizing attempts to control her, as well as Bond's acknowledgement that Honey is a dominant and independent woman, can be read to signify Jamaica's political and national autonomy from Britain, and as a telling concession to the newly emergent political order of post-war, postcolonial geopolitics. Again, that the novel concludes with Honey telling Bond to 'do as you're told' suggests something of Fleming's authorial endorsement of Honey's emergent authority and of the couple's inversion of traditional political, racial, cultural and social power dynamics. On the other hand, the repeated emphasis placed throughout the narrative upon Honey's childliness is connotative not of a potentially transgressive or iniquitous sexuality on Bond's part but of a rather specific metaphoric economy. The implied legal, moral, ethical and philosophical question of Bond's sexual interest in the childlike Honey is also a political one, in this context, but it is Honey's childliness and not (for once) Bond's sexuality that is important, here. We have already seen Fleming's strategic attempts to ameliorate British fears of West Indians through his loving presentation of Quarrel, whose kindliness and childish qualities, it is implied, is indicative of Britain's (and specifically Bond's) parental management of its (figurative) unruly child – its Jamaican colony. Like Quarrel, Honey, too, is shown to possess knowledge which Bond himself does not have: 'Anyway, what do you think you know about animals and thing? ... you're just city folk like all the rest' (ibid.: 121). However, unlike Quarrel, Honey's obedience is much less a condition of her relationship to Bond. That is to say, if Honey is a child, then she is a wayward one. The narrative makes it clear that she is neither servile nor tameable. When Bond notes that 'there would be no dropping the leash until he had solved her problems for her' (ibid.: 171), it is implied, firstly, that Bond's efficacy as a problem-solver is tied (indeed, invariably leads at the close of each narrative) to his conquest of the female body; and secondly, that Honey's animality, though presented in questionably racialist terms, belies a fierce independence that is in no need of Bond's control. Robert A. Caplen's assertions that 'Bond must save [Honey] from herself' and that 'Honey has only herself to blame for the entanglements in which she finds herself' (2012: 70) strike me, therefore, as reductive and not a little misogynistic. Far more accurate is Christine Bold's argument that 'Bond frequently depends on women to guide him through enemy territory' (1993: 315), and that Honey's knowledge of Jamaican tides and her navigation of the island terrain of Crab Key suggest a considerably independent character. Indeed, Bond notes that Honey has 'the face of a girl who fends for herself' and that she is 'far more capable of taking care of herself than any girl of twenty Bond had ever met' (Fleming [1958] 2012f: 115, 171). The narrative's insistence on labelling Honey as childish, then, is part of the text's ambivalent political economy: Fleming's ambivalent presentation of Honey as both independent adult and dependent child is demonstrative of the narrative's (and, arguably, his own) internal ambivalence concerning Jamaican independence from Britain at the time.

That Honey can be read as the personification of Fleming's political ambivalence with respect to Jamaican independence can be seen most explicitly in the narrative treatment of her nose, in particular, which becomes the corporeal focal point of the novel's ambivalent politics. There has been much critical discussion about the ambiguities embodied in Honey, little of which has focused on the political territory of her nose.[24] When Bond first encounters Honey on the shores of Crab Key, he notices that her nose is 'badly broken, smashed crooked like a boxer's'. Bond, we are told, is so repulsed by Honey's marred appearance that he 'stiffened with revolt' at her 'shame' (ibid.: 115). Honey later tells him that her nose was broken during an attack when she was younger, when a man by the name of Mander knocked her unconscious and raped her. Her nose is, apparently, so strikingly deformed that even Dr No comments upon it during their first encounter, calling it a 'misfortune' (ibid.: 220). Honey's nose, then, poses a particular concern to a number of characters throughout the narrative, highlighted repeatedly as a problem in need of fixing. In particular, it becomes a point of contestation between Honey and Bond. While Honey is adamant that she is going to have corrective surgery to fix it ('all I wanted to do was save up money to get my nose made good again ... Do you think the doctors can put it back to how it was?' (ibid.: 166)), Bond's position on the issue shifts from the surety of simple concordance with Honey's wishes to something altogether much more ambivalent. Early on in the narrative, Bond wonders why Honey has not already had her nose mended: 'It was an easy operation,' he muses to himself (ibid.: 154). Here, Bond is in agreement with Honey's assessment of her own disfigurement. Indeed, as he makes clear, the superlativeness of Honey's beauty is contingent precisely upon her undertaking corrective surgery: '*Then* [when she gets a nose operation] she would be the most beautiful girl in Jamaica' (ibid., my italics). As she is, Honey presents something of a physically desirous paradox to Bond: she is a 'beautiful, ravishing, Ugly Ducking' (ibid.). The narrative implies that it is only through Bond's beneficent aid (Bond offers to pay for the surgery) that Honey can be assured of completion. Throughout the course of the narrative, however, Bond's opinion softens: he notes variously that 'he had almost forgotten her broken nose' and that 'the beautiful face smiled at him ... the broken nose seemed appropriate in its animalness' (ibid.: 117, 138).

He reassures Honey that she is 'one of the most beautiful girls [he has] ever seen', and he reflects to himself that he even 'loved the broken nose' (ibid.: 160, 204).

If we accept that Honey personifies or in some way embodies Fleming's political ambivalence regarding Jamaica's emergent political autonomy and its independence from British governance, then we might read Bond's fluctuating responses to the issue of Honey's nose (i.e. the feature of her body upon which most emphasis is laid within the text) as indicative of a further political ambivalence. Within the context of the narrative, Honey's nose becomes a symbol of Britain's ongoing political management of the increasingly nationalist, independent Jamaica. If Honey's body represents the politically emergent Jamaica, caught in the historical interstices of the period between British colonial governance of the island and Jamaica's own national autonomy, Bond's encouragement of Honey's corrective surgery suggests, on the one hand, that Britain's continued control of Jamaica is figuratively exercised through Bond's (re)construction of Honey's apparently broken or deformed body. In other words, Bond's (and Fleming's) management of Honey's body is tantamount to Britain's continued management of its colonial enclave in Jamaica, the 'deformation' of which, it is implied, is the country's desire for political nationalism (i.e. the *de-formation* of empire). But, on the other hand, as Dr No's trans-corporeal enhancements are presented as threatening to the bounds of human nature itself, and, moreover, because they are self-administered, Honey's desire for surgical enhancement is ultimately threatening to and ultimately discouraged by Bond precisely because of the implicit symbolic alignment in *Dr. No* between Honey's bodily autonomy and Jamaica's political autonomy. That Bond ultimately strives, towards the end of the narrative, to discourage Honey from undertaking surgery ('D'you really want to have that operation? I love your face – just as it is. It's part of you. Part of all this' (Fleming [1958] 2012f: 326)) is indicative of his desires to preserve the political status quo in Jamaica. Bond's insistence that Honey's nose remain exactly as it is illustrates not only his will to exercise control over her body (thus further depriving her of agency) but also the narrative's political conservatism with respect to emerging British-Jamaican political relations. Indeed, when Bond tells Honey that her broken nose is 'part of all this', the narrative explicitly configures Honey's physicality as a synecdochal part of Jamaica's overarching cultural ethnoscape. In this moment, Jamaica's political landscape is figuratively transposed onto Honey's 'disfigured' body, and her body itself becomes activated within the narrative as a metonymic substitution for the island of Jamaica – the 'ills' of which Bond is also attempting to police and 'fix'.

The metaphoric transposition of Honey's body and the Jamaican landscape is made all the more explicit by the fact that it is among the literal ruins of her (broken) family home that Honey first receives her broken nose. She is raped in the crumbling ruins of her parents' old colonial plantation settlement at Beau Desert and subsequently raised by her Black nanny following her parents' death in the Great House fire. That Honey lives in the cellar of the old ruin (i.e. below ground level) further implies a connection between her body and the island's geographic terrain: she is brought up *in* the earth. Moreover, that Honey is raped by Mander, the 'white overseer for the people who own the property' (ibid.: 164), signifies a correlation between her body and those violent acts of ecocide committed by or in the name of Jamaica's colonial plantocracy. The aggravated sexual and racial assault of her Creole body among the ruins of the plantation house – an act both of literal penetration and of figurative colonization – is also configured as an act of environmental despoliation. That Honey releases a black widow spider into Mander's bed in recompense indicates a further symbiosis between her and the natural environment. Mander's death by spider poisoning constitutes an act of both ecological vengeance and reverse colonization; he, too, is literally penetrated (bitten) and ultimately dies a violent death. Honey's rape is very much tied to her complicated position as a colonial subject. As a white Creole born on the island and raised, for the most part, by an Afro-Caribbean nanny, she is a cultural and social native of Jamaica. But, as the daughter of settled British plantocrats, she is ethnically and racially European. Bond's desire for Honey to have her nose repaired, then, suggests that Honey's ideological and political realignment is configured in terms of physiognomic aesthetics, preconditioned by Bond's wish for her to *appear* more British than Jamaican. That the name of Honey's rapist (Mander) is both a visual and aural rhyme with the official naval rank held by Bond (Commander) also underscores the point that Bond's desire to 'fix' Honey is neither wholly aesthetic nor simply altruistic, but an expression of Britain's anxieties concerning the imminent loss of control over its acquired Caribbean territories and its need to 'put right' (or to command) its colonial affairs. Both Bond and Mander desire Honey physically, and their shared desire is conditioned not simply by personal lustfulness but by their more rapacious instincts to imperialize her. Mander's rape of Honey represents a literal conquest of her body-territory, while Bond's desire for Honey to have her nose realigned signifies his attempts to metaphorically repatriate her.

Moreover, Bond's figurative repatriation of Honey mirrors Mander's attempts to literally rehouse her, which she recounts to Bond earlier in the text. She tells

Bond that '[Mander] wanted me to move up to his house near Port Maria' (ibid.). Bond's symbolic alignment with Mander and with the rapacious threat of the white colonizer is emphasized further by Honey's revelation that the ruins of her parents' Great House are in the Beau Desert estate, where, coincidentally, Bond and Quarrel have taken up temporary residence for the duration of the mission. In effect, Bond can be said to have stepped into the role of the plantation's white overseer, while Honey performs the role of an indentured labourer of sorts, his figurative subordinate whose adopted family, her nanny, worked the breadfruit and sugar cane crops on the estate. Honey's symbolic subordination to Bond on the plantation is further emphasized through Bond's insistence on Honey's atavism. Surprised not to have seen her at Beau Desert before, Bond jokingly asks her, 'Do you live up a tree?' (Fleming [1958] 2012f: 158). And, later, when Honey shows Bond where she lives among the ruins, Bond notes, 'What a lovely room. From what you said I thought you lived in a sort of zoo' (ibid.: 326). Here, Bond's attempted colonial subjugation of Honey is configured through oblique references to her animalism, which underline, once again, the character's trans-corporeality – and, by extension, Bond's comparative humanity or civility. Finally, Honey's subjugation to Bond becomes fully realized through one simile in particular that Bond uses to describe her: he notes that 'she looked like a principal girl dressed as Man Friday' (ibid.: 118). This comment not only aligns Bond with the absolutist mythos of Britain's colonial greatness as figured in the eponymous hero of Daniel Defoe's 1719 novel *Robinson Crusoe*, but it also configures Honey's subordination in specifically racial terms, since Defoe's original 'Man Friday' was a Black Caribbean to whom Crusoe taught the ways of British culture and society. Thus, it is implied that Honey's intention to 'come back to Jamaica and buy Beau Desert' (ibid.: 168) after a period of employment as a sex worker in the United States is but wishful thinking. As with the character of Friday in *Robinson Crusoe*, Honey's desired repatriation to her native Jamaica is presented as an impossibility within the ideological economy of the text, and at odds with Bond's efforts to reposition her within a post-war Anglo-Saxon cultural, social and political context.

Thus, the narrative's treatment of Honey is much like the overarching political significance of the novel *Dr. No* itself. The question of whether Honey is a subordinate child in need of Britain's parental guidance or an independent and autonomous woman capable of directing her own fate is reflective of the immanent political anxieties of British-Jamaican relations in 1958 which the novel belies. The political, social, cultural and racial consequences of the immediate post-independence period in Jamaica, following transfer of sovereign powers from Britain to the island's national government, is retrospectively addressed in Fleming's third and final Jamaica-set novel, *The Man with the Golden Gun*, which was published after Fleming's death, in 1965. The underlying political concerns of *Dr. No*, though, are made explicit through the novel's repeating motifs of corporeality, and their meanings are apparent. Where in *Live and Let Die* Fleming's Jamaica was simply a static, exoticized backdrop for the commencement of patterned action, the narrative of *Dr. No* makes it abundantly clear that the island, like Honey, is a mobilized ethnoscape transfused with political and corporeal agency.

3

Mobility, memory and touristic modernity in *The Man with the Golden Gun*

By the time *The Man with the Golden Gun* was published in 1965, a great deal had changed with respect to Britain's political landscape. Two months prior to the release of Fleming's final novel, Sir Winston Churchill had died of a stroke (on 24 January). The death of this beloved elder statesman was, in David Cannadine's words, 'self consciously recognised as being a requiem for Britain as a great power' (1979: 46). Cannadine further notes that

> a changing conventional morality [in Britain of the mid-twentieth century] was accompanied by an unprecedented rise in living standards, which encouraged the most puritanical critics of 'decline' to liken England to the degenerate days of the later Roman Empire or early 17th-century Spain – obsessed with sex and self-indulgence, and turning its back on the more Spartan modes of life which had been the foundation of former greatness. (ibid.)

Moral 'decline' on British shores, Cannadine argues, was 'mirrored in international "decline" abroad, as the tropical African empire was wound up, the white Commonwealth was severely shaken by the departure of South Africa, and Britain's standing in the eyes of the world was irretrievably damaged as a result of the Suez fiasco' (ibid.). By the time Fleming had finished writing *The Man with the Golden Gun*, Britain had undertaken further decolonization in Kenya, Cyprus, Uganda, Sierra Leone and in many other places, including, of course, Fleming's beloved Jamaica in early August 1962. Britain's (neo)imperial posturing on the global stage and Bond's delusional political fantasies concerning his own relevance within the context of Jamaica's emergent nationalism were no longer credible in real terms. In *The Man with the Golden Gun*, Fleming strives to maintain the reader's credulity in a fantastical world wherein Britain has retained both its political and economic pre-eminence in post-war global affairs. Certainly, the later Bond novels suffer under the strain of this delusion.

The invention of SPECTRE, the depoliticized criminal enterprise headed by Bond's nemesis, Ernst Stavro Blofeld, permits Fleming to divert Bond's concern away from the historical contexts of real-world geopolitical issues and towards the unreality of those imagined villainies of Fleming's particular fictive universe. From *Thunderball* (1961) onwards, Fleming's novels undergo a shift in focus away from Cold War conflicts between the Eastern and Western blocs and towards the expressly apolitical criminality of the capitalist machine SPECTRE, whose members are concerned more with financial remuneration than they are with advancing a specific political agenda. With respect to Fleming's British-Jamaican geopolitics, Jeremy Black is quite clear that the 'global scope' of Bond's adventures (and of Britain's political influence) which was last to be seen in *Thunderball* has well and truly vanished in *The Man with the Golden Gun*. Moreover, that Britain 'played only a marginal role in the Cuban Crisis of 1962' (Black 2005: 78) suggests that Bond's discovery by accident that Scaramanga is hiding in Jamaica and not in Havana (as he previously suspects) is part of the revisionist political economy of the text, whereby Fleming's relocation of narrative action from Cuba to the familiar territory of Jamaica is an attempt to imbue British-Jamaican relations in the post-independence period with ongoing and continued significance, thereby reinscribing Britain's relevance within a historical conflict (and an alternate political topography) to which it was by that stage, in reality, largely unconnected. That Scaramanga turns out to be working for Cuban communists – Bond's red enemy of old – further evidences the novel's anachronisms. Bond's intercession on behalf of Britain's faded empire into the economic affairs of postcolonial Jamaica conflates the political landscape of the contemporary Caribbean with those fears encroaching communism long foretold in Fleming's previous Jamaica-set novels, as far back as *Live and Let Die* in 1954. It is, perhaps, precisely because of the confused political context of *The Man with the Golden Gun* that Simon Winder has declared that, while the novel is 'not so much good [it] still became a vast, nostalgic bestseller' (2006: 208). Of course, *The Man with the Golden Gun* conveys a certain nostalgia for the displaced Bond, who is (not unlike Fleming himself) uncomfortably positioned within the political, social and cultural interstices of British-Jamaican relations. Bond is positioned between the illegitimacy of Britain's (neo)imperialization of the island and the patronage afforded to the national police by his unofficial, retroactive secondment to the Jamaican government at the end of the story.

Moreover, Fleming's final Bond novel is also something of a nostalgic paean to Fleming himself, who 'died before he could revise, polish, and add the rich detail he always incorporated after he had completed the first draft' (Benson

1984: 140). Fleming died of a heart attack on 12 August 1964, some eight months before the publication of the novel, which was 'finished' by Glidrose Productions (now Ian Fleming Publications) and released posthumously. When compared with the vastly superior works of *Live and Let Die* and *Dr. No*, in particular, *The Man with the Golden Gun* simply does not measure up to its literary forebears. As Raymond Benson notes, 'it doesn't seem as if one is experiencing Fleming's world through Bond, as one usually is. This time, the narrative voice speaks more often in the third person. Gone is the identification with the character which succeeded in giving Bond the well-rounded traits that has become so familiar' (141). Lars Ole Sauerberg has also noted that Fleming's transition in his later works 'from uneasy realism towards pure romance' represents a literary failure, largely because 'the simplicity of Bond's predicament was no longer possible' (given the political climate into which Fleming forcibly wedges the anachronistic Bond) and partly because Fleming's style in his final novel is 'downright bad' (1984: 169). It is reasonable to conclude that Fleming himself was not unaware of these issues. In a 1963 interview for the *Gleaner*, Jamaica's local newspaper, Fleming's response to the question of whether or not he would write another Jamaica-set novel was characteristically glib: 'I can't go on plugging Jamaica like this or my public will think I have shares in the Jamaican Travel business' (qtd in Parker 2014: 293–4). While Fleming did (inevitably) elect to set his subsequent novel in Jamaica, his approach to what would be his concluding offering to the Bond canon was anything other than frivolous. On the contrary, Fleming was deeply anxious about the fate of his protagonist. In a 1963 letter to his editor William Plomer, Fleming ponders, 'What the hell am I going to do with Bond now?' He confesses to 'feeling horribly lethargic' about his own literary creation and 'very inclined to leave him hanging on his cliff in Vladivostok' (Fleming 1963b: n.p.), where the preceding novel, *You Only Live Twice*, concludes. Fleming informs Plomer almost a year later that he has 'somehow managed to write a, nearly, book [*sic*]', but that the writing process has left him feeling as 'empty as a Jamaican gourd' (Fleming 1964a: n.p.). It is clear from Fleming's correspondences that *The Man with the Golden Gun*, which Fleming refers to as his 'stupid book' (Fleming 1964c: n.p.), suffers from a great number of stylistic defects. Indeed, he inquires of Plomer whether together they might 'give it another year's working over so that we can go out with a bang instead of a whimper' (ibid.). Moreover, Fleming further confesses that he is 'not enthusiastic' about his final effort (Fleming 1964a: n.p.), while his good friend Maurice Cargill noted that 'poor Ian was in a terrible state over that last book of his' (1965b: n.p.). Much like his protagonist in *The Man with the Golden*

Gun, whom Kingsley Amis refers to as 'more of a man without qualities than ever before' (1965: 33), it is apparent by the time he has come to write his final Bond novel that Fleming is something of a hollow vessel of his former assured and mocking self, harbouring much greater ambivalence towards his own (and Bond's) fictional enterprise.

In terms of narrative, the opening of *The Man with the Golden Gun* expressly signals to the reader that something is unthinkably wrong within (and with) Fleming's fictive universe. Bond has been 'turned' by the Soviets and is poised to assassinate his once-beloved M; the very foundations of Britain's national defences – not to mention its patriotic self-image as rendered in the personage of Bond himself – have been compromised.[1] Clearly, these are exceptional times for both Fleming and Britain – the former of whom is literally dead by the time the novel is published, and the latter of which has been rendered politically and economically impotent as a result of both the Second World War and the fallout of decolonization. The conceit of Bond's brainwashing at the hands of Russia's KGB does, however, afford Fleming a rare opportunity to level directly against Britain's political history charges of imperial warmongering. In a scene of finely wrought tension rendered hardly as well in even those of Fleming's earlier, more superior novels, Bond is shown to express for the first time in his career (and, fittingly, only at the very end of it) an explicit resistance to the political machinery he himself is employed by and operates within. Granted, Bond is under the influence of Soviet reconditioning, but, nevertheless, from his own mouth, M's crimes (and Britain's) are rendered plain: 'You've been making war against someone or other all your life. You're doing so at this moment. And for most of my adult life you've used me as a tool', he says to M (Fleming [1965] 2012m: 19). Were British Intelligence to demobilize its own apparatus, Bond intimates, the Russians would comply and demobilize their KGB. While this is undoubtedly to be understood as a misguided ruse on the part of his addled brain, the implication of what Bond is saying is clear enough. As the historical purveyor of global terror masquerading as colonialism's civilizing mission, Britain itself is to be blamed for a great deal of the world's ills it purports to manage and police – while M, specifically, is to be blamed for Bond's own personal disaffection and psychological maladjustments. This moment is a rare instance of Fleming's uncommonly brazen (and unambivalent) indictment of Britain's imperial heritage, so often overlooked within the corpus of his writings. At the very least, it offers a check to the reductive arguments of those who insist on reading Fleming as 'simply' colonialist. That Bond himself purports to be completely *compos mentis* throughout this sequence (when it is very apparent to

M and to the reader that he is brainwashed) is not to be read strictly as evidence as to why we should dismiss his sentiments as deluded ramblings, either. On the contrary, Bond's strident insistence on his own mental capacity only further underscores his damning excoriation of Britain's imperial history.

Consider, too, Fleming's trajectory as a writer. As I have already outlined, *The Man with the Golden Gun* represents something of a nadir in the Bond canon (leaving aside the altogether derisible *The Spy Who Loved Me*). Fleming himself was grossly displeased with the novel, and the writing of it coincided with (indeed, almost assuredly precipitated) the fatal decline of his own physical health, which lead to his eventual death shortly after completing the first draft. Bond's accusation to M ('for most of my life you've used me as a tool') might just as easily be read as the damning repudiation of an ailing author wearied by his most notorious literary invention, a character who enabled Fleming to accrue a great deal of personal wealth but very little artistic satisfaction and to whom he felt burdensomely beholden. Indeed, as far back as 1954, when the third Bond novel, *Moonraker*, was to be published, Fleming admitted to Michael Howard, his publisher at Jonathan Cape, that 'I have a horrible feeling that I have begun to parody myself, which is obviously a great danger when one is writing of characters like James Bond *in whom one doesn't believe*. (qtd in Fleming 2015: 55, my italics). At the end of Fleming's writing career, then, when both his body and the character James Bond seem to be failing him, Bond's confrontation with M (and all that he stands for) is really a proxy for Fleming's renunciation of the much-beleaguered formula of his own increasingly anachronistic Bond novels, as well as, in part, a renunciation of Bond himself (and some – if not all – of what *he* stands for). The dramatic opening of *The Man with the Golden Gun* represents not simply Fleming's reorganization of the (by now) staid structural formula he laid down in *Dr. No* (see Pearson 1966: 286); it also signifies a significant structural ambivalence with respect to the novel's internal politics. On the one hand, Bond's mission in *The Man with the Golden Gun* is restorative – both of Bond's capabilities as an agent and of his political and national allegiance to Britain, as well as of Britain's 'rightful' management of its former colonial enclave in Jamaica. M makes this much perfectly clear in his musings on Bond following the assassination attempt. Bond's assignment (to assassinate Francisco Scaramanga) is overtly about testing Bond: 'If he succeeded, [Bond] would have regained his previous status. If he failed, well, it would be a death for which he would be honoured' (Fleming [1965] 2012m: 29). More implicitly, it represents a barely coded endorsement of Britain's continued surveillance of its former Jamaican colony as well as its ongoing ideological war against eastern communism. On the other hand, that Fleming elects to open the novel with an unmistakably scathing reproach of Britain's imperial politics, embodied in the tense face-off between Bond and M, suggests that Fleming is as tired of Bond's politics in real life as Bond is of M's in the novel. As Paul Stock argues, it is precisely because James Bond is 'Britain and Britishness incarnate' (2000: 35) that the narrative is at great pains to insert Bond within a geopolitical context upon which he cannot reasonably be expected to have any plausible bearing in the postcolonial period. As an 'icon of national identity', Bond's continued presence in the Caribbean 'promotes a particular geopolitical framework through which the world should be viewed' (Dittmer 2008: 16). The narrative is also at great pains to stress Bond's – that is, Britain's – restorative glory. Apart from a few descriptive lines on Bond's electroshock therapy, Fleming's narrative elides any substantial discussion of Bond's rehabilitation and his recovery from the Russians' brainwashing.[2] After the first few chapters of *The Man with the Golden Gun*, it is merely assumed that Bond's reassignment to active duty is preconditioned by his restoration to full psychological health. (M is remarkably accommodating, if not flagrantly irresponsible, in his expediency and in his trust in Bond, here.) But while the remainder of the novel is ostensibly concerned with the central questions raised by the opening few chapters (Is Bond actually medically qualified to carry out his duties as before? Will he restore his former glory or will he die in pursuit of Scaramanga?), Fleming's decision to withhold from the reader any insight into Bond's inner psychological and emotional life results in a complete lack of narrative tension. Rather, the narrative's lack of elaboration on these issues suggests that Bond's psychological well-being is ultimately immaterial to Fleming. By the time Fleming comes to write *The Man with the Golden Gun*, Bond is, like Fleming, an ailing cipher of himself. Jamaica is what matters (as it always has to Fleming), and it is Jamaica over which Fleming can be said to wage one final ideologically ambivalent war.

Mobility and (re)memory in post-independence Jamaica

In *Dr. No*, Fleming employs a number of images of bodily transgression in order to convey to his readers a sense of the seismic political, cultural and social transformations that had commenced in earnest on Jamaica and within British-Jamaican relations as a result of increased nationalist agitation on the island. A number of different cultural borders, territorial boundaries and socially imposed margins – between white Britons and Black Jamaicans, between Black

Jamaicans and Chinese immigrants and between humans and animals – are shown to be variously corrupted, broached, transgressed or erased throughout the course of the narrative. In *The Man with the Golden Gun*, Fleming extends these metaphors further. Britain's much-weakened political standing in the Caribbean basin following the commencement of territorial decolonization (Jamaica and Trinidad and Tobago in 1962; Guyana and Barbados shortly after, in 1966) is signalled to the reader primarily through metaphors of embodied (im)mobility and (im)potency. Within the narrative, political supremacy over the textual Jamaica is decidedly metonymic of the body politics at play between Bond and Scaramanga. That is to say, Bond's bodily displacement – his out-of-placedness – within the topography of post-independence Jamaica in the novel is correlative to the emphasis placed within the narrative upon the potency and mobility of Scaramanga's body. Geopolitics and bodily territory are aligned in *The Man with the Golden Gun*; Britain's weakened political position in the Caribbean (the decolonization of its former territories and its loss of political influence to communist Cuba) is narratively configured through Bond's implied bodily impotence and stasis. In comparison to the incapacitated Bond, who must undergo neurological surgery to reverse the effects of his brainwashing before being reassigned to active duty, Francisco Scaramanga is presented as an almost supranaturally virile entity. His hands are described as 'very large and powerful' and his ambidexterity suggests a superior ability to comport himself in combat (both with weapons and in a hand-to-hand match); while his third nipple is, as the text underlines, 'considered a sign of invulnerability and great sexual prowess' among 'Voodoo and allied local cults' (Fleming [1965] 2012m: 32). This comment puts the reader in mind of Bond's other great adversary affiliated with Caribbean Voodoo: Mr Big, from Fleming's first Jamaican novel, *Live and Let Die*. It is also strongly implied that Scaramanga's redoubtable skill as a marksman is tied to his sexual potency, for we are told that he 'invariably has sexual intercourse shortly before killing in the belief that it improves his "eye"' (ibid.).[3] It is telling, then, that, in the commentary by 'C.C.', the cover identity of the former Regius Professor of History at the University of Oxford whom British Intelligence has employed to profile persons of interest, Harold L. Peterson's *The Book of the Gun* is quoted at length. 'C.C.', quoting Peterson, notes that the 'possession of a gun and the skill to use it enormously augments the gunner's personal power, and extends the radius of his influence and effect a thousand times beyond his arm's length' (qtd in Fleming [1965] 2012m: 40). He adds the following annotation to his report: 'In the Freudian thesis, "his arm's length" would become the length of the masculine organ' (ibid.). Scaramanga's golden gun, therefore, is explicitly aligned with phallic fetishism. That Bond has tried and failed to assassinate M with a poison-filled pistol at the novel's opening underscores the unfavourable sexual and bodily comparison between him and Scaramanga; the crude suggestion is, perhaps, that Bond is 'firing blanks' in more ways than one. Moreover, in the context of Peterson's point (quoted by 'C.C.') that 'more than any other implement, the gun has shaped the course of nations and the destiny of men' (ibid.), Bond's phallic impotency signifies his ultimate failure to shape or redirect the course of British history – which has, in Fleming's eyes, in the aftermath of the Second World War and following the commencement of wholesale decolonization of former territorial holdings, been economically crippled and politically disgraced.

Conversely, Scaramanga is variously described as having 'complete freedom of access' to the Caribbean territories (ibid.: 31). We are told that he has 'travelled the whole of the Caribbean area' on various passports, including a Cuban diplomatic passport, which has given him 'legitimate access' and 'complete freedom of movement and indemnity from interference in "his" territory' (ibid.: 33–4). Thus, the textual Jamaica upon which the majority of narrative action transpires is roundly aligned with Scaramanga (the Caribbean is 'his' territory), whose supremacy over this space is seemingly naturalized by the freedom of movement afforded him. Scaramanga's mobile navigation of the political, cultural and social geographies of the postcolonial Caribbean is presented in stark contrast to Bond, for whom, as an emissary of the former colonial power of Britain, such mobility and freedom of access is no longer accommodated. Long gone are Bond's (and, indeed, Fleming's) halcyon days upon Jamaica, as in *Live and Let Die*, in which Strangways 'was at the airport to meet him and [to usher him] quickly through the Customs and Immigration and Finance Control' (Fleming [1954] 2012b: 214). While Jason Dittmer is correct in his acknowledgement that 'Bond's mobility is one of his key attributes' (2008: 16), this simply cannot be said to be the case in *The Man with the Golden Gun*. Rather than demonstrating 'the ease of [Bond's] movement throughout the world', Fleming's final novel 'seems overanxiously to illustrate the global scope of Britishness' that once was (ibid.). Though Bond still behaves as if he were the gentleman colonialist of old, he is patently not the figure of mobility he was in *Live and Let Die* or even in *Dr. No*. While Bond has, in Travis L. Wagner's words, '[moved] through the world as a colonizing agent' (2015: 52), such mobility was a condition of the former 'political unity of Britain and its empire' (Dittmer 2008: 17). As Paul Stock notes, 'Bond's presence on the margins of empire [i.e. on the sovereign Jamaica of *The Man with the Golden Gun*] is an attempt to retain a paternalistic and empowered position in a "post-colonial" era' (2000: 42). For Stock, it is clear that both Bond and the vestiges of empire exist only 'in the traces of outposts' upon which Fleming insists on setting his narrative (ibid.).

In contrast, it is intimated that Scaramanga's mobility is a condition of his dubious political liminality.[4] Whereas Bond's mission in *The Man with the Golden Gun* is concerned (implicitly, at least) with the authentication of his ideological repatriation to Britain following his brainwashing at the hands of the Russians, the narrative also makes it abundantly clear that Scaramanga's motivations, in contrast, are simply financial – neither ideological nor patriotic. Having settled in Havana in 1959, the reader is told, 'while remaining ostensibly a Batista man, [Scaramanga] began working undercover for the Castro party' (Fleming [1965] 2012m: 33)[5] – a comment which signifies both his ideological capriciousness and his political opportunism, two qualities that are anathema to the fervently nationalistic Bond. Scaramanga's ability to effectively navigate the fluctuating political climate of the increasingly communist Caribbean basin to secure his own advantage only shores up Bond's and Britain's contrasting political short-sightedness in the postcolonial period. Scaramanga's political protection suggests that his claim to Jamaica is more 'authorized' than Britain's illegitimate claim to its continued policing of the island, as Britain's weakened imperial and political position on Jamaica is symbolically configured, initially, through Bond's comparative impotency. Bond's eventual defeat of Scaramanga, then, represents in the context of the narrative not only the suppression of ideological communism (Scaramanga works for the communist Batista) and criminal opportunism within the newly independent Jamaica, but also the reassertion of Bond's phallic potency. If, as Fleming has already made explicit through the report by 'C.C.', the gun equates to the male sex organ, then Scaramanga's death at the hands of Bond's pistol shot ('the iron in his hand cracked viciously again and again – five times' (ibid.: 192)) suggests that he has been bested by Bond both ideologically and sexually.[6] Bond's sexual supremacy over Scaramanga is further confirmed as an act of bodily and territorial reclamation; in shooting him dead, Bond quite literally puts an end to Scaramanga's mobility.

As in *Dr. No*, nowhere are the political restrictions placed on Bond's mobility – as well as Fleming's ambivalent concessions to Britain's post-imperial status on the island – made more apparent than in the novel's airport scene. But whereas in *Dr. No* his transit through Kingston International Airport conveys the loss of Bond's privileged identity as a white Briton on the island, Bond's passage through the airport in *The Man with the Golden Gun* is, conversely, concerned with his attempts to relocate that identity in the political context of post-independence Jamaica. The airport sequence of the latter novel cannot be said to be either strictly necessary or even apparently logical within the context of the narrative's structure. It is by absurd chance and coincidence that Bond, who is in transit between Trinidad and Cuba, discovers by way of a written message on the display board for incoming and outgoing passengers that his quarry, Scaramanga, is in Jamaica. Based on this information, Bond reroutes his plans and the rest of the narrative takes place in Jamaica. Unlike in *Dr. No*, the Kingston Airport sequence in *The Man with the Golden Gun* appears to serve no discernible narrative purpose. The scene begins in medias res with Bond already ensconced in the transit lounge. Crucially, we see Bond neither enter nor leave Jamaica; he is simply just *there*, as though in preset tableau, inert and bound to the island. It is made clear to the reader in the novel's opening sequence that Bond has lost his memory while undergoing torturous interrogation and reconditioning by the Soviets, and it is during the Kingston Airport sequence that Fleming illustrates to the reader Bond's pains to recollect memories of his lost personal identity. I would argue that the Kingston Airport sequence, here, functions as a particular plot device which enables Fleming to link together the restoration of Bond's personal identity with the reconstruction and recovery of Britain's imperial presence on the island, as the process of Bond's identity reformation (and, indeed, Britain's geopolitical identity in the novel) is shown to be inextricably tied to his imperial rememory and conceptual recolonization of Jamaica. Fleming's conceit of Jamaica is shown to be essential to the narrative's restoration of both Bond's personal memory and Britain's national and cultural heritage as a former imperial power; the structural relationship between Bond and Jamaica is configured through Fleming's narrative choices as perhaps the defining factor in negotiating pre- and postcolonial British-Jamaican relations in the period. Consider Bond's musings on Jamaica: he spends most of the Kingston Airport sequence either recalling details of his own past on the island or making comparisons between present-day Jamaica and the historical Jamaica that he has known. For instance, the narrator opines that 'there are few less prepossessing places to spend a hot afternoon than Kingston International Airport in Jamaica' (Fleming [1965] 2012m: 42). The authority with which this statement is delivered is, of course, predicated entirely on the diegetic assumption that it is Bond himself who recalls previous instances of his own personal discomfort while in the transit lounge. This sentiment is to be understood as meaningful within the context of the narration *only* if it is assumed that Bond is drawing an equivalence between his own past experiences of Kingston Airport and his current discomfort (the 'hard bench' on which he is sat, for one). Bond's metaleptic reflections are further underscored by his condemnation of Jamaica's burgeoning mania for commercial modernity. The transit lounge of Kingston Airport is less than prepossessing, he believes, precisely because 'all the money has been spent on lengthening the runway out into the harbour to take the big jets' (ibid.). He bemoans the 'expensive scents, liquor, and piles of overdecorated native ware' that line the commercial outlets in the airport's concourse (ibid.), an observation which highlights Bond's unfavourable comparison of new- and old-world Jamaica – his disdain for the cultural commercialization of mass tourism as an egalitarian pursuit, on the one hand, and his mourning for the loss of those refined luxuries of the genuine (gentleman) traveller, on the other. In Matthew Parker's words, 'Bond complains that Kingston airport has sacrificed volume for comfort' and that such commercial concessions 'have attracted the likes of Scaramanga to the tourism business' (2014: 304). Tellingly, Bond is shown to be something of a man out of step within this new global infrastructure. His inability to profitably capitalize on the expediencies of commercial air travel ('for six weeks, Bond has been chasing [Scaramanga] around the Caribbean and Central America. He had missed him by a day in Trinidad and by only a matter of hours in Caracas' (Fleming [1965] 2012m: 44)) suggests that his mobility is frustrated by the fluid modernity of a post-imperial world that increasingly outpaces him.[7]

It is no small irony, then, that Bond's longing for the charms of 'old' Jamaica not only puts him on to Scaramanga's trail in Jamaica but also facilitates a rather complex textual process of personal and metatextual rememory. Scanning a copy of the *Gleaner*, Bond notes an advertisement for the public auction of a particular property: No. 3½ Love Lane, Savannah La Mar. Bond appraises the style of the advertisement as being 'so typically "old" Jamaica', and he delights in the 'splendid address and the stuff about chains and perches and the old-fashioned abracadabra', which, he claims, recalls to his mind 'all the authentic smell of one of the oldest and most romantic of former British possessions' (ibid.: 45). That this property is also the site of Bond's first meeting with Scaramanga is not insignificant, for the narrative seems to advocate the view that the progress of Bond's mission (his moving *forward* in the hunt for Scaramanga) is predicated – somewhat paradoxically – on personal retrospection (his looking *backwards* over his past experiences on the island of Jamaica). It is no coincidence, then, that in this moment Bond recalls his adventures with Honey Rider in *Dr. No*, a novel that is set prior to Jamaica's independence from Britain: 'James Bond smiled to himself as the dusty pictures clicked across his brain. How long ago it all was! What had happened to her? She never wrote' (ibid.: 46). Here, Bond's wistful contemplation of Honey Rider not only serves to further anchor Bond's reclamation of his own erstwhile identity in the present (an identity which, Fleming makes abundantly clear, is firmly entwined with Jamaica itself) but also this moment represents a double act of metatextual rememory. On the one hand, Fleming's invocation of Honey Rider recalls the events of *Dr. No*, placing *The Man with the Golden Gun* firmly within the same fictive universe as that novel and situating Bond's reconstruction of his own identity within the familiar environs of his 'old' Jamaica; that Honey 'never wrote' affords Bond the psychological illusion that 'his' Jamaica has remained as it once was, in his memory. But, on the other hand, this invocation also functions conversely to underline the historical, political and contextual alterity between the colonial Jamaica of *Dr. No* and the postcolonial Jamaica of *The Man with the Golden Gun*. Bond's act of rememory (in looking backwards to Honey Rider and forwards to Scaramanga) positions him in some sort of liminal temporal stasis – between his latent desire for the pre-independence coloniality embodied in Honey and his ambivalent regard for Jamaica's postcolonial independence embodied in Scaramanga.[8] Indeed, Fleming further hints at the complex political liminality embedded within the novel when he has Bond note that 'for all [Jamaica's] new-found "independence" he would bet his bottom dollar that the statue of Queen Victoria in the centre of Kingston had *not* been destroyed or removed to a museum, as similar relics of an historic infancy has been in the resurgent African states' (ibid.: 45–6, italics in original). Fleming's wry dismissal of Jamaican independence, his suggestion that Britain is still the de facto ruler of the island, is configured in the image of the monument to Britain's queen that remains intact. That the statue has not (yet) been torn down in violent resistance to British colonial rule, Fleming implies, suggests something of an ambivalence over decolonization on the part of Jamaican locals, who are, the narrative wishes to stress, seemingly unsure of their own nationalism. Like the monument of Queen Victoria, Bond's identity, too, is positioned in this scene as liminal, caught in the indeterminate space between history and memory. Bond's musing on historical Jamaica and the country's political liminality is also configured in the text as an act of personal memorialization: it is through and by way of the recollection of his own time on the island that Bond is shown to fully recover his own identity.

Indeed, the narrative lays much emphasis on Bond's remembering. When he discovers Scaramanga's whereabouts in Kingston, Bond decides that he must avail of the High Commissioner's assistance in apprehending his foe. '[Bond] remembered the name of Head of Station J', the narrative tells us (ibid.: 48) – a point that is at once innocuous but also indicative of Bond's ability to recall the details of his former life on the island, thus reorienting himself within the intelligence community through which he has come up. When Bond is put through to Commander Ross's office, he recognizes 'something vaguely familiar in the lilt of the voice' of Ross's female assistant, who answers the call. But before Bond can put his finger on quite who it is he is talking to, we are told that 'the voice broke in excitedly' in recognition of Bond himself (ibid.). Significantly, it is only after the speaker has identified Bond (calling him by his familiar first name) that Bond's memory of the voice is prompted. He realizes that he is, in fact, talking with Mary Goodnight, the former secretary to the Double-0 section who appeared previously in the novels *On Her Majesty's Secret Service* and *You Only Live Twice*, and who is now employed in the Secret Service's Kingston station. Thus, it is through the recollection of Bond by others that Bond, too, recalls himself: 'Now he'd got an ally, someone *he knew*' (ibid.: 49, my italics). In this simple exchange, Bond is shown to pick up right where he left off with his former colleague; it is without any question of doubt as to his foregoing mental psychosis ('I heard you were back, but I thought you were ill or something' (ibid.: 48)) that Goodnight puts at Bond's disposal the resources of her office. Bond's psychological and professional restoration is presented in the narrative as a matter of course, and it occurs to no one to question either his trustworthiness or his motivations. This is not narrative oversight on Fleming's part. Rather, these seeming omissions are fundamental to the political economy of the text as a whole: Fleming's anxious desire to reinstate the political status quo within the fictive geography of 'his own' Jamaica by securing Bond's a priori professional status on the island. In a somewhat clumsy exchange between Bond and Goodnight, Fleming further assuages any lingering doubts the reader might have as to Bond's character: 'You've established your identity,' Goodnight intones rather sardonically when Bond instructs her to wear 'something that's tight in all the right places' (ibid.: 49). Bond's misogyny in this scene is employed not (just) as a function of his prospective seduction of Goodnight (the narrative is actually largely ambiguous as to whether Bond and Goodnight eventually sleep together or not) but as a correlative to Fleming's reconstitution of Bond's recognizable personality as a known philanderer. The meaning of this exchange could not be made more explicit: Bond's identity has, in part, been re-established precisely through his tendency towards misogyny. Given that Bond's confrontation with Scaramanga is configured in both ideological and sexual terms, with the battle for political supremacy and geographical mobility within Jamaica mapped onto the phallic potency of both men's gun arms, the exchange with Goodnight serves as an unambiguous reminder of Bond's once redoubtable sexual potency – a potency that he will only fully recover in his defeat of Scaramanga and in his symbolic acquisition of the equally symbolic golden gun.

Goodnight's reappearance 'from the old days' (ibid.), and the fact that the proprietor of the hotel in Port Royal where Bond stays 'had once been in Intelligence himself' (ibid.: 50), suggests that the political landscape of Jamaica which Bond occupies in *The Man with the Golden Gun* is a reactionary one, an anachronistic geography of British imperial resurgence, the unsubtle implications of which point to an unofficial sleeper network of British Intelligence officers which continues to operate on the island even after Jamaican independence. Indeed, the hotel owner's quip to Bond ('What is it this time? Cubans or smuggling? They're the popular target these days' (ibid.)) underlines the irony at the heart of the text's political and historical displacement. Fleming is only ostensibly concerned with Cuban communism ('the popular target these days'), for, in reality, *The Man with the Golden Gun* is actually about reinscribing Britain's old imperial dominance of Jamaica, rather than actually addressing in any meaningful way the pressing contemporary political concerns within the Caribbean basin. 'It's so wonderful to have you back' (ibid.: 53), Goodnight tells Bond – a confession that speaks at once to Bond's personal rehabilitation as well as to the text's more nefarious overarching politics: the apparent advocacy of Britain's continued administration of its former Jamaican colony even after sovereignty has been granted. Equally, Bond's favourable appraisal of Goodnight is premised largely on the fact that, to his eyes, 'she hadn't changed' (ibid.) – a comment which underscores something of the imposed, exoticized timelessness of the Jamaican backdrop against which their meeting is set. This point is somewhat ham-fistedly underscored by the fact that Goodnight makes available for Bond's use the old Sunbeam Alpine that previously belonged to Strangways, the former Section Chief of Jamaica who was murdered in the opening chapter of *Dr. No*. In that novel, Bond was very much aggrieved by the ineptitude of the Colonial Office, whose choice to give Bond use of the Sunbeam 'certainly put the finger on him and on what he was doing in Jamaica if anyone happened to be interested' (Fleming [1958] 2012f: 48). In *The Man with the Golden Gun*, however, Bond seems entirely unconcerned by the fact that he is using the same vehicle: 'That's fine' is all he says of Goodnight's report on the car (Fleming [1965] 2012m: 57). The difference in Bond's attitude is as much political as it is practical for Fleming. In *Dr. No*, Bond did not want to be seen in Strangways' old car precisely because it revealed his identity as a figure of law enforcement and signalled to his enemies his purpose on Jamaica. In *The Man with the Golden Gun*, though, Bond's attitudinal nonchalance towards Strangways's old car (which, after three Jamaican novels, must surely be recognized by locals the whole island over as a government vehicle) implies that, rather than dissembling his intentions, Bond covets ostentation. Practically, this is poor spycraft. In terms of Fleming's narrative politics, though, Bond's comparative brazenness signifies his political allegiance. Unlike in *Dr. No*, Bond evidently desires to flaunt his Britishness and the power of the (once mighty) political infrastructure behind him. This cannot, presumably, be for Scaramanga's benefit, since Bond does adopt the guise of one 'Mark Hazard', a contractor for the West Indian Sugar Company, in order to get close to Scaramanga's operation (thus concealing who he is). Rather, Bond's ostentation represents something of a show of political force against the people of Jamaica and against national Jamaica itself. As a part of Bond's process of remembering, the recovery of his personal identity following his brainwashing at the hands of the Russians, his Britishness, his national and cultural identity, is shown to be showily leveraged against the islanders' Jamaicanness through his self-conscious alignment with the iconography of British imperialism (i.e. Strangways' car). Bond's conduct on Jamaica in *The Man with the Golden Gun* can be said to resemble far more closely that of his time on the island in *Live and Let Die* than it does in *Dr. No* – a curious parallel, not least of all because of the disparity in political context between Fleming's first Jamaican novel in 1953 and his final one in 1965. In *Live and Let Die*, Jamaica was very much presented as a colonial enclave of the British Empire; and *Dr. No* illustrates vividly the effects of increasing nationalist agitations on the island, which Fleming could hardly be said to have ignored. Though Jamaica had been granted official independence only two years prior to the novel's publication, in *The Man with the Golden Gun*, however, Bond's ostentatious display of Britishness belies a certain ambivalence regarding the handover of sovereign power and suggests something of an inclination to reverse the effects of British decolonization. Even though he is shown at various points throughout the novel to muse favourably on Jamaica's changing political landscape, Bond's conduct on the island represents, to all intents and purposes, a reinscription of those British imperialist values seen in *Live and Let Die* rather than a considered adaption to the island's postcolonial condition, which Fleming seems much more cognizant of in *Dr. No*. In effect, Bond's efforts to pick up where he left off on the island signifies (in an uneasy fashion, it must be said) the narrative's efforts to reorient British-Jamaican relations in the post-independence period. The emphasis placed on Bond's recollection of his old life in Jamaica, prior to his brainwashing at the hands of the Soviets, enables Fleming to orient the reader's conception of independent Jamaica *through* the pre-independence politics of Bond's memory. Indeed, certainly for avid readers of Fleming's novels at the time, the pre-independence period of Fleming's James Bond oeuvre can be read as something of a romantic throwback to a time in which, among other things, the Bond novels themselves were a far sight better than Fleming's unsatisfying, final offering. Thus, Bond's nostalgia for pre-independence Jamaica is also a metatextual correlative to the reader's nostalgia for the golden age of Bond himself – more *Goldfinger* than *The Man with the Golden Gun*.

Ruination and (re)construction: Tiffy's Bordello and Scaramanga's hotel

In *The Man with the Golden Gun*, Fleming's ambivalent reconception of post-independence Jamaica as an imperial *lieu de memoire* is also an exercise in spatiality, as his efforts to reinscribe Britain's (geo)political significance on the island (as well as his meditations on Bond's political function in the emergent postcolonial period) are configured within the text through metaphors of spatial geography. If the site of the run-down bordello on Love Lane (with its implied squalor and physical degradation) represents the geospatial 'ruination' of imperial Jamaica, then the site of Scaramanga's new hotel, the 'Thunderbird', is equally representative of the (literal) reconstruction of Jamaica's economic infrastructure from the ruins of empire. Both locations are essential to the narrative economy of Fleming's post-imperial Jamaica within the text. Much like the temporal paradox I noted earlier – in which Bond's progress (moving forward) is predicated on and framed around scenes of personal retrospection (looking backwards) – the bordello and the hotel together symbolize the spatio-temporal interstices in which Bond finds himself within this particular narrative, poised on the threshold between ruination and reformation – between the figurative death of 'old' Jamaica and the reconstitution of a 'new', independent Jamaica, and between imperial nostalgia and post-imperial progress.[9] Bond's occupation of these various locations thus signifies a form of spatial ambivalence; his spatial practice of these topographical spheres replicates, in part, the politics of tourism, a practice which attempts to secure the individual's meaningful identification with/to a particular location while at the same time stressing the difference and newness of that space. Indeed, at one point during his reconnaissance of Love Lane, Bond even deliberately apes the habits of a lolling tourist: 'He slit open the packet [of Royal Blend] with his thumbnail and lit a cigarette to help the picture of an idle tourist examining a corner of old Jamaica' (Fleming [1965]

2012m: 60). Note, here, the syntagmatic alignment of Bond's touristic practice with 'old' Jamaica. Like the tourist, Bond's energy is directed almost exclusively towards the recovery of an anachronistic conception of a bygone Jamaica, the Jamaica of pre-independence. Bond's traversal of such liminal spatio-temporal geographies – two particular sites which are commonly associated with sex (bordello) and leisure (hotel) tourism – emphasizes his own transience and dislocation within the text. Bond is decidedly *dis*placed within this post-imperial world, and Fleming's narrative is unable to meaningfully reconcile Bond's occupation of colonial space with those defamiliarizing landscapes he inhabits in *The Man with the Golden Gun*.

Firstly, the bordello. Having intercepted a message for Scaramanga at Kingston Airport, Bond makes his way to the location in Love Lane of a supposed exchange between Scaramanga and an associate of a sample of what he later discovers to be ganja. The narrative emphasizes not only Bond's alterity within Savannah La Mar's geospatial landscape (i.e. Bond's idle tourist routine) but the contextual otherness of the location itself. Savannah La Mar is described as 'not a typically Jamaican town' and 'most un-Jamaican' (ibid.: 59–60); it is an enclave of difference within Jamaica's cultural landscape. As the text implies, it is through this defamiliarized topography that Bond must pass in his symbolic quest to recover the 'real' history of pre-independence Jamaica in Love Lane. Savannah La Mar, then, is a zone of both spatial and temporal liminality surrounding 'the old quarter on the waterfront' (ibid.: 59), which is the object of Bond's focus in this sequence; it is a veritable time capsule within which 'old' Jamaica is seemingly preserved. While Savannah La Mar is configured as a space of alterity and difference, the narrative suggests that Bond is figuratively transported to the recognizable colonial landscape of pre-independence Jamaica when he enters Love Lane. The other-worldliness of Savannah La Mar (that is, its *un*Jamaicanness) is contrasted in Bond's eyes with the comfortingly familiar images of Jamaica's old-world imperial charm: the fishing canoes on raised stilts, the lignum vitae root that has overrun the colonial-style property and the assortment of branded advertisement for Red Stripe, Royal Blend, Four Aces and Coca-Cola that adorn the window of the café – all of which signify the island's history of economic and corporate imperialism. Tiffy, the pretty octoroon who manages the front desk of the bordello, even tells Bond that Love Lane has an 'atmosphere … [l]ike sort of old Jamaica. Like it must have been in the old days' (ibid.: 65) – a comment which, in terms of narrative geography, explicitly aligns Bond's nostalgia for imperial Jamaica (the quest for history) with the politics of desire (the quest for sex). Tiffy's intimation that the girls in the bordello will 'do it for free if the man's a good feller' (ibid.: 66) further emphasizes the seeming ease of Bond's access to the erotic landscapes of imperial Jamaica. Conversely, though, the narrative seems to imply that the old-world charm of imperial Jamaica is also lost to Bond. Love Lane is described as 'brokendown' (ibid.: 60), and the bordello itself is referred to as 'broken in many places' (ibid.: 61). The colouring of the 'silvering shingles' on the building suggests an ethereal spectrality (ibid.), while the '*vulturine*-necked chickens' and the '*skeletal* Jamaican black-and-tan mongrels' in the yard around the bordello also strongly connote death and deathliness (ibid., my italics). On the one hand, the text naturalizes such images of dilapidation and decay of which the 'real' Jamaica is seemingly comprised; on the other, that Fleming should elect to present old-world Jamaica to the reader through this particular assemblage of death imagery would seem to suggest that such a world is also irretrievably lost (or dead) to Bond, too. Indeed, this sequence is very much framed as a narrative meditation on a Jamaica that once was but which now no longer exists: 'It must once have had importance' (ibid.), Bond notes of the building which houses the bordello. The sign over the entrance to the bordello ('Dreamland Café') is also perhaps an ironic, self-referential nod to the impossibility of Bond's desires in the context of postcolonial Jamaica. In addition to its allusion to the fantasies of sexual excess which are promised within the walls of the bordello, the sign also disclaims as pure fantasy Bond's wish to return to the Jamaica of pre-independence he once knew, the place of sexual and capital excess he last encountered in *Dr. No*. This point is seemingly endorsed through Bond's interaction with Tiffy. The promise of sex that is, at first, hinted at in her eyes – and by the 'quick glimpse of fine bosoms' (ibid.: 62) she affords Bond as she retrieves a bottle of Red Stripe from an icebox – quickly subsides when she laughs, as Bond is immediately put off by the sight of her teeth that 'had been sharpened by munching raw sugar cane' (ibid.: 63). The implication here, of course, is that the eroticist façade and charming allure of old-world, imperial Jamaica is no longer accessible to Bond within the emergent political and economic geographies of post-imperial British-Jamaican sexual relations. Thus, when the narrator notes that the 'quick glimpse of fine bosoms' which Tiffy gives to Bond is 'not dictated by the geography of the place' (ibid.: 62) he is suggesting not only that Tiffy is a practiced tease but that the spatial and sexual geographies of British-Jamaican relations have been fundamentally altered in the post-imperial period – an ironic point, for sure, given that this exchange takes place in perhaps the most sexual of Bond's textual geographies: a bordello. Behind Bond's initial fantasy of sexual conquest over Tiffy, conditioned both by his own heterosexual desires and, predominantly, by his imperial agency, lies the reality of Britain's comparative impotency within post-imperial Jamaica (an impotency first glimpsed in the personage of the ineffectual Acting Governor in *Dr. No*). Bond's implied disgust at Tiffy's marred physical appearance – a disgust which the narrative seems to advocate: 'Tiffy's pretty face was no longer pretty. It was a taut skull' (ibid.: 70) – is thus symbolic of the impossibilities of Bond's own acclimation to the altered cultural, social and, in particular, sexual geographies of post-independence British-Jamaican relations.

It is, perhaps, precisely because of the impossibility of Bond's nostalgic longing for a British-Jamaican cultural geography that no longer exists (for all its subtle charm, Love Lane is in ruins) that Fleming should choose to set most of the narrative action on the construction site of Scaramanga's new Thunderbird Hotel project in Bloody Bay. If the bordello signifies through its images of dilapidation and decay the impracticality of Bond's return to high imperialism (the death of old Jamaica), then the hotel signifies through its half-finished façade of 'lath and plaster' (ibid.: 92) the problematics of neo-imperial modernity and the birth of a new commercialist Jamaica. After their initial encounter in the bordello, Bond (in the guise of Mark Hazard) is taken into Scaramanga's employ as his personal bodyguard and brought to the hotel development site in Negril, west Jamaica. There, he is instructed to protect Scaramanga and to ensure that the various meetings which Scaramanga has arranged with his business associates and stockholders remain private to the other guests. Within *The Man with the Golden Gun*, the hotel is arguably the most complexly ambivalent of Fleming's psychogeographies. As Parker points out, the development is representative of 'the fallout from the Cuban revolution, in terms of both American gangsters looking for a new playground, and a "Redland" looking to duplicate the establishment of a communist regime in the United States' back yard' (2014: 302). While financial backing for the development has been provided by a combination of European and American funds, and by what Scaramanga refers to as 'Caribbean money' (Fleming [1965] 2012m: 96), it becomes apparent that the beneficiaries of the Thunderbird project are communist foreign powers: the USSR and, specifically, Castro's Cuba. This revelation explicitly underlines for the reader, once again, Fleming's gravest political concern: the implication, here, is that without British 'protection', Jamaica would, indeed, seem to fall prey to communist insurrection. From what can be discerned of Fleming's rather confused plot, Scaramanga's hotel project is but one of a number of far-reaching political schemes designed to instigate political unrest within the Caribbean. As John Gilbert notes, Scaramanga and his criminal cohort 'plan to sabotage the island's bauxite trade, deal arms to Castro, smuggle narcotics into America, and ruin the Jamaican sugar industry by setting the cane fields ablaze, thus increasing the value of Caribbean sugar' (2012: 412). In essence, Scaramanga is at the centre of a Cuban- and Russian-backed plot against the Jamaican economy, a threat so apparently all-encompassing, with supposed 'links between the KGB, the Mafia, Black Power, terrorism and drugs' (Black 2004: 298), that it is hard not to dismiss it as patently absurd. Clearly, for Fleming, Jamaica has never been at greater risk of political subversion – an ideological position which further augments the novel's configuration of Bond's (and Britain's) neo-imperial ministration of the island in the post-independence period.[10] Conversely, Daniel Ferreras Savoye is much more balanced in his consideration of Fleming's political hyperbole: he asserts rather wryly that the 'dastardly plot which Bond uncovers is a rather perfunctory collection of routine crimes against humanity – marijuana smuggling, the burning of Jamaican sugar-cane fields to boost the price of Cuban sugar, and the like' (2013: 53).

But aside from the (however hyperbolic) threat of political communism which pervades the narrative, Scaramanga's hotel also typifies the worst excesses of tawdry cultural modernism, the likes of which Bond first encounters in the transit lounge at Kingston Airport. As Parker notes, the new threat to Fleming's Jamaica comes not solely from insurrectionist political ideology but 'from a desire for self-promotion and "modernity"' (2014: 302) brought about by an increase in the tourist trade. The politics of new commercialism in Jamaica (which have come about, it is implied, as a result of lenient tax laws on the island) are readily apparent through the spatial topography of the hotel itself, the marked artificiality of which connotes not simply its hurried completion but the dissimulation of its criminal proprietors. Bond notes that 'with the *theatrical lighting* and the surrounding blackness to conceal any evidence of halted construction work, the [hotel] made a brave show [of appearing to be what it was]' (Fleming [1965] 2012m: 85, my italics). Here, the very staginess of Scaramanga's enterprise underscores the performative nature of tourism itself, largely an industry of pretence.[11] Like the practice of tourism, which is designed both to *reveal* sites of cultural interest and to *conceal* those elements of national heritage which detract from the tourist's wilful exoticism, the 'sudden blaze of brilliant yellow illumination' (ibid.) draws attention to both the touristic hyper-object (the hotel itself) and, by contrast, its absence within the 'surrounding blackness' (the criminal ploy behind it). For all of the supposed opulence of the hotel's 'aristocratic frontage', with its 'tall Regency windows' and the 'black-and-white marble flooring beneath blazing chandeliers' (ibid.), the property is, as Bond discovers on a walk around the grounds in daylight, a 'mockup'. Like mediocre amateur theatre, the hotel's restaurant, nightclub and living rooms are, to Bond's mind, 'stages for a dress rehearsal, hastily assembled with the essential props, carpets, light fixtures, and a scattering of furniture, but stinking of fresh paint' (ibid.: 92). Bond even overhears a Kingston calypso combo in rehearsals towards the rear of the building. While Scaramanga's labourers work at 'tacking up curtains, vacuuming carpets, [and] fixing the electricity', it appears to Bond as though 'no one was employed on the essentials – the big cement mixers, the drills, the ironwork that lay about behind the hotel like the abandoned toys of a giant. (ibid.). As Parker notes, Scaramanga's hotel enterprise is 'all tacky, hollow and fake' (2014: 302). The distasteful artifice of Scaramanga's scheme is augmented by Bond's musings on the swampland which borders the hotel compound: 'No doubt, if the hotel got off the ground, all this area would be turned into an asset. There would be native boatmen, suitably attired as Arawak Indians ... [and] guests could view the "tropical jungle" for an extra ten dollars on the bill' (Fleming [1965] 2012m: 93–4). Bond's observations, here, underscore his disdain for yet another common facet of Jamaica's touristic modernity: that is, the misuse of indigenous cultural heritage for private commercial benefit.

But for all of his ardent concerns over the nefarious threat to Jamaica of cultural modernity, Bond is nevertheless shown to replicate precisely the practices of commercial exoticism which he ostensibly critiques elsewhere in the novel. In order to ensure that Scaramanga's criminal syndicate are properly lubricated for business dealings, Bond takes it upon himself to liven up the evening's entertainment in the hotel – 'to blind [Scaramanga's] guests with pleasure' (ibid.: 92). Set against the background of the hotel's dining room, which is converted into a crudely improvised '"tropical jungle" with the help of potted plants, piles of oranges and coconuts, and an occasional stem of bananas' (ibid.: 123), Bond orchestrates what can only be described as an orgiastic spectacle of cultural exoticism. He plies the calypso six-piece combo with rum and marijuana and instructs the exotic dancer to 'come up close [to Scaramanga's cronies] and sing "Belly-Lick" very clearly with the blue words', insisting that, by the end of the show, the female dancers 'have got to end up stripped' (ibid.: 126). What follows is a somewhat nasty cabaret of lewd and erotic excess in which the 'hasty beat' of the calypso box keeps time with the 'quickened pulse' of the room – the collective sexual vitality of Scaramanga's men, who are teased and goaded towards both musical crescendo and figurative climax by the sight of a young female dancer who is 'totally naked and shining with palm oil', gyrating, swooning and jerking around the giant statue of a six-foot outstretched black hand (ibid.: 127–8). Fleming's narrative seems to take excessive pleasure in describing the 'languorous, but explicit and ingenious, acts of passion [the dancer engages in] with each of the fingers in turn', as well as the 'well-simulated ecstasy' the girl achieves having finally 'mounted the thumb [and] slowly [expiring] upon it' (ibid.: 128). Unlike a similar such scene in *Live and Let Die*, during which Bond witnesses G. G. Sumatra's erotic striptease in Mr Big's nightclub, the exotic floorshow in *The Man with the Golden Gun* is not meant as a collectivizing expression of a shared cultural and sexual experience into which Bond has inadvertently stumbled. Rather, in this scene, the narrative patently lays emphasis upon the orientalizing gaze of the male observers (who are all tourists, it should be noted) and on the visual discourse of exoticism through which the sequence is presented. Bond, we are told, is 'aroused' by the spectacle, while Scaramanga watches the dance 'with rapt attention, his eyes narrow slits' (ibid.). Unlike the rapturous audience of G. G. Sumatra's striptease in *Live and Let Die*, who are described as 'panting and grunting like pigs at the trough', and whose verbal interactions – 'Cmon, G-G. Take it away, Baby. Cmon. Grind, Baby, grind' (Fleming [1954] 2012b: 72) – are presented as synergistic, the erotic display by the unnamed dancer in *The Man with the Golden Gun* is clearly meant to be savoured voyeuristically, and in silence. Moreover, while it is implied that G. G. Sumatra is unconcerned by (almost unconscious of) her audience during the nightclub sequence in *Live and Let Die*, the dance in *The Man with the Golden Gun* is framed specifically as a self-conscious performance of Jamaican sexuality and cultural exoticism. At the dance's commencement, the girl 'moves into the pool of light round the hand' as though to better facilitate the men's view of her. Her dance (or 'scene' or 'act', as it is variously described) is 'well-acted' and 'well-simulated', and when she concludes, as in all well-regulated performances, 'the lights [come] on and everyone, including the band, [applauds] loudly' (Fleming [1965] 2012m: 127–8). But if hers is a performative display, then Bond is certainly the de facto director. By assuming directive control over the performance of the native female body, Bond himself can be said to reinscribe within the narrative the historical subjugation of indigenous femininity to white, male coloniality. Moreover, that the female dancer is not a Black Jamaican but a Creole with Chinese blood (in the narrative, her skin is described as being 'almost white against the black hand' (ibid.: 128)) suggests that, while Bond, Scaramanga and the others certainly desire her, their desire is also conditioned by fears of miscegenation represented by her racial hybridity. These fears are dictated by those broader discourses of race from the period which intimate that it is the purview of the white man to rescue white women from the (in this case, literal) grasp of the metonymic black hand. We have already seen this in *Live and*

Let Die, when Bond rescues Solitaire from Mr Big. Thus, Bond's earlier musings on the artifice of tourism with respect to the 'native boatmen, suitably attired as Arawak Indians', as well as his disgust at Tiffy's marred physical appearance in the bordello, are placed into cruel, ironic relief against his own reliance upon the most cynical stratagems of neo-imperialist, touristic modernity – the racial and sexual exoticization of the native body.

Of course, the fantasies of sexual excess which are played out in Bond's direction of this erotic sequence are predicated upon the more aggressive imperial fantasies of racial dominance, commercial ownership and political control. Unlike the bordello in Love Lane, in which Bond believes he will find traces of 'old' Jamaica, it is within Scaramanga's hotel that Bond fully recovers his own coloniality. Take, for example, the nightmare Bond has during his first night's sleep at the hotel. In it, Bond sees himself 'defending a fort' from a cannonball attack by Scaramanga (ibid.: 90). If we are to read Bond as an allegorical cipher for Britain itself (as we have done), then the dream can certainly be read as a parable. Bond's defence of the symbolic fort represents variously his defence of Britain's national security and its beleaguered imperial status in post-independence Jamaica, as well as his protection of the interests of Britain's property class against the commercial and political welfare of communist modernity represented by Scaramanga (which is, the text makes clear, anathema to the cultural and social life of modern Britain). But given that this dream sequence takes place during Bond's stay at the Thunderbird Hotel – a veritable monument within the text to neo-imperial commercialism – it could be argued that Bond's symbolic defence of British interests (the fort) becomes conflated with his defence of Scaramanga's own commercial interests (the hotel). Ferreras Savoye notes that the Castle Perilous theme which we saw most demonstrably in Bond's assault of Dr No's island fortress, Crab Key, 'appears weakly in Scaramanga's unfinished Thunderbird hotel' (2013: 53). But unlike *Dr. No*, in which Bond deliberately sets out to destroy the eponymous villain's underwater lair, in *The Man with the Golden Gun* Bond's energies are purportedly directed towards the preservation of Scaramanga's enterprise. He accepts the role of Scaramanga's personal bodyguard in order to get close to him, and, for most of the novel, he masquerades as a defender of Scaramanga's commercial venture. Indeed, before ever learning about Scaramanga's business interests in the Thunderbird hotel, Bond himself muses that one of his potential covers on the island might be that of 'a rich man looking around for a building site' (Fleming [1965] 2012m: 52). He even names the Thunderbird as one of the prospective sites he would mention if pushed on his identity, a point which also firmly aligns the psychogeography of Scaramanga's hotel with Bond's recovery of his own imperial agency. Moreover, that 'Thunderbird' was Ann Fleming's nickname for her husband following his purchase, for himself, of a car of the same name (Parker 2014: 300) suggests that the construction site of the hotel in *The Man with the Golden Gun* is a complex and personal topographical metaphor for Fleming's reconstruction of both Bond (following his brainwashing at the hands of the Soviets) and the political context of anachronistic imperial Jamaica – not to mention an attempt on the part of the author (who is, during the writing of this novel, suffering from declining physical health) to figuratively 'rebuild' himself. Thus, the Thunderbird hotel represents something of an ambivalent spatial metaphor: on the one hand, it connotes the encroaching threat of political communism and commercial modernity; on the other, it signifies something of Fleming's efforts to reconstruct within his fictive universe the imperial legacy of Britain's empire. As a topographical symbol, the hotel is also reflective of Jamaica's status as a newly independent country – a nation undergoing political, cultural and social reconstruction.

The Jamaican cover-up; or, Fleming's last words?

Although Fleming's three Jamaican novels can, for the most part, be read as politically ambivalent documents concerning fluctuating British-Jamaican cultural relations in the postcolonial period, *The Man with the Golden Gun* is perhaps the most reactionary. Whereas the racial geographies of both *Live and Let Die* and *Dr. No* can be said to connect to real-world geopolitical events during the period of nationalist agitation on the island (fears of racial miscegenation and hybridity; the growing threat of communism and Asian technocracy), by the time Fleming came to write his final Bond novel, 'British fantasies of a willing and compliant empire' had been significantly undermined (Dittmer 2008: 24). Jason Dittmer argues that 'the evolution of the representation of Jamaica between [*Live and Let Die* and *The Man with the Golden Gun*] illustrates the racial anxieties of Fleming as a Briton living on the island during the period of independence' (ibid.). As such, Bond's reinscription of British imperial practices and his promotion of cultural exoticism (his desire to locate 'old' Jamaica in Love Lane, or his direction of the dancer's highly eroticized performance at the Thunderbird Hotel, for example) within the racial, cultural and political geographies of new Jamaica suggests that Fleming's final novel is something of a revisionist work. Like Scaramanga's hotel, the narrative itself is reconstructive, attempting to elide almost altogether the historical effects of decolonization on the island. The novel sets aside real-world geopolitics, dissimulating for the reader a world in which racial anxieties and the cultural conditions of post-coloniality can hardly be said to be noticed at all. For example, as Parker notes, given that Britain's handover of power to local Jamaican governance occurred over two years prior to the publication of the novel, 'it is striking in the book how the people in authority Bond encounters are actually still British' (2014: 308–9). Moreover, Parker points out that Fleming's 'dismissal of independence in *The Man with the Golden Gun* is in stark contrast to the edginess of *Dr No*' (ibid.: 310), in which Fleming's narrator predicts that the 'stubborn retreats' of Britain's colonial culture 'will not long survive in modern Jamaica. One day [the Queen's Club] will have its windows smashed and perhaps be burned to the ground' (Fleming [1965] 2012f: 2). That it 'never seems to occur to either the British or Americans to involve local authorities in their investigation on Jamaican soil' (Parker 2014: 308) during *The Man with the Golden Gun* is expressly the point of Fleming's final novel: within the postcolonial geographies of Bond's Jamaica, it is strongly implied that local Jamaican governance is not up to much.

This is seen most clearly in the novel's final chapters, during which the reader is given some insight into the political administration of the island after empire. Firstly, the 'extremely smart policeman from the wrecking squad' (Fleming [1965] 2012m: 193) who is the first Jamaican officer on the scene following Scaramanga's death. While this man's conduct is certainly dignified, the narrative nevertheless underlines his relative ineptitude within the context of the novel's broader geopolitical conflict. Indeed, much like Fleming's presentation of Quarrel in *Live and Let Die* and *Dr. No*, for all this man's invaluable knowledge of the swamplands ('he had been born not far away, at Negril, and as a boy he had often used his gins and his slingshot in these marshes' (ibid.: 193–4)), he is presented as yet another 'kindly' and 'childlike' Jamaican (Mills 2010: 107). For one, the narrator is positively scornful of this man's professional abilities. We are told that 'Felix Leiter ... had said [to him] that a good man was after a bad man in the swamp and that there might be shooting' (Fleming [1965] 2012m: 193) – a comment which, in its self-conscious derision of the policeman's facile grasp of the situation at hand, reduces the plot's complex politics to the simple moralism of childhood *fabula*. Moreover, so assured is this man by the uncomplicated morality of the law ('to kill a policeman was a capital offence without the option. He only hoped that the good man and the bad man knew this too' (ibid.: 194)) that he actually 'saunter[s] cautiously off on his own' to intercept Bond and Scaramanga (ibid.: 193), which, apart from anything else, underscores his professional incompetence. Note, too, the 'desperately conspicuous' attire of his black-and-blue uniform (ibid.: 194), an observation which further suggests how out of place this man is within the landscape he occupies. Indeed, the man's pretence to power is emphasized when the narrator notes with biting irony that he swings his police baton with 'assumed jauntiness' (ibid.) – the suggestion being, of course, that the impression of authority which this man cultivates is altogether unsubstantiated. Though he appears for just three paragraphs in the novel and is never seen again, this minor character succeeds in reinforcing within the text 'the British view of Jamaica as a place still in need of tutelage, perhaps in the form of the British Commonwealth' (Dittmer 2008: 24). That the man acknowledges to himself that 'no Jamaican policeman ever breaks into a run' because '*he has been taught* that this lacks authority' (Fleming [1965] 2012m: 193, my italics) underlines precisely the text's ideological assumptions regarding Britain's 'parental' management of Jamaica's political, cultural and social 'childliness' in the period immediately following independence. Certainly, the narrative encourages the reader to draw unfavourable comparisons between those methods of the internationalist Bond (the British parent-figure) and the idiosyncratic parochialisms of this local policeman (the Jamaican 'child' who is in need of tutelage).

In spite of the fact that Bond has assassinated a foreign agent on Jamaica's sovereign territory (an act which should necessitate legal intervention on the part of the Jamaican government), Jamaica's administration is shown to acquiesce entirely to Britain's 'metropolitan superiority' over the matter (Dittmer 2008: 24) – a point which simply and conclusively underscores the neo-imperial ideology at the heart of Fleming's text. Nowhere is this more apparent than in the scene of the judicial inquiry held towards the end of the novel, during which Jamaica's new government attempts to save face with the Jamaican public by claiming sole responsibility for Scaramanga's takedown, thereby officially disavowing both British and American interference in the case. It becomes apparent that this cover-up routine is part of the Jamaican government's efforts to assuage both local and international public relations concerns over its own efficacy as a newly independent nation. As the police commissioner informs Bond, 'there are many rumours running around the island and abroad, and Sir Alexander Bustamante [Jamaica's first democratically elected prime minister] is most anxious to have them dispelled for the sake of justice and of the island's good name' (Fleming [1965] 2012m: 198). But, given Scaramanga's earlier admission to his criminal conspirators (which Bond overhears) that 'a certain [Jamaican] Minister has been in touch with me' (ibid.: 153) regarding the introduction of illegal gambling revenue to the island, it appears as though Fleming's narrative moves to vindicate Britain's political anxieties regarding Jamaica's potential for self-governance. Scaramanga's admission seems to imply a pre-existing relationship between an anonymous government minister and the foreign gangsters and communists against whom Bond wages battle. This is a particularly inflammatory insinuation, the implications of which are clear enough: without Britain's protection, the novel implies, the island of Jamaica has, indeed, become overrun with criminals. Moreover, the suggestion that Jamaica's leadership is now potentially corrupt, as well, can be seen to go some way towards ameliorating (through favourable contrast between a pre- and post-independence Jamaica) Britain's colonial administration of the island prior to independence. In the final chapters of *The Man with the Golden Gun*, Fleming makes nothing less than a mockery of Jamaican independence, painting the island out to be a corrupt modern economy susceptible to bribery and gambling. Ironically, the police commissioner's efforts to secure Bond's official silence on the scandal by conferring upon him the 'Jamaican Police Medal for gallant and meritorious services to the Independent State of Jamaica' (ibid.: 201) further underlines not only the propensity of the Jamaican government within the text for political corruption but also the inability of independent Jamaica to manage their own affairs without the assistance of foreign intelligence services. The commissioner's obvious delight 'with his rendering of all this rigmarole' (ibid.) is also suggestive of the selfsame theatrical staginess which characterizes Scaramanga's hotel – a further point of equivalence between the gangsters' enterprise and the new Jamaican government within the text. Equally, Leiter's characterization of the inquiry as 'the neatest wrap-up job I've ever lied my head off at' (ibid.: 202) also underlines the connection between pretence and Jamaican self-governance. Jeremy Black has argued that 'unlike at the close of *Dr. No*, the officials are no longer British and praise has now to be distributed at the behest of the independent government of Jamaica' (2005: 78). But although the police commissioner and the other official figures who appear in the judicial inquiry scene are indeed Jamaican, their textual function within Fleming's representative political landscape is entirely reactionary – they are certainly not meant to be read sincerely as either respectable or dignified Jamaican lawmakers and governors, and the text is knowing in its encouragement of the reader's derision of these figures. David Cannadine notes of Jamaica's purported independence in *The Man with the Golden Gun* that the 'regrettable reality of change' brought about by decolonization is 'ignored' in Fleming's final novel, and that Fleming 'successfully takes us within him into this world of fantasy where the *Pax Brittanicus* has never ended', and where the 'consequences [of independence] were minimal' (1979: 54–5). Throughout *The Man with the Golden Gun*, Fleming never quite manages to reconcile his love for Jamaica with the cultural politics of post-imperial Britain, and his derisive narrative treatment of those figures of Jamaican authority which appear in the judicial inquiry seems to imply that he has been ultimately unable to come to terms with the postcolonial transformations of British-Jamaican cultural relations at large.

4

After Fleming: Jamaica on screen

In 1962, former US secretary of state Dean Acheson proclaimed that Britain had 'lost an empire' but that it had 'not yet found a role' in post-war, post-imperial global affairs (qtd in Robertson 2015: 57; qtd in Frenk and Krug 2011: 3–4). Economically destitute and politically disgraced following the Suez Canal crisis of 1956, modern Britain can be said to have rediscovered something of its former imperial glory (and, certainly, a new culturally nationalizing identity) with the release of the first of James Bond's cinematic adventures, *Dr. No* (1962), directed by Terence Young, produced by Albert R. Broccoli and Harry Saltzman, and starring the now-iconic Sean Connery as the infamous spy. The producers had originally intended for the most recent novel (at the time, *Thunderball*) to be the first Bond film, but a legal injunction by film producer Kevin McClory, whom Fleming had first approached in 1958 to make a Bond film and with whom he had collaborated on an initial screen treatment (which Fleming later novelized as *Thunderball* without acknowledgement), meant that the producers were forced to borrow from elsewhere in Fleming's canon. Much like *Thunderball*, the novel *Dr. No* is set in the Caribbean (Jamaica, as opposed to Nassau in the Bahamas), and, indeed, one of the very great appeals to the producers of Fleming's sixth novel was its romantic and exotic location (Parker 2014: 272). Moreover, that Jamaica was Bond's cultural birthplace made the choice of *Dr. No* an altogether more fitting one for the first film. But the choice to adapt *Dr. No* as the first film was as much a fortuitous one as it was a politically astute one. Location shooting on the film had commenced in January 1962, and the film premiered on 6 October later that year – exactly two months after Jamaican independence, which had been granted on 6 August. Thus, the film's production can be said to trace the emergence of Jamaican nationalism and the island's attainment of self-governance from Britain over a particular condensed period of time.

According to Keith Q. Warner, the film was one of the first shown in the post-independence period to portray the anglophone Caribbean (2000: 49). *Dr. No* also happened to be screening in cinemas during the brief, thirteen-day Cuban Missile Crisis between the United States and the Soviet Union in late October 1962, during which it was discovered that Russian ballistic hardware had been installed in Cuba to deter American invasion into communist territory.[1] As James Chapman has noted, 'the very real danger of nuclear war between the Superpowers ... created the sort of atmosphere in which a film about the "toppling" of American space rockets acquired sudden topicality' ([1999] 2007: 71). The fraught geopolitical resonances of Dr No's scheme within the film (to interfere with American test rocket launches for the strategic military benefit of his shadowy Russian paymasters) was a complete coincidence,[2] but it proved an early indication of 'the degree to which Bond's career would continue to tap into the *Zeitgeist*' (Barnes and Hearn 1997: 6). Young, the film's director, called *Dr. No* 'the most perfectly timed film ever made', asserting that 'we arrived [in] not only the right year, but the right week of the right month of the right year' (qtd in Chapman [1999] 2007: 53), a grandiose claim which must nevertheless be given some credence by the timeliness of those real-world historical events surrounding the film's release. As James Robertson notes, *Dr. No* captured 'current transitions as Jamaica sought to comprehend the shift from life in a minor British colony to citizenship in an independent state that would need to fit into the unequal power relations of the cold war' (2015: 61; see also Hall 1972). Indeed, *Dr. No* succeeded in capturing viewers' imaginations not simply because it was a 'fast-paced thriller with beautiful location shots' but because it 'engaged with current [political] concerns before offering its viewers consolingly clear resolutions' (Robertson 2015: 57).

Much like reviewers' responses to Fleming's source novels, the critical heritage of the filmic *Dr. No* has been both divisive and ambivalent (see Haining 1987). Unsurprisingly, much of the film's criticism has been levelled at the representation in *Dr. No* of postcolonial race relations. Certainly, the cinematic universe of Bond's Jamaica endorses a discomfortingly familiar racial hierarchy in which the Black Jamaican is presented in all respects as inferior to the white Anglo-Saxon Britisher, but as superior to those members of the Black Chinese community. The film is replete with (uncomfortably casual) racialist power dynamics, especially in those scenes in which a somewhat peremptory Bond barks orders at Quarrel ('Cover it up', 'Fetch my shoes', 'Get her, Quarrel, and the camera'). Played by American actor John Kitzmiller, the filmic Quarrel is but a pastiche, a caricature of his soulful literary counterpart. As James Chapman notes, Kitzmiller's characterization 'marks a regression from the book: Fleming's Quarrel commands Bond's respect and even his affection, whereas in the film he has become little more than a menial sidekick' (Chapman 2018: 216). Most stereotypically, Quarrel's base superstitions and fearful regard for the dragon which supposedly roams the island of Crab Key are shown to be quelled by his casual reliance on alcohol, and composer Monty Norman's underscoring of the scene in which Quarrel swigs from an oversized bottle of rum with the instrumental leitmotif of Diana Coupland's song 'Underneath the Mango Tree' is deliberately mocking in tone. Moreover, so assured of the Black Carib's vices must Young's audiences be that, in the scene at the docks in which Bond first encounters Quarrel, it can hardly go unnoticed that the large cigarette which Quarrel purports to smoke is actually glued to the side of Kitzmiller's mouth. According to Cynthia Baron, Kitzmiller's 'bulging eyes invite the character to be read as the stereotyped "spook"', whose 'innocent' and 'eternally loyal' ([2003] 2009: 159) attachment to the imperialist Bond suggests rather worryingly that, firstly, the Black man's fearfulness is a 'natural' condition and, secondly, that the white Briton's gallant resolution of the Black man's fears are an equally 'natural' consequence of imperialism. Remember, Quarrel's misgivings about Crab Key (which he vocalizes) is precisely the catalyst for Bond's reconnaissance of the island, which leads to Quarrel's death. The film's implicit racial message is that the 'islanders are so naive that they would believe just about anything, eventually paying dearly for their gullibility' (Warner 2000: 50). But because Quarrel also 'embodies the "proper" relationship between British imperial power and the Other' (Baron [2003] 2009: 159), the film further implies that Bond's infiltration of Crab Key and the success of his mission is predicated on the emotionality and fears of its Black characters. The promise of vengeance for Dr No's murder of Quarrel's sailor friend (which occurs off-screen, prior to the commencement of the narrative) is undermined by the fact that Bond himself leads another of the islanders to his premature death on Crab Key. In his state of almost perpetual fearfulness on Crab Key, Quarrel 'stutters' his way around the island after Bond (ibid.). Thus, Bond can hardly be said to save the Black man from his own fears, for, a few moments after he dispels Quarrel's superstitions and fears of the dragon, Quarrel nevertheless ends up dead. Indeed, one need only think of the 'silence' (Wagner 2015: 53) of the Black woman with whom Bond interacts at the docks when looking for Quarrel (she points to the shoreline and responds with an almost unintelligible 'him'), or the fact that voice-over actors were used for a number of the leading actresses in the film (Caplen 2012: 72), to conclude that Bond's triumphalism – not to mention the success of the film – is predicated largely on the depreciation of minority voices.

Certainly in the cinematic Bond's pursuit of imperial civility, neither Black lives nor, it seems, Black fears matter all that much.

Dr. No also activates on screen a particular imperial ethnoscape. The film's title sequence serves as both a visual and aural interlude, symbolically denotative of Jamaica's transition from colonial outcrop to independent nation state. The brassy flourish of Monty Norman's signature James Bond tune (played over the sequence) dissolves into a recognizable Caribbean calypso beat, an auditory cue designed to signal to the viewer an exotic turn in the film's cultural landscape, while the images of stylized dots and traditional '007' iconography gradually give way to the colourful overlapping silhouettes of multiple Jamaican bodies shimmying and dancing along to the calypso music. Moreover, as the darkened silhouettes of the 'Three Blind Mice' appear on screen, the colour scheme of the graphic background against which they are contrasted is reminiscent of the colours of Britain's Union Jack flag (approx. at the 2:29 mark). The horizontal movement within this continuous shot of both the characters and the filmic frame (from left to right), as well as the cross-fade of this sequence into the film's first live-action shots of Kingston, indicates that the implied viewer, too, is in something of a figurative transition, moving away from the oppressive symbolism of Britain's empire (the red, white and blue of the background) and into the full-coloured liveliness of the real Jamaica.[3] Nevertheless, as Matthew Parker notes, the shots of Kingston which follow the title sequence (and which the 'Three Blind Mice' trace along their route) constitute 'a walking tour of colonial statues' on the island (2014: 282). Moreover, the geospatiality of the filmic Kingston is seemingly confused, as the arrangement of each successive tracking shot of the characters' movements through the city suggests a navigational route that is theoretically coherent but practically impossible. As Parker argues, this sequence constitutes a 'touristic portrayal' rather than a logical representation of topographical Kingston (ibid.).

The post-title sequence (in which, much like the source novel, Strangways is murdered in cold blood) reaffirms the white man's traditional fears of 'the colonized subject as animalistic' (Wagner 2015: 53). Indeed, these scenes also reinforce that particular facet of Fleming's novels which suggest through stereotype that the indigenous Jamaican is more childish or childlike than his European counterpart – an aspect emphasized through the particular choice of musical nursery rhyme ('Three Blind Mice') that accompanies this sequence (Baron [2003] 2009: 157). Far more crude is the film's insistence on the rapacious threat of Black Jamaicans. During the scene in which Strangways's secretary, Mary Trueblood, is murdered, the initial sight of the Black men outside the windows of Strangways's cottage (who have, it is implied, strayed across landed, cultural and social boundaries) is enough to elicit her screams of fear. Once Trueblood is dead, her body is roughly manhandled: the men roll her over and rummage in her skirt for her keys before lifting her bodily out of the cottage. The unambiguous implications of this moment underline the fearful 'transgressive sexual unions between white women ("true-bloods") and non-white men', whose rapaciousness is presented as 'pathologized' (ibid.: 158). Indeed, as Christine Bold points out, even though Mary Trueblood's superior has, in the preceding scene, been murdered by the same team of assassins, her death conditions a particularly gendered act of violence. The framing of this scene, with its building tension, is predicated on the audience's *anticipation* of her murder (Bold 1993: 322), the inevitability of which is signalled by the previous shot of the black hand swinging open the gate to Strangways's cottage to the ominous creaking sound of rusting hinges.[4]

But, for its many scenes depicting problematic British-Jamaican cultural and racial relations, *Dr. No* also configures certain spatial geographies in which racial tensions are deliberately played down, and in which the colour divide is presented as seemingly inconsequential. Such ambivalent ethnoscapes are usually characterized by their transience or by their function within the leisure industry. For instance, though Kingston Airport is presented in the film as a site of potential treachery for Bond (he is surveilled variously by the photographer, Annabel Chung, and his chauffeur, alias 'Mr Jones', both of whom work for Dr No), the air traffic control tower is also the first site of racial integration presented in the film. Here, both indigenous Jamaicans and white Britons work alongside one another without the film calling its audience's attention to it. This is in distinct contrast to those scenes set in the Queen's Club (not a tourist spot but a social organization for Kingston's expatriate white community), in which it is very apparent that people of colour appear only as servants and waiters, and never as leisure seekers themselves. Another site of racial integration within the film is the nightclub owned by Pussfeller, Quarrel's associate, in which both indigenous Jamaicans and British expatriates can be seen to enjoy the ska and calypso stylings of the popular Jamaican musical group Byron Lee and the Dragonaires. Like the airport, Pussfeller's club, too, is something of a post-racial haunt, with indigenous Jamaicans and white tourists alike dancing wildly to the music without comment. *Dr. No* seems to insist upon the view that spaces of leisure tourism seemingly unhampered by issues of racial conflict exist simultaneously alongside those geographies of racialized violence we have already seen in the murders of Strangways and Mary Trueblood at the hands of Black Jamaicans.

The film, then, operates a kind of selective racism, intimating, on the one hand, that its ideological reactionism is a precondition of the (apparently) ubiquitous threat to white people on the island of racial violence and, on the other, that such cultural dilemmas are eradicated entirely through the 'simple' post-raciality of touristic modernity. The latter view is certainly endorsed through the film's alignment of Bond with not only touristic but also technological modernity. Having flown Pan Am commercial airlines to Jamaica, the cinematic Bond is shown variously throughout the film to be modern and internationalist, a man in step with the historical times. This is very much in contrast to the Bond of the literary *The Man with the Golden Gun*, who is largely frustrated with the infrastructure of global modernity. In the scene in which he first meets Quarrel, for instance, Bond's out-of-placedness (in contrast to the locals, he is dressed in a full suit in sweltering Jamaican heat) represents a certain anti-provincialism, and the huge cruise ship that can be seen in the background of this scene serves as a metonymic foil for Bond's own modernizing mobility. And while some critics have dismissed the imperialist Bond of *Dr. No* as outmoded,[5] Robertson argues that 'British filmgoers saw [in the filmic Bond] a courageous agent working with the latest equipment rather than … an unscrupulous operative from post-war Britain's imperial rear-guard' (2015: 57). Indeed, though the filmic *Dr. No* does retain insights from Fleming's novel regarding shifting cultural and political relations on the island in the period of Jamaican independence, there are a number of differences between the film and its source novel which 'demonstrate how the verities of the cold war and the glamour of high technology encouraged the overwriting of elements in [Fleming's] original plot' (ibid.:56) – such as the film's employment of the latest communicational gadgetry, Bond's Geiger counter reader and Mr Jones's cyanide-encased cigarettes.

One striking difference between novel and film is the representation of Government House in Jamaica, which is afforded far greater deference by the film-makers than by Fleming. In the novel *Dr. No*, Fleming portrays the Acting Governor as a 'nincompoop' (Maudling 1965: n.p.), the consequence of which was that the producers were later denied access to the real Government House for filming in 1962.[6] In contrast, Young's film portrays Jamaica's Principal Secretary, Pleydell-Smith, as shrewd and sensible. Unlike in the novel *Dr. No*, in which the Governor inadvertently signals Bond's purpose on the island by making available to him Strangways's old Sunbeam Alpine (a government car), the Principal Secretary of the film is much more cautious: 'I didn't think you wanted an official reception,' he tells Bond over the telephone – a comment which not only alerts Bond to the duplicity of Mr Jones (the chauffeur who identifies himself as having been sent from Government House but who, in reality, is working for Dr No) but which also offers a comparatively favourable revision of the Acting Governor as he appears in Fleming's novel. When Bond later drives up to the Governor's residence with the dead Mr Jones in the back seat of his car, the Principal Secretary barely seems to register the fact at all. There are no apparent legal ramifications for Bond's nonchalant murderousness, the point of which serves to underline with audacity the presumptuousness of Britain's imperial presence on the island, seemingly endorsed by the Principal Secretary's silent complicity. However, that another of Dr No's associates, Miss Taro, should have successfully infiltrated the island's colonial administration (she works undercover as Pleydell-Smith's secretary) says much for the implied threat of the so-called 'Asian invasion' of Western democracy and very little for the security of Jamaica's Government House itself. (This point is also subtly implied in the novel *The Man with the Golden Gun*, when Scaramanga insinuates that he has loyal contacts working for him from inside the Jamaican government.) Miss Taro – whose very name has mystic connotations – is very much presented, in Lisa Funnell's words, as a 'Dragon Lady, a racial stereotype of Asian femininity' (2015: 80), a veritable honey trap for the white Britisher Bond and an exoticist threat to the ordered masculinity of Britain's administration of the island – though it might be said, perhaps, that Pleydell-Smith's apparent blindness to both Miss Taro's race and beauty is indicative of the restrained orderliness required of the proper colonial administrator: a colour-blind sexual ascetic. Miss Taro's sexual and racial visibility, however, is at once both emphasized and played down in the film, as she is but one of a number of Asian characters who populate the filmic Jamaica. Professor Dent's secretary is Asian, as are Dr No's matronly concierges Sister Rose and Sister Lily, along with a host of other servants and henchpeople, all of whom speak with curious British accents, either affected or because the actors themselves are British and made up to appear Asian. (This is certainly the case with Zena Marshall, the British actress who plays Miss Taro.) In terms of local geopolitics, the film certainly exploits Jamaican cultural memory of the anti-Chinese riots of 1918 and 1938, which occurred largely as a result of the disaffection of indigenous Jamaicans over the expansion and relative economic prosperity of the island's Chinese communities.[7]

But *Dr. No* is also concerned with American and Chinese relations. As Lisa Funnell and Klaus Dodds note, 'China was considered a growing political threat [the concerns of which] were far more pressing in the United States than in Britain' (2015: 360) – a point which may account for the tentative geopolitical footsie which Bond and Leiter engage in throughout the film. Bond can be seen to court American anxieties over Chinese (communist) insurrectionism in the Caribbean, and, in return, Leiter plays along with Britain's fantasies of imperial relevance. Even though Dr No is toppling *American* missiles, it is made abundantly clear to Leiter by Bond, on their approach to Crab Key, that the mission is Bond's 'beat'. Moreover, Leiter gladly acquiesces to Bond's authority and returns to Kingston, reappearing only at the close of the film with reinforcements. As Robertson notes, Leiter's command of the Royal Navy conveys 'more of a British military presence' than the original script, in which Leiter was initially accompanied by the Jamaican police force (2015: 16). This scene does not simply imply a fluid transfer of Anglo-American jurisdictional power in the Caribbean; rather, it suggests that American authority in this region is bolstered through Leiter's cheerful concession to British naval might. Leiter does not even appear in Fleming's source novel *Dr. No*; the inclusion of Bond's CIA counterpart in the narrative, not to mention the casting of charming American actor Jack Lord in the part, was a calculated attempt to curry favour for the film in the American market. Of historical Anglo-American political relations at the time, Jeremy Black notes that 'relations between the two powers had improved since the Suez crisis of 1956' and that 'America's public image as [a British] ally benefited from Kennedy's election and from his popularity' (2005: 94). In reality, though, as James Chapman argues, 'the Americans have rarely shown such deference to the remnants of British colonialism in the Caribbean' ([1999] 2007: 62) as does Felix Leiter to Bond in *Dr. No*. The 'special relationship' which the film configures between British and American forces is, in actuality, far more unequal (and not in Britain's favour) than the Bond universe suggests (ibid.).

While *Dr. No* certainly takes somewhat fantastical liberties with post-war Anglo-American allegiances, local Jamaicans responded positively at the time to depictions of their cultural homeland, enjoying the film's display of Jamaica's 'new nation[al] potential' and the fact that it 'touched on issues current in the place where it was filmed' (Robertson 2015: 57). Marguerite LeWars, the Jamaican actress who plays the bristly photographer Annabel Chung in *Dr. No*, recalls that the film was an accurate reflection of Jamaican life and that many Jamaicans took great pride in its representation of Kingston and the island at large (Parker 2014: 281; Warner 2000: 50). However, West Indian critics have tended, on the whole, to be somewhat less positive. While *Dr. No* does show 'ordinary Jamaicans' going about their lives in Kingston, the film's 'sub-conscious messages' on hierarchical racial and cultural relations, as well as the fact that 'principal action was probably conceived elsewhere and [Jamaican] personnel were shipped in for the convenient backdrops', suggest that it is not designed to be as complimentary of Jamaica and Jamaicans as many locals believed (Warner 1992: 47–8). Indeed, Robertson goes so far as to argue that *Dr. No* 'short-changed Jamaica's music, dance, and people' (2015: 61). That said, the film's afterlife was profoundly impactful on Jamaica's cultural life. The film remained in cinemas in Kingston for fourteen months and can be said to have first promoted the development of ska music on the island and the reputation of the band Byron Lee and the Dragonaires, more specifically. On the level of national symbolism, *Dr. No* showcased to Jamaican audiences 'their island as the British Empire was departing', helping local islanders to come to terms with their own shifting and emergent cultural and national identities (ibid.: 73). Reflecting on the film's impact fifty years after its release, Robertson concludes that *Dr. No*'s success at a particular historical moment can be attributed overwhelmingly to the fact that when the film 'touched on difficult issues [such as Soviet interventionism, Chinese insurrectionism and British-Jamaican race relations] it offered simple solutions' to its European viewership (ibid.: 75). More specifically, the film appealed to Jamaican audiences precisely because it 'highlighted an independent Jamaica's possibilities', however 'limited' an understanding of local political, cultural and racial concerns it evinces (ibid.). Ultimately, Robertson contends, one of the principal elements of the film's success – and which subsequent iterations of Bond's adventures have failed (or have been unable) to capitalize on – is precisely its engagement with local Jamaican concerns at a particularly pregnant historical juncture (ibid), and through the precise popular cultural form by which the 'influence that decolonization produced' (ibid.: 60) was made discernible to and interpreted by cinematic audiences across the globe.

While James Chapman acknowledges that '*Dr. No* would be the only Bond film whose narrative is set at the historical moment of the end of Empire', his assertion that 'subsequent films in the series distanced themselves from the colonial trappings of *Dr. No*' is somewhat less accurate (2018: 217). Fleming's *Dr. No* was adapted for the screen and introduced Sean Connery as the very first cinematic incarnation of James Bond, but it is noteworthy that the first two Roger Moore Bond films are adaptations of Fleming's other two Jamaican novels, *Live and Let Die* and *The Man with the Golden Gun*. Though neither film is set in Jamaica – *Live and Let Die* (1973) is set in New York and on the fictional Caribbean island of San Monique, while *The Man with the Golden Gun* (1974) takes place in South East Asia – both are, to various degrees, positionally aligned with narratives of empire and with *Dr. No*'s Jamaican psychogeography. The wreckage of the RMS *Queen Elizabeth* liner that is seen foundered in Hong Kong's Victoria Harbour in *The Man with the Golden Gun* proves an interesting counterpoint to Dr No's island compound. Whereas Dr No can be said to have infiltrated one of Britain's most important colonies in the Caribbean by (inexplicably) establishing a secret missile toppling base offshore of Jamaica, in *The Man with the Golden Gun* it is the British who are seen to have penetrated communist China and Hong Kong by setting up a mobile intelligence outpost disguised by and contained within the hull of the wrecked liner – itself a rusting steel inversion of Dr No's exotic island hideaway. It is also clear from the sequence set aboard the liner that the British are engaged in ongoing and clandestine intelligence operations: between the 'Chinese fleet on one side and the American fleet on the other', the British naval men aboard the ship are shown to be salvaging sunken Chinese fighter planes from the harbour beneath them and secretly harvesting their technologies for gain. The paradigmatic alignment between *Live and Let Die*'s setting and *Dr. No*'s Jamaican psychogeography is much more apparent: the island of San Monique is an imaginary reworking of the novel's original Jamaican setting, which, in 1973, over a decade after Jamaica's independence, was no longer seen as an appropriate landscape for the imperialist Britisher Bond. The filmic *Live and Let Die* even includes the character 'Quarrel Jr', the son of Bond's long-time ally Quarrel, the Cayman Islander who appears in the novels *Live and Let Die* and *Dr. No*. Quarrel Jr is the creation of screenwriter Tom Mankiewicz, introduced to ensure continuity between the cinematic universes of Connery's first screen outing as Bond and Moore's.[8] *Live and Let Die* is, as James Chapman asserts, 'a transitional film in the Bond series' ([1999] 2007: 141); its overt purpose is to introduce Moore's Bond, but, perhaps more implicitly, it succeeds in forging connections for the viewers between the political ethnoscapes of the fictional San Monique and the real Jamaica. While neither *Live and Let Die* nor *The Man with the Golden Gun* are expressly set on Jamaica, their cinematic landscapes can be read, in Tim Waterman's words, as 'propagandistic allegories and situating narratives' which 'represent both the overarching goals and the explicit practices and representations' (2018: 185) of Fleming's original Jamaican psychogeography. They are symbolic geographies, metonymic stand-ins for the historical Jamaica about which Fleming wrote but that were, in the contemporary climate of Jamaican autonomy, politically 'off limits' to the films' producers.

As a result of the momentous political and cultural changes that had taken place in British-Jamaican relations after decolonization and Jamaican independence, there are a number of differences between the literary and filmic versions of each text. Of course, Fleming's source novel is practically unrecognizable in the filmic version of *The Man with the Golden Gun*, as so little of the original material was adapted for screen. Consequently, on that film I have relatively little to say. Conversely, *Live and Let Die* is a much more discernible adaptation of the novel on which it is based. The film retains the basic plot structure of Fleming's novel, curtailing the Harlem and New York sequences and extending those parts of the narrative that are set upon San Monique, the film's fictional reimagining of Jamaica. In the simple act of 'renaming' Jamaica, the film affords Britain a 'reprieve on past colonial legacies' as the 'centuries-old construction of white supremacy were silenced' by the invention of the 'ambiguously Spanish-French sound "San Monique"' (McClure 2011: 293). Thus, Jamaica's imaginary reinvention as San Monique, another Caribbean small island state, 'allows British and U.S. action in the world – via Bond – to manifest itself as defensive in nature, and not as a continuation of the maintenance of centuries old colonial power relations' (ibid.: 295). As a marker of changing global geopolitics, and as something of a salute by the filmmakers to the first decade of Jamaica's independent status, the film opens on a scene set during a United Nations pan-island unity conference, in which the delegates from San Monique (who, it transpires, are the film's primary antagonist, Dr Kananga, and Bond's eventual romantic interest, Solitaire) are afforded a prominent diplomatic position during the discussions. San Monique's seat at a high-level United Nations council meeting suggests its elevated status and, more implicitly, its political legitimacy. If we are to read San Monique as a metonymically displaced Jamaica, then the implication of this scene is that the now-independent island enjoys full and acknowledged diplomatic status in the post-imperial period. This view is somewhat augmented by the numerous shots we see of Kananga in San Monique's New York embassy and in his official presidential residence on the island, where he is shown at his desk signing official documentation. Indeed, during one of Kananga's speeches at the embassy (pre-recorded for the benefit of the CIA, who have wired the building for sound), Felix Leiter notes to Bond that 'Kananga's knitting a flag in there', a comment which ostensibly refers to the passion of Kananga's political rhetoric during the speech but which also connotes the image of a newly independent nation state in the process of realization: Kananga is 'knitting a flag', figuratively or rhetorically patching together the island's symbolic nationhood. Moreover, the tenor of Kananga's recorded speech concerns the need for more powerful island nations in the Caribbean to redouble their efforts to protect their smaller counterparts from being 'bullied' by US industry in the region, a point which is conspicuous in its elision of any mention whatsoever of British colonial interventionism.

But while *Live and Let Die* does tacitly acknowledge San Moniquean/Jamaican independence, it also undermines the political and diplomatic credibility of

Caribbean self-governance in the post-independent period. During the United Nations conference, the delegate for the UK is murdered on Kananga's orders,[9] and, later, a British agent is strung up and killed during an orgiastic Voodoo ceremony on the island of San Monique. The implication of these events is clear enough: Caribbean island states (and Jamaica in particular) cannot be trusted to govern themselves either lawfully or civilly.[10] The murders of British diplomatic and intelligence personnel in foreign territory carries the fearful prospect that the Caribbean's 'erstwhile colonial subjects might take over and make white men obsolete' (Daub and Kronengold 2015: 106). That Kananga (literally) gets away with murder on the floor of the United Nations' council chamber implies in no uncertain terms the ruthlessness and efficacy of violent Caribbean resistance to US democratic doctrine, the implication being that 'a failure to control both black neighbourhoods and small Caribbean islands could undermine America' and the highest levels of its political democracy (Black 2005: 134). As Adrian Daub and Charles Kronengold note, this sequence certainly suggests something of a 'discomfort with non-white visibility (and audibility)' within the political sphere (2015: 98). No longer is it the case that the filmic Bond simply ventures out to pacify marginalized imperial cultures; rather, his missions are more overtly concerned with suppressing acts of 'reverse colonialism' by 'formerly subjugated nations and peoples' who desire to '[sink] their talons into the metropole' (ibid.). In this case, it is the United Nations, the very heart of Western diplomatic relations. This shift is somewhat in keeping with certain cultural and social trends that emerged in Britain in the late 1960s and which carried over into the next decade. The film's images of 'black urban criminality' and Caribbean Voodoo coalesced in Britain's cultural imagination of the period, during which 'British anxiety towards black migrants to Great Britain gained momentum' (McClure 2011: 291).[11] The film was released to a climate of 'increasingly loud … and explicitly racist' demands in Britain to 'halt black immigration' to British shores, as the film's many Black characters embodied for British audiences 'the link between blackness and criminality' in much the same way that the 'connection of Jamaica to Harlem linked Great Britain to the increasing urban problems in the United States' (ibid.: 293).

When considered against the volatile social, political and historical context of 1970s Britain, critics' defence of the issues of race and racialism in *Live and Let Die* are troublingly ambivalent. Writing for *Time*, Richard Schickel argued that there is a 'dubious rationale' for Bond's racism, and that 'it is just a matter of equal rights to let [African Americans] have their chance to play masochists to [Bond's] pseudo-suave sadist' (1973: n.p.). Arguably, Bond is undiscerning in his attitudes to race: he discriminates equally. Nevertheless, Schickel himself cannot help but ponder why the film's African-American characters are 'either stupid brutes or primitives deep into the occult and Voodooism' (ibid.). Dilys Powell in the *Sunday Times* asserts that *Live and Let Die* is an 'anti-white' film, and that it is actually 'slanted against the incompetence of the whites' (1974: n.p.). Much later, critic and Bond continuation author Raymond Benson has argued that the accusations of racism directed at the film are unwarranted, precisely because the film-makers 'decided to create a high-class criminal organization as opposed to Fleming's group of second-rate crooks' (1984: 207). While Benson's declaration that 'Fleming's original story was thrown out' is somewhat inaccurate (ibid.; *Live and Let Die* is a reasonably faithful adaptation), it can be argued that the film's all-Black criminal organization somewhat improved upon Fleming's characters (though this may not be saying much). Much more recently, James Chapman counters common charges levelled against *Live and Let Die* and argues that the film is not necessarily blaxploitation, 'given that its hero is a white male and that is set only partly in a black *milieu*' ([1999] 2007: 138).[12] But he also acknowledges the 'rather uneasy tension' between the themes and motifs of blaxploitation pictures and stereotypical representations of African Americans and Black Caribbeans (ibid.; see also Alexander 2020). Aside from the film's many instances of casual, racialized violence (in the credit sequence, for example, we are presented with the repeating image of a terrorized Black woman's head exploding into flames), *Live and Let Die* is replete with superficial African-American stereotypes and suspect racialist imagery. For instance, Kananga plans to turn impoverished communities across the United States into his own zombified army of heroin dependents by distributing free samples of the drug throughout the country. Though his scheme may not be said to be overtly racist in intent (Kananga claims that his product is for 'man or woman, black or white, I don't discriminate'), it is strongly implied that unilateral drug addiction will amalgamate various socio-economically underprivileged Black communities, in particular, thereby implicitly connecting North America's growing crime rate (i.e. to feed the drug habit) with the rise of Black power movements and the fearful prospect of a racial revolution or uprising against white 'civility'.

This point is endorsed by the film's overwhelming dismissal of almost all Black people as untrustworthy criminals. Besides the duplicitous Rosie Carver, who pretends to be a CIA agent but who is, in reality, working for Kananga, virtually every person of colour who appears in the Harlem sequence (from waiters to street-side shoeshiners, and from retail assistants to taxi drivers) is shown to be in the employ of 'Mr Big', Kananga's nom de guerre. This is, of course, Mr Big's extensive network of spies brought to life in the film. But when it is later revealed that one of the ostensible members of this network is, in fact, the undercover CIA agent Strutter (a colleague of Bond's ally, Felix Leiter), we realize that the film has deliberately stoked its audience's fearful regard for the African-American male, in particular, in order to deliver a moment of brief narrative jouissance. Whereas the colour of Strutter's skin (he is played by African-American actor Lon Satton) seemingly aligns him with the pervasive Black threat of Mr Big/Kananga's urban empire, the revelation that he is, in Jason Dittmer's words, a 'collaborationist' rather than a 'dangerous' Black (2008: 24) underscores the fact that the film deliberately elicits from its audience a distinct racial paranoia, predicated on the belief that it is impossible to distinguish 'good' African Americans from 'bad' ones, as well as the assumption that 'while you can take white American figures at face value, all black American characters are suspect' (Funnell and Dodds 2015: 363). Moreover, Strutter's revelation to Bond of his real identity is to be understood as an effective narrative 'twist' only in the context of the audience's implied distrust of African Americans, which has been inculcated within the narrative from the film's opening moments, when the white British UN delegate is murdered by the anonymous black hand who operates the plunger of the sonic blaster. The audience's enjoyment of this narrative 'twist' – the tinge of relief that is felt by the revelation that Strutter is a Black ally and not a Black foe – is predicated entirely on the complicity of the viewer's own prejudicial assumptions about the (inherent) criminality of urban Black men. Though the narrative jouissance of this particular moment hinges upon audiences' recognition of their own decidedly uncomfortable assumptions about what Strutter's Blackness signifies, as well as the surprising inversion of superficial racial misreadings, the film nevertheless fails to offer a 'credible critique of white racism' (McClure 2011: 298–9). And while 'Strutter's understanding of the racial geographies of New York helps to bolster the perception of his professional competence' (Funnell and Dodds 2015: 363), his later death at the hands of Big/Kananga's network in New Orleans only undermines his credibility as an effective agent – thereby reinforcing, in this case, the stereotypical vision not of the Black man's criminality but of his incompetency.

With respect to the more pernicious representations of Caribbean cultural and religious practices, the film's commercialization of the occult and the orgiastic spectacle of the numerous Voodoo ceremonies showcased throughout suggest a racialized frenzy of exotic excess in which the prospect of Black-on-white violence is imminent. The inclusion of the occult, of course, 'helps reinforce the audiences' identification of the black characters with images of a "savage" Africa'

(McClure 2011: 295). The primary difference between the film and the novel's representation of obeah is the film-makers' decision to incorporate Baron Samedi as an actual character within the narrative. Whereas Fleming makes it clear in his novel that Baron Samedi is a guise adopted by Mr Big in order to strike fear into his network of informers, in the film he is a literalized figure (played with great poise by the Trinidadian-American choreographer Geoffrey Holder), first seen leading the dance of a touristic floor show put on for guests of the San Moniquean hotel at which Bond is staying. The film also strongly suggests that Baron Samedi is, indeed, a supernatural being; his appearance at the front of the train on which Bond and Solitaire are travelling at the end of the film implies that he survives the poisoning by multiple snakebites he receives after Bond tosses him into a coffin full of deadly reptiles during the climactic battle on San Monique. The film itself seems to neither understand nor know what to do with the supernatural figure of Baron Samedi. Such absurd concessions to the supernatural (not to be found anywhere else in the filmic Bond canon) are part of what Martha Mary Daas refers to as the film's 'Disneyfication of Voodoo' or the ways in which the film's 'treatment of Voodoo and African-American culture … demonstrates a tendency towards the denigration of a culture and a mythology that is neither white nor Western' (2011: 167, 162).

We see something similar in the film's treatment of Solitaire's Voodoo powers. As with the portrayal by Swiss Ursula Andress of the Jamaican Creole Honey Rider in the filmic *Dr. No*, the casting of British actress Jane Seymour as Solitaire eradicates from the narrative those concerns regarding the character's cultural hybridity (in the novel *Live and Let Die*, Solitaire is French-Haitian), thus marking her realignment by Bond in politico-ideological and not racial terms. While Solitaire's religious and spiritual practices are discernibly non-Western (and therefore threatening to the ordered rigidity of British Christendom), Seymour's whiteness does much to mitigate such fears in the viewers' eyes: her whiteness aligns Solitaire's powers of the obeah less with Black primitivism and more with a sublimated Christian religiosity. That said, Seymour's whiteness is counterbalanced throughout the film by a confusing mélange of cultural and racial signifiers designed to connote otherness. As Joyce Goggin notes, 'Solitaire's ethnicity is given a considerably more fluid and polyphonic twist': 'she pronounces her name *à la française* and wears a red silk tunic which suggests Indian origins, while her hair and make-up signal the Orient' (2018: 150). Curiously, though the character's racial and ethnic origins in the novel are whitewashed on screen, the 'multiple ethnicities' (152) of the costume and design aesthetic of the filmic Solitaire suggests a much more troubling inclination not just towards cultural denigration but cultural appropriation too. The central act of sexual conquest, Bond's veritable assault of Solitaire (he uses her own deck of tarot cards to trick her into believing that the loss of her virginity to him is fated), can also be read as metonymic of the film's figurative assault on non-white, non-Western cultural mythology configured through the female body – the full racialized and imperial effects of which are, again, only partly shielded by Seymour's whiteness. The film sanctions such an assault (Bond's trickery is played for laughs) precisely because the alternative sexual match between Solitaire and Kananga connotes the unthinkable: 'the white fear of black contamination of the [female] vessel of whiteness' (McClure: 295). Both in terms of Bond's actions and the film itself, as a frame for that character's actions, *Live and Let Die* betrays an insidious desire 'to demean all that is not western and all that is not part of a Christian mindset' (Daas 2011: 165). Solitaire's sexuality is precisely the object of that debasement, as her powers of the obeah are explicitly tied to her remaining virginal.

Ironically, while the question of Solitaire's ethnic and racial hybridity is played down in the filmic version of the character, *Live and Let Die* marks the first time in the series in which Bond becomes romantically involved with a Black woman, Rosie Carver, played by African-American actress Gloria Hendry.[13] While Carver initially declines Bond's sexual overtures – which, according to Charles Burnetts, 'signals a morality that runs counter to neo-colonialist constructions of libidinous black femininity' (2015: 63) – the character is otherwise presented in trite stereotypical terms. While Quarrel's superstition of dragons in *Dr. No* is affectionately absorbed and only mildly disparaged by Bond, in *Live and Let Die* Bond positively derides Carver's irrationality over her fear of Voodoo iconography: her piercing wails at the sight of the top hat with bloody chicken feathers stuck to it, or the scarecrows in the poppy fields, for instance, elicit not sympathy but ridicule. Later, when Carver stumbles upon the radio communications equipment and weapons cache aboard Quarrel Jr's boat, she mistakenly identifies him as an enemy agent and holds him at gunpoint – only to be ridiculed for her incompetence once more by Bond, who reveals to Rosie that Quarrel Jr is the son of Bond's much-loved ally, Quarrel. Much like the revelation earlier on in the film that Strutter is a CIA agent, the narrative reveal of Quarrel Jr's identity (a nostalgic callback to Bond's first cinematic outing and to the franchise's Jamaican heritage) is predicated on the viewers' shared racialist assumptions about the professional incompetency of people of colour (in this case, a Black woman's inability to correctly assess a particular situation), as well as the rather more pernicious shared desire for women of colour to be repeatedly disparaged and mocked. In a moment of pronounced discomfort for the modern viewer, Carver addresses Quarrel Jr as though he were an inarticulate oaf: 'Me ... clothes off ... where?' she mouths to him, assuming him to be incapable of understanding her. Here, Carver can be said to perpetuate the selfsame racialist, imperial mythos concerning the perceived unintelligence and 'savagery' of people of colour that she herself is subject to by the film's framing of her own incompetence as a humorous fait accompli. The narrative takes something of a nasty relish in purposefully undermining and embarrassing Black professionals, and Carver in particular, a point which (rather more uncomfortably) is seemingly proven justified by the later reveal that Carver is, herself, an enemy agent working for Kananga – though, again, not a particularly competent or effective one. Kananga has her murdered before she reveals too much of his operation to Bond. Carver's ineptitude, the film suggests, is marked by her own 'fear and implicit belief in the Other's exoticised culture' (Burnetts 2015: 63). It is precisely her inability to 'embody Bond's atheist cynicism' (ibid.) over the iconography of Caribbean Voodoo (the bloody top hat, the scarecrows) that renders her both politically and professionally misaligned – a point Bond makes abundantly clear to Quarrel Jr in his dismissal of Carver as a 'lousy agent'.

Concluding thoughts

Much like Daniel Defoe's Robinson Crusoe, Arthur Conan Doyle's Sherlock Holmes and Bram Stoker's Dracula, James Bond has 'transcended the novels and films which brought him to life' and has now become a transglobal figure 'known by many who never read or saw the "original" texts' (Denning 1987: 91). Almost everything about Fleming's fictive universe is superlative and unequivocal. As David Cannadine notes, 'nothing is mundane, and there are no half measures' in Bond's world; everything is 'the biggest, loveliest, best, fastest (or most horrible and sinister) on the planet' (2002: 288). Even the very mythoi upon which Fleming built his most famous creation are some of the grandest in British literary and cultural tradition. Through Bond, 'myths of espionage, patriotism, and masculinity are made to converge' (Bold 1993: 314) and the novels 'encompass ideologies of nationhood, national concerns with regard to territorial dominance and the prevalence and preference for tradition in the collective British psyche' (Goodman 2016: 10). But for all of the grand ideological assurances promised to British readers by the superlativeness of Bond's political and social milieu, neither the novels nor their later filmic adaptations ever quite resolve the issue of Fleming's ambivalence regarding Caribbean and, specifically, Jamaican topopolitics. Fleming's good friend on the island, Morris Cargill, described Fleming as 'a great friend of Jamaica', as someone who 'sang the praises of Jamaica' and as someone who 'through his books, films and articles ... did more perhaps than any other single person to give [Jamaica] extensive and favourable publicity abroad' (qtd in Parker 2014: 307). However, it is somewhat difficult to reconcile this personal assessment (which, owing to the two men's friendship, may certainly be considered biased, anyway) with the representational politics that we have seen throughout Fleming's major Jamaican novels. Fleming's writings can be said to offer a less than favourable vision of Jamaica than Cargill claims. Indeed, to borrow a phrase from Mimi Sheller, Fleming's Jamaican psychogeography constitutes 'an ambiguous place in the realm of Western imagined geographies', a place whereupon his own 'paranoid fantasies of discovery' are played out in colonial and imperial terms (2003: 107). As Parker notes, Fleming could not but be aware of the fact that Jamaica was 'the most brutal of all the British slave colonies' and that this history left upon the island 'a legacy of violence and resentment' towards the 'vicious tyranny' of colonial slave owners (2014: 121). The 'sanitized racialism' (Richler 1972: 81) which Fleming employs in his Jamaica-set novels, then, does little to redress this violent imperial history. In spite of Fleming's oft-reported love and affection for Jamaica and Jamaican peoples, his novels actually service those 'Little Englanders who believe they have been undone by dastardly foreign plotters [by pandering] to [Britain's] continuing notion of self-importance' in the Caribbean and the wider world (ibid.).

Notes

Introduction: Ian Fleming and the politics of ambivalence; or, From Jamaica with love?

1 For a selection of enlightening literary and film trivia on all things James Bond, see Sterling and Morecambe (2002), Cork and Scivally (2002), Smith and Lavington (2002), Field and Chowdhury (2015) and Egan (2016).
2 For a discussion of the pre-history of the term 'ambivalence', see Montaigne (1938: 333–4).
3 For more information on the concept of postcolonial ambivalence, see James (1963), Taussig (1993) and Belnap (1993).
4 There is a somewhat limited catalogue of specifically Jamaican and/or British-Jamaican films that have reached wider British audiences. Notable titles include Perry Henzell's enormously influential *The Harder They Come* (1972), Theodoros Bafaloukos's *Rockers* (1978), Don Letts's *Dancehall Queen* (1997), Rick Ellgood's and Don Letts's *One Love* (2003), Tony Jenkins's *Glory to Gloriana* (2006) and Mary Wells's *Kingston Paradise* (2013).
5 For more information on the politics of tourism and the touristic gaze, see Leed (1991), MacCannell (1999), Huggan (2001), Holland and Huggan (2002) and Urry and Larsen (2011).
6 In the interest of parity, it should be noted that *Yardie*'s director, Idris Elba, is not himself Jamaican; he is of Sierra Leonean and Ghanaian heritage.
7 For more information on the historical practices and cultural representations of cannibalism in the colonial context, see Arens (1979) Sanday (1986), Lestringant (1997), Avramescu (2011) and Earle (2012).
8 Turner is incorrect. See endnote 4, above.
9 Indeed, much of the myth about Fleming and Bond has grown up around the notion that Fleming himself was a crack spymaster, someone who had *lived* the very experiences he was writing about. See, for instance, Lett (2013).
10 In *Live and Let Die*, for instance, Fleming copies at length from one of his favourite authors (and his good friend) Patrick Leigh Fermor, whose 1950 book *The Traveller's Tree* James Bond pores over as something of an authoritative guide to Caribbean Voodoo practices. Fleming's reliance on Fermor's travelogue puts one in mind of R. M. Ballantyne, an earlier writer of adventure fiction (and one of Fleming's favourite childhood authors), whose 1885 novel *The Coral Island* borrows extensively from early-nineteenth century Pacific Island travelogues – in particular,

John Williams's *Narrative of Missionary Enterprise* (1837). The difference between Fleming and Ballantyne, of course, is that whereas Ballantyne never visited the Pacific and thus relied entirely on the accounts of other travellers and writers of fiction for his descriptions, Fleming himself lived and wrote in Jamaica. For more on Ballantyne's plagiarism, see Dutheil (2001: 105–22) and Edmond (1997: 146–8).

11 See, for instance, Hall (2013).
12 For further information on mediatization and media and communication theory, see Strömbäck (2008: 228–46), Friesen and Hug (2009: 64–81), Adolf (2011: 153–75), Couldry and Hepp (2013: 191–202), Hjarvard and Peterson (2013: 1–7) and Hepp, Hjarvard and Lundby (2015: 314–24).
13 For a more expansive treatment of the mediatization of the Caribbean through film and photographic reproductions, see Thompson (2006).
14 Halloran argues that 'the Caribbean constitutes the one physical and ideological space in which displaced, racially hybrid characters – both villains and heroes – feel at home' within Fleming's fictive universe. She draws on Mary Louise Pratt's concept of the 'contact zone' to describe the Caribbean as the site upon which European, American, Asian and African cultures converge seeking political supremacy in the post-colonial, post-war period of the mid-twentieth century (2005: 160). For a discussion of cultural contact zones, see Pratt (1992).
15 Simon Winder notes that '[Fleming] also provided a very strange link between old Jamaica and new in his long-running affair with Blanche Blackwell, a white woman resident there'. He says: 'I never tire of thinking about the strangeness of Fleming, perched in his house in the Caribbean tapping out the novels that were to have such a vast influence and which so beautifully articulated the pains of Britain's post-war predicament, sleeping with the woman who provided the fundamental link with the new ganja and dreadlock Jamaica [Blanche's son, Chris Blackwell, was the founder of Island Records, which gave Bob Marley and many other Jamaican ska and reggae artists their start in music] – one that would have horrified and baffled Fleming' (2006: 140).
16 For a history of British-Jamaican relations (and Euro-Caribbean relations more broadly) see Williams (1964), Craton (1983), Campbell (1988), Carey (1997) and Brown (2008).
17 For a more detailed account of the overlaps between the histories of Britain and James Bond, see Winder (2006).
18 Fleming dedicates his novel *Goldfinger* (1959) to Cuneo, whom he jokingly refers to as his 'muse'. 'Ernie Cuneo' is also the name of a taxi driver character who appears in *Diamonds Are Forever* (1956).
19 The title of Parker's 2014 biography of Fleming – *Goldeneye: Where Bond Was Born: Ian Fleming's Jamaica* – suggests that Jamaica is key to interpreting the James Bond mythos. Fleming was 38 years old in 1946 when he purchased land in

Oracabessa (on Jamaica's north coast) and built what would eventually be his home, Goldeneye. Though Fleming spent relatively much less of his life in Jamaica than he did in Britain, Parker employs Jamaica as a framing device in his recitation of the whole of Fleming's life. His title indicates just how significant that Caribbean island was in the creation of James Bond. Coincidentally, in August 1952, when Ian submitted the final manuscript of his first James Bond novel, *Casino Royale*, Ann gave birth to their son, Caspar Fleming. Thus, the gestation period of Fleming's child was also roughly equivalent to that of the character he created (Benson 1984: 6).

20 For instance, in the first James Bond adventure, *Casino Royale* (1953), the narrator makes a point of noting that 'Bond knew Jamaica well, so he asked to be controlled from there and to pass as a Jamaican plantocrat whose father had made his pile in tobacco and sugar and whose son chose to play it away on the stock markets and in casinos' (Fleming [1953] 2012a: 26). In *Live and Let Die*, the reader is told that '[Bond] had been there [Jamaica] on a long assignment just after the war when the Communist headquarters in Cuba was trying to infiltrate the Jamaican labour unions. It had been an untidy and inconclusive job but he had grown to love the great green island and its staunch, humorous people' (Fleming [1954] 2012b: 224). Thus from the very beginning of Fleming's novels, Bond's efficacy as a spy is tied to Jamaica; his knowledge of the island means that he can more effectively pass himself off as someone else.

21 Godfrey is long rumoured to have been the inspiration for the character M.

22 For a more detailed description of Fleming's first encounter with Jamaica, and for further insight into Fleming's local relationships on the island, see Bryce (1975).

23 Christine Berberich notes that 'the 1950s and 1960s were turbulent decades in Britain, a nation slowly emerging from the shock and privations of the Second World War. Britain had entered the war in 1939 as a world power; it emerged, severely shaken, six years later, confronted by its decreasing status in the world and the almost immediate dissolution of the Empire. On the home front, the 1950s and 60s saw similar groundbreaking changes once the immediate postwar austerity years had been overcome: the creation of the Welfare State promised a fairer, less class-ridden society; employment, and with it individual affluence, rose steadily, and consumerism increased; the arts became seemingly more liberated – more (for want of a better word) expressive – and sexuality more emancipated. ... The old structures, old values and old certainties which for over a century had made Britain a disciplined, deferential society, were increasingly derided and rejected. Violence, profanity and sexuality, hitherto rigorously suppressed by puritanical social and legal codes, were unleashed and became prominent in both high culture and low. Personal style, cool, chic, cynical and consumerist, became the ideal – self rather than service, immediate gratification rather than long-term spiritual or intellectual development' (2012: 13, 15).

24 During a dinner party at Allen Dulles's house in 1960, Kennedy reportedly asked Fleming for advice on how best to topple Fidel Castro's regime in Cuba. With characteristic flair and imagination, Fleming 'argued that simply killing Castro was not enough. He had to be humiliated as well. To do this, Fleming suggested flooding the streets of Havana with pamphlets explaining that radioactive fallout from nuclear testing caused impotence and was known to be drawn to men who had beards. As a result, Cuban men would shave off their facial hair, thus severing a symbolic link to Castro and the revolution'. Equally absurd as Fleming's facetious suggestion was the decision, in 1961, when the Kennedy brothers took office, to implement 'Operation Mongoose', a 'covert action program aimed at stimulating a rebellion in Cuba' along the same lines as Fleming's idea (Moran: 2013: 142–3; see also Pearson 1967: 24). As laughable as his suggestion might seem (and is), Fleming's opinion carried weight with those present: military leaders actually took seriously his thoughts on political matters. Indeed, a number of government agencies in the United States have sought to reproduce the spyware technologies from Fleming's James Bond novels. For a good account of James Bond's influence on the Central Intelligence Agency's (CIA) technologies, see Moran (2013: 119–47).

25 It is an irony not lost on Lietta Tornabuoni that while Fleming was a favoured author of President Kennedy, and *From Russia with Love* a favoured novel, Lee Harvey Oswald, the man who assassinated Kennedy in 1963 (the same year as the film version of *From Russia with Love* was released) was also known to have borrowed and read all of Fleming's novels from the public library in Dallas (1966: 17).

26 Within Fleming's own particular parish of St Mary's, the indigenous Jamaican Taínos (Columbus had rechristened them 'Arawaks') had been settled for 2,500 years prior to Columbus's arrival. For a summation of Spanish history in Jamaica as it pertains to Fleming and to Goldeneye, see Parker (2014: 18–19).

27 Simon Winder is particularly critical of Britain's and Spain's economic ravishment of Jamaica, a country, he notes, 'whose entire native population (the Tainos) have been exterminated ... which had then been populated by the Spanish and British entirely with people bought or stolen and then in effect crushed to make sugar for generations after generation'. He is also scathing of the extent to which Fleming and his ilk took advantage of the market economics of the island: 'When Fleming and his friends sat here, slurping their drinks in heavy cut-glass tumblers, Jamaica had stabilized as an almost entirely pointless place. Like the rest of the West Indies, its days of wealth and success ... were gone more than a century ago ... As a colony it had been run on a neglectful shoestring for years and people like Fleming could snap up substantial amounts of land for very little' (2006: 136–7).

28 Parker further notes that, for some locals, 'the "evil empire" of the wealthy and idle tourists was threatening to "de-Jamaicanize" the population' and that 'while the

economic benefits of tourism were meant to mitigate the problems of Jamaica's colonial past … the industry actually shored up many core features of that original condition and trapped the island in the grip of neocolonialism'. Jamaica's tourist boom, then, very much became 'a trade-off between dignity and much-needed dollars' (2014: 87–8).

29 Christine Berberich has asserted that 'the Suez fiasco marks a decisive moment in Britain's post-war history. In many ways, it publicly signalled the end of Britain's international clout – a death rattle from the British Empire. As Suez made clear, in the geopolitical reshuffle that followed the end of World War II, Britain lost out to its more influential wartime ally, the US. And with its Empire contracting rapidly, Britain was rapidly losing its remaining spheres of influence to what was diplomatically termed "decolonisation"' (2012: 24). For more information on the Suez Canal crisis, see Adamthwaite (1988: 449–64), Pearson (2002), Varble (2002), Verbeek (2003) and Dietl (2008: 259–73).

30 Goldeneye seemed the obvious choice for Eden's recuperation for a number of reasons. Apart from the personal connection between the Edens and the Flemings, John Pearson notes that 'the weather would be perfect, the populace loyal, [and] the visit could be arranged at a moment's notice with a minimum of fuss and protocol' (1966: 290). To all intents and purposes, Eden's visit to Goldeneye was an unofficial one. However, Sir Hugh Foot, captain general and governor-in-chief of Jamaica in 1956, did not want it to appear to the public that the prime minister was the private guest of Fleming. Foot insisted that Eden be the official guest of the Government of Jamaica. In consequence, a makeshift office was set up in the summer house of Goldeneye, with emergency telephones and typewriters, and dispatch writers were deployed several times daily between Goldeneye and Government House (ibid.: 292–3).

31 Fleming's close friend, Noël Coward, who also knew the Edens, considered Fleming's decision to host them at Goldeneye 'a most terrible mistake' and acknowledges that 'they must have had a perfectly ghastly time there'. He continues: 'Considering the fuss Ian used to make about Goldeneye you'd have thought it was Knole [country house estate in Sevenoaks, West Kent, and one of Britain's largest great houses] and I suppose Anthony and Clarissa came expecting that it was. I had no idea of what was going to happen, so although I knew both of them very well, I kept firmly away' (1965: n.p.). Coward's admission suggests that he recognized in the Edens' visit to Jamaica the potential for political scandal and the need for careful diplomacy, which, in his absence, Fleming was neither able to mitigate against nor plan for.

32 Indeed, the title of Fleming's 1959 article for the *Spectator* – 'If I Were Prime Minister' – further underlines his drive towards power. Fleming's *Spectator* article was characteristic of the author's style: mocking, derisive and largely self-effacing.

Fleming explains that: 'I am a totally non-political animal. I prefer the name of the Liberal Party to the name of any other, and I vote Conservative rather than Labour because the Conservatives have bigger bottoms, and I believe that bigger bottoms make for better government than scrawny ones.' He does, eventually, allow for more conventional sincerity: 'My own particular hero is Sir Alan Herbert ... And of course I have the affectionate reverence for Sir Winston Churchill that most of us share' (1959: n.p.).

33 Fleming is characteristically ambivalent in his response to both Bustamante and Manley: in his *Horizon* article on Jamaica for Cyril Connolly's 'Where Shall John Go?' series, he refers to the former as a 'gorgeous flamboyant rabble-rouser' and to the latter as 'the local Cripps [after magnanimous British philanthropist Sir Cyril Humphrey Cripps] and white hope of the Harlem communists'. He further notes that '[one] would like both of these citizens although they would both say that they want to kick you out' (qtd in Parker 2014: 60). Fleming is, of course, addressing the implied British reader for whom both Bustamante and Manley represent a considered threat to imperial rule in Jamaica. At the same time that Fleming wishes to entice his readers and to champion the beauty of Jamaica, his article can also be read as something of a cautionary lesson in incendiary Jamaican politics.

34 Morris Cargill is deeply critical of Fleming's tendency to 'infantilize' Caribbean peoples (and Jamaicans more specifically). He notes with vehemence that 'we have to stop being colonials and start being Jamaicans ... The umbilicus which attached us so sadly to Mother England was as much a fantasy as a reality and had to be cut'. He further asserts that the 'need for independence' and 'the need to cut ourselves away from a deadening childishness was, and is, a profound psychological need' (qtd in Parker 2014: 192–3).

35 This is most apparent in Fleming's presentation of the Cayman Islander, Quarrel, who aids Bond in his missions in Jamaica in the novels *Live and Let Die* and *Dr. No*. Charles W. Mills notes that Quarrel is presented in these novels 'not so much [as] a man as he is a friendly animal – perhaps one of those big, loyal, helpful dogs, like a Saint Bernard. ... As blacks go, however, Quarrel is fit to be a (properly deferential) companion of Bond because – in the racial logic that structures the text – he too is of mixed blood, having "dark grey eyes that / showed descent from a Cromwellian soldier or a pirate of Morgan's time" (34). But the rest of his features remain undescribed: this genetic combination is a benign one, so that his Negro-ness is best left unemphasized, as an unfortunate handicap that, between friends, Bond and Fleming will generously overlook' (2010: 107–8).

36 See, for instance, the magnificently rendered underwater sequences in the novels *Live and Let Die* and *Thunderball* (1961), as well in as the short stories 'The Hildebrand Rarity' in the collection *For Your Eyes Only* (1960) and 'Octopussy' in the collection *Octopussy and The Living Daylights* (1966). As Parker argues,

'Fleming's adventures underwater on his Goldeneye reef – a place of both beauty and danger – inspired some of the very best Bond scenes. More than that, the spirit of the island – its exotic beauty, its unpredictable danger, its melancholy, its love of exaggeration and gothic melodrama – infuses the stories' (2014: 6).

37 According to Sam Goodman, Fleming's fascination with 'the exotic' is also part of a much more complex discursive relationship between territory and identity (personal, national and sociocultural) (2016: 11). Goodman argues that 'Bond's "England" is one constructed from the imagery of privilege … an unformed and porous idea of national identification' (54). I would contend that Fleming's vision of Jamaica is constructed in much the same way: much like this vision of England, so too is Fleming's Jamaica a fictive (albeit limited) construct; the fantasy of Fleming's Jamaican psychogeography is very much tied to Fleming's privileged status as a wealthy white British writer living and working on the island. For instance, Goodman notes that 'to read Fleming's novels … is to enter a fiction world in which little has changed since the high-water mark of imperial propaganda in the 1920s …. continued British governance of the West Indies [appears] a given' (146). The privilege which affords Fleming's maintenance of Jamaica's imperial pretext within his novels is inextricably linked to his British identity. In Fleming's conceptualization of his Jamaican psychogeography, the socio-economics of 'real' Jamaica are subsidiary to his much-preferred and imagined realities of the island.

38 Pankratz further notes that 'the play with signifiers of Britishness [within Fleming's writings] correlates with Bond's equally ambivalent adaptability. [Bond] regularly demonstrates that he could go native if he wanted to' (2007: 137). Here, Pankratz is referring to Bond's adaptability to the many cultures he encounters during the course of his adventures. Though ostensibly the epitome of British nationalism, Bond's proximity to the racially-other cultures and contexts of the non-anglophone world in which he often carries out his missions is viewed as threatening precisely because he is exposed to these cultures for prolonged periods of time – the implication being that he might grow accustomed to their ways and stray from Britain. Much of the fear underpinning British imperial ideology during the age of empire has centred largely on the belief that the Anglo-Saxon race is superior to all other races, and that Britain, in particular, must protect itself against the perceived disorder of racial miscegenation and the dissolution of genetic 'purity'. Thus, the relative ease with which Bond assumes the guise of a Japanese in the film *You Only Live Twice*, for instance, or his ability to disguise himself as one of the Mujahideen in the filmic *The Living Daylights*, is suggestive, on the one hand, of his efficacy as a spy but, on the other, of the threat to Britain's image of itself as racially boundaried and separate to the rest of the world.

39 Fleming's estate in Jamaica, Goldeneye, was very much the architecture of his childhood dreams of adventure made manifest. John Pearson notes that

'[Fleming's] ghost is stronger here than anywhere else. Jamaica, and particularly his bit of it, is still sort of treasure island, a tropical Cornwall with everything that would appeal to his romantic schoolboy sense of adventure, and none of the social or intellectual intrusions that troubled him so much in England. Here he could relax, be as much of himself as there was, go on treats, expeditions' (n.d.: n.p.). It is clear from Pearson's account that Jamaica replicated for Fleming in his adult life the kinds of adventures he had discovered from his childhood reading habits.

40 For an extensive list of Fleming's literary interests, see Gilbert (2012: 616).
41 Fleming was undiscerning in his casual xenophobia and was not known for his delicacy of expression when commenting upon non-Anglo-Saxon races and nations. Fleming noted in a 1939 report entitled 'Russia's Strengths: Some Cautionary Notes' that the Russians are 'grey-faced little men' and that Russia 'would be an extremely treacherous ally. She would not hesitate to stab us in the back the moment it suited her' (qtd in Fleming 2015: 5–6). In a *Sunday Times* article he had written while attending the International Police Conference in Istanbul in 1955, Fleming remarked that Turkey is 'built upon those hatreds that fester between neighbours in a suburban street a lead to fisticuffs and end up in court and a shameful half column in the evening paper – the hatreds that gather and come to a head between two families or even two generations in the same house' (Fleming 1955: n.p.). While in a letter to William Plomer, his editor at Jonathan Cape, Fleming wrote of his experiences in Japan, which he visited in 1963 to carry out research for his eleventh Bond novel, *You Only Live Twice*: 'I have just spent the morning with an absolutely idiotic Japanese trying to get some of my oriental kultur right before having my new typescript cleaned up for your eagle eyes' (Fleming 1963a: n.p.).
42 Orientalism is defined broadly as the 'corporate institution for dealing with the Orient … by making statements about it, authorizing views of it, describing it, teaching it, settling it, [and] ruling over it'. It is, in other words, a 'Western style for dominating, restructuring and having authority over the Orient' that is predicated on a 'complex dialectic of reinforcement by which the experiences of readers in reality are determined by what they have read [which] in turn influences writers to take up subjects defined in advance by readers' experiences' (Said 2003: 94). Most importantly, in the case of Fleming, orientalist texts 'create not only knowledge but also the very reality they appear to describe' (ibid.). This is precisely the case with Fleming's construction of his Jamaican psychogeography, which appears, in his writings, to augment a particularly exoticist vision of his Jamaican life that ran somewhat perpendicular to reality.
43 Indeed, one need look no further than the response within mainstream media of the conservative-right to the contemporary European migrant crisis and the virulent racialism of anti-immigrant, pro-Brexit politics which have largely been defined by the essentialist rhetoric of orientalism.

44 Christine Berberich has argued that Fleming's 'upholding and celebration of a quintessential Englishness would not be quite so problematic if it did not always come at the expense of the "Other" or the subaltern' (2012: 25).

45 As Baron further notes, 'the power of Bond's "secret intelligence" depends on a type of knowledge that is, like Orientalism, "a form of paranoia". … This is precisely 007's "language", for as a secret agent, he is by definition engaged in watching, enumerating, and particularising, and his exploits mobilise a knowledge of the Other that exists for the sake of controlling it' ([2003] 2009: 159).

46 John Kitzmiller's Quarrel (Cayman Islander) is burned alive in *Dr. No*; Pedro Armendariz's Kerim Bey (Turkish) is tortured to death in *From Russia with Love*; Akiko Wakabayashi's Aki (Japanese) is poisoned in *You Only Live Twice*; Gloria Hendry's Rosie Carver (African American) is the object of ritual humiliation and derision (before being killed) in *Live and Let Die*; Lon Satton's Harold Strutter (African American) is, it is heavily implied, stabbed to death, also in *Live and Let Die*; Vijay Amritraj's Vijay (Indian) is sawn in two in *Octopussy*; and Frank McRae's Sharkey (African American) is killed and hung up in *Licence to Kill*. Even Naomie Harris's Moneypenny (Black British) is, arguably, subject to professional humiliation and near redundancy in *Skyfall* and (especially) *Spectre*.

47 Some fans of the film franchise have called for a Black actor to take over the role of James Bond, with Idris Elba long associated with such speculation. See, for instance, Hyde (2016). With the twenty-fifth Bond film, *No Time to Die* (2021), the series' producers have been able to have their proverbial cake and eat it by casting Black British actress Lashana Lynch *not* as James Bond but as Nomi, an MI6 agent who has inherited the '007' code number from a retired Bond.

48 On more than one occasion, the films present Judi Dench's M as incompetent and as a woman misruled by her emotions. For instance, M's misjudgement of Elektra King nearly brings about the nuclear devastation of the West's global oil supply in *The World Is Not Enough* (1999); and in *Skyfall* (2012) it is difficult to ignore the implication that the film's central conflict is, arguably, entirely M's fault. Her death towards that film's end, and her replacement as Head of the Secret Service by Ralph Fiennes's Gareth Mallory, signals not just the realignment of conservative patriarchal values but also an attendant admonishment of female authority figures. See Dodds (2014: 116–30); Krainitzki (2014: 32–40); and Pua (2018: 94–107). More problematically, Jeffrey Wright's Felix Leiter services *Casino Royale* as a one-dimensional plot device whose sole function it is to prop Bond up financially after a devastating gambling loss to the film's villain, Le Chiffre. In exchange for the money, Leiter secures Bond's assurance that the CIA (the agency for whom Leiter works) will take credit for Le Chiffre's arrest. Given that Bond has played a much more active role in the pursuit of Le Chiffre throughout the poker game, the film's attempt at mild humour in this scene rests uncomfortably on the audience's awareness of Leiter's complete uselessness as a character: Bond benefits not from

Leiter's skills as an agent (or as a card player), but from the 'Marshall Aid'-type financial support of the government agency whom Leiter represents. Moreover, in *Quantum of Solace*, the character is even more maligned: he spends virtually all of the film being chastised by the CIA Section Chief for South America, Gregory Beam, who questions his capabilities and who micromanages his field affairs in Bolivia. Thus, even the more recent Bond films, those in which the representation of cultural, gender and racial conflicts is apparently more nuanced, fall short, doing no justice, on the whole, to its female and Black characters.

49 Mordecai Richler has been particularly punishing in his disregard for Fleming. Not only was Fleming an 'appalling writer', in his estimation, but he considered Fleming as having 'no sense of place that scratched deeper than Sunday supplement travel articles or route maps' – a comment which no doubt would have irritated Fleming greatly, who put great stock by his descriptive abilities of place and location. Richler also denounced James Bond as 'a Little Englander … a meaningless fantasy cut-out' (1972: 70, 62). Raymond Durgnat was equally scathing of Fleming; he noted that Fleming's novels were a 'mish-mash' of 'Blachin-type verisimilitude with a streamlined, air-conditioned Gothic grotesque' (1970: 152).

50 Contrary to Fleming's protestations, Christine Berberich argues that the Bond novels 'seem to respond to and comment on the socio-political context of their time: regardless of the author's intentions, they do have a political and even potentially ideological message that, from a contemporary viewpoint, makes them into highly charged and problematic texts' (2012: 15). As far as the present study is concerned, Berberich's point is in need of little qualification.

51 Rosenberg and Harlemann Stewart note that Bond categorizes certain foreigners as 'safe' individuals. The Cayman Islander Quarrel, for instance, who appears in *Live and Let Die* and *Dr. No*, is one such figure in whom Bond confides. Of course, as Rosenberg and Harlemann Stewart underline, 'racial others are not racial equals', and it is clear that Bond's trust in Quarrel is also a marker of condescension: he treats him as a sounding board for his own ideas and regards it is safe to do so precisely because Quarrel is mixed blood (1989: 120). In the novel *Dr. No*, Quarrel is described as having 'dark grey eyes that showed descent from a Cromwellian soldier or a pirate of Morgan's times' (Fleming [1958] 2012f: 47). Thus, Quarrel is 'white' enough to garner Bond's trust but 'Black' enough that Bond is assured of his positional superiority in relation to him.

52 Another, Guido Piovene, has conceded that matters of race are certainly present within Fleming's writings but believes Fleming's readers to be disinterested in such things. He says: 'The purveyors of popular amusement … are in the habit of inserting … a pinch of political mythology of their own … [but] I do not believe that the spectators of 007 greatly mind those commonplaces of political mythology, discredited from the first by an obvious and complete lack of moral intentions' (qtd in Rosenberg and Harlemann Stewart 1989: 94).

53 Amis notes that 'even if Mr. Fleming is encouraging his readers to think unkindly of Rumanians and plain Turks, I can't see the danger. The opportunities of translating such thoughts into action will be rare. Perhaps, again, group sentiment per se is catching and likely to escalate, so that a French liver complaint sneered at today will mean a Pakistani stomach kicked tomorrow. But why should this not work the other way round – a sympathetic Cayman Islanders [here he is talking about the character Quarrel who appears in two of Fleming's novels, *Live and Let Die* and *Dr. No*] read about this morning not lead to a Jamaican being asked into the bar-billiards league this evening? Enough. Some forms of prejudice are sinister, but not these. These are no more than fascinating expressions of chauvinism at once smartened up and on its last legs' (1965: 76–7).

54 To be precise: Cayman Islander, Turkish, Corsican and Japanese, respectively.

55 Fleming's editor, William Plomer, also defends the James Bond novels on the grounds of innocence. He considers Fleming's novels to be 'brilliant, romantic fairy-tales in which a dragon-slaying maiden-rescuing hero wins battle after battle against devilish forces of destruction and yet is indestructible himself: an ancient kind of myth skilfully recreated in a modern idiom. They are, like life, sexy and violent, but I never thought of them as corrupting. Compared with some of the nasty stuff that gets in to print, they have a sort of boyish innocence' (qtd in McCormick 1993: 191).

56 Lisa M. Dresner notes that the James Bond novels 'appear about five years into the surge of immigration (mainly from its former colonies) into Great Britain after World War II, particularly immigration from the Caribbean. Starting with the arrival of several hundred workers (many of them former British soldiers during World War II) on the *S.S. Empire Windrush* from Jamaica in 1948, Britain began to gain a growing permanent population of Caribbean ancestry ... Yearly immigration to Britain from the Caribbean increased from the first small group to much larger numbers in the mid-1950s and early 1960s – 66,000 in 1961 alone – and eventually led to the Commonwealth Immigration Act, which severely limited Caribbean to Britain ... Clearly, this restrictive legislation reflected – as did the Nottingham, Notting Hill, and Notting Dale race riots of the late fifties – deep British anxieties about national, ethnic, and racial mixing, in part brought on by the growth in immigration.' Dresner also notes that 'just as the wave of Caribbean immigration was coming to England, Fleming himself was doing a "reverse immigration" to Jamaica' (2011: 282–3). John G. Cawelti and Bruce A. Rosenberg also argue that 'racist ambivalence' and a combination of 'fear and fascination' with exotic, foreign cultures (such as Fleming's obsession with Jamaica) were 'important component[s] of the early twentieth-century heroic spy story' which underline the complex relationship between spy fiction and race and ethnicity (1987: 44).

57 Alex Adams, for instance, notes that 'Fleming does not uncritically valorise the UK; rather, he praises a certain emerging form of British masculinity as the solution to

its decline ... As Britain loses its Empire, Bond remains guarantor of the continued quality of British national character through his multiple varieties of masculine prowess, including factors such as his physical appeal to women, his athleticism, his skill at cards and his almost parodically generous capacity for the pleasures of food, tobacco and alcohol. Bond is located in the literary tradition of the British lover, in which heterosexuality, national security and justice form as associational complex' (2017: 144).

58 Certainly, Bond functions as a signifier of both past and present, antiquity and modernity, but the present-day incarnation of Bond in the Daniel Craig-era films is very much anachronistic (see, for example, *Spectre*'s clunky portmanteau of outdated set pieces or its retroactive sexism) as well as beholden to the defining sobriety of early twenty-first-century cultural anxieties (*Skyfall* and *Spectre* are both iterations of the same ubiquitous theme of the fears of technocracy).

59 Fleming's ambivalent politics can also be traced through the dubious ethical regard in which he (and his narrator) holds a number of characters within the Bond universe. Darko Kerim in *From Russia with Love*, Enrico Colombo in the short story 'Risico', and Marc-Ange Draco in *On Her Majesty's Secret Service* are all examples of the type of morally suspect men for whom Fleming (and Bond) evidently harbours great affection. Kerim is the head of Britain's Secret Service station in Turkey, ostensibly a respectable fellow, but who nevertheless enjoys chaining young Bessarabian women up under his kitchen table, after winning them from local gypsies; Colombo, garrulous and charming, is the coordinator of an extensive drug-smuggling operation in the Mediterranean; while Draco is the head of the Unione Corse involved in organized crime, who becomes, for a very short time, Bond's father-in-law when Bond marries Draco's daughter, Tracy. Each of these men are portrayed as dependable, larger-than-life characters who adopt a pseudo-paternal role towards Bond. Umberto Eco, for one, has noted that characters such as Kerim, Colombo and Draco serve as 'ambiguous' figures within the Bond universe, precisely because they possess 'many of the moral qualities of the Villain, but [they use] them in the end for good' (1979: 150). Katharina Hagen notes that the ambiguity at the heart of these characters 'serves only to underline the moral question at the heart of James Bond's actions', and that 'the question of [these characters'] morality is narratologically resolved by the implicit assumption that as long as [their] actions are beneficial to the completion of Bond's (and Britain's) mission, these actions, however objectively unscrupulous they may be, are deemed to be useful and beyond reproach' (Hagen 2018: 6). Hagen further notes the 'fine ethical line which Bond himself threads between government-sanctioned agent and terrorist threat'; she argues that one of the most important features of Bond's friendship with these suspect father-figures is the strong personal codes of honour which each man seems to possess. For instance, while Colombo makes his

living from smuggling drugs, his personal code of good conduct forbids him from ever sampling his own material (7). Moreover, Jeremy Black argues that Colombo and Draco, in particular, can hardly be regarded as straightforward criminals because they have been awarded military honours in service of Britain's national cause (2005: 59). For a discussion of ethical philosophy and the James Bond franchise, see Bradley (1963: 35–46).

60 For a comprehensive discussion of the politics of postcolonial Britain in the immediate aftermath of the war, see Ward (2001), especially Richard Jeffrey's chapter on 'Imperial Heroes of a Post-Imperial Age: Films and the End of Empire' (128–44), which discusses Fleming and Bond, specifically; and Cannadine (2002). Daniel Ferreras Savoye offers an excellent survey of most of the significant works of scholarship published on James Bond since the mid-twentieth century, and, though there are a few factual slippages, this is a good place to start for a scholarly overview of the franchise. It is also worth noting that Lisa Funnell and Klaus Dodds's *Geographies, Gender, and Geopolitics of James Bond* (2017), one of the most brilliant contemporary critical works on James Bond to be published, owes much to Ferreras Savoye's discussion of 'primal forces' within the Bond universe. See Ferreras Savoye (2013).

61 Berberich further notes that 'Fleming's reaction to the diminution of British power and influence in the world was not only (largely) to ignore it, but, far more proactively, to create a British super-spy who claims to be the best in his field and is indeed acknowledged as such by the rest of the world. In this way the novels comment not only on the state of Britain overall but help create a new notion of Britishness that continues to advocate British dominance over the rest of the world. More specifically, the fact that it is a particular Englishness that the novels seem to celebrate is even more problematic in the social and political context of the time, as it highlights not only a misguided belief in British supremacy but also one in English superiority over the United Kingdom as a whole' (2012: 24).

62 Cannadine offers a comprehensive account of the shifts that took place in British cultural life during the 1950s, which, he contends, greatly informed Fleming's ambivalent politics. He notes that, 'in Britain at the time, a changing conventional morality was accompanied by an unprecedented rise in living standards, which encouraged the most puritanical critics of "decline" to liken England to the degenerate days of the later Roman Empire or early 17th-century Spain – obsessed with sex and self-indulgence, and turning its back on the more Spartan modes of life which had been the foundation of former greatness. And moral "decline" at home was mirrored in international "decline" abroad, as the tropical African empire was wound up, the white Commonwealth was severely shaken by the departure of South Africa, and Britain's standing in the eyes of the world was irretrievably damaged as a result of the Suez fiasco. Elizabeth's coronation, at

the time of the first full-length Bond novel, was a retrospectively unconvincing reaffirmation of Britain's continued great-power existence' (1979: 46).

63   In his 1959 article for *Spectator*, 'If I Were Prime Minister', Fleming outlines some of the changes he approved of with respect to British society's sexual mores: 'I should proceed to a complete reform of our sex and gambling laws, and endeavour to cleanse the country of the hypocrisy with which we so unattractively cloak our vices ... I would consult with my Minister for Leisure about the possibility of turning the Isle of Wight into one vast pleasuredome ... This would be a world where the frustrated citizen of every class could give rein to those basic instincts for sex and gambling which have been crushed through the ages ... Since it is impossible to suppress the weaknesses of mankind, I would at least put an honest face on the problem, and do something to release the *homme moyen sensuel*, or *femme*, for that matter, from some of their burden of shame and sin' (Fleming 1959: n.p.). Indeed, Cannadine argues that Fleming's novels actually 'prefigured the sexual liberation of the "permissive society"' of the late 1950s and early 1960s (2002: 300).

64   Cannadine notes that 'Fleming was the champion and successor of the clubland heroes in a degenerate age who, like M, was opposed to the domestic decline, and to the softening of the national backbone, which he believed had been ushered in by the post-war Labour governments, the Welfare State and the emancipation of women. But that was not how all of his contemporaries regarded Fleming, or received his novels. For his critics believed that his work did not deplore Britain's decline at all: on the contrary, it seemed to them to depict it graphically, and to welcome it ... Fleming deserved the blame for encouraging the very trend he affected to lament' (2002: 299). Furthermore, Cannadine attributes much of the confused political rhetoric of the James Bond books to Fleming's internationalist outlook: '[Fleming] had grown up when Britain was the greatest power in the world; but, as foreign manager of Kemsley Newspapers, he was fully aware of Britain's lessened standing after 1945; and this tension between past glories and present uncertainties was never resolved in the novels. In the early Bond books, Fleming paid scarcely any attention to Britain's weakened international position; halfway through the series, he was obliged to recognize that Bond was operating against the "canvas of a diminishing England"; yet to the very end, he also tried to pretend that the British nation and Empire were still strong' (303). One of the principal ambivalences within Fleming's writings which critics objected to most vehemently was the author's emphasis on materialism, on the 'detailed descriptions of places and gadgets and meals' which, to many critics, seemed to parade and endorse the very materialism that, elsewhere in his writings, Fleming claimed to abhor and condemn'. Such materialism was argued to '[glorify] consumer spending and consumer culture'. 'Fleming seemed to his critics to be encouraging individual

greed and personal gain – shallow and selfish (and godless) activities which were incompatible with the sterner imperative of national greatness' (299–300). The irony of such a conflict is expressed particularly well by Anette Pankratz, who claims that 'cheerful consumerism as extension of the discerning taste of the British gentleman are juxtaposed with both the anti-capital threat of the Soviet régime and the gigantomania of American capitalism. [Fleming's novels] thus endorse a capitalist world view and criticise its underlying principle. They have their martini and drink it, too' (2007: 134).

65 That said, it is, perhaps, worth noting that, of the six actors to play James Bond in the Eon film series, only three (Roger Moore, Timothy Dalton and Daniel Craig) are, in fact, British. The others are from Scotland (Sean Connery), Australia (George Lazenby) and Ireland (Pierce Brosnan) – three nations, in particular, which have had (and, in the case of Scotland and Northern Ireland, continue to have) complex and fraught historical and political relationships with (post)colonial Britain.

1 Imagined identities and the Black body politic in *Live and Let Die*

1 Bond and Leiter's respective national identities are not insignificant when considering the geopolitics of the James Bond series. Leiter, as the American agent, is often shown as subservient to Bond, whose prowess is held up in contrast to Leiter's perceived disabilities as an agent. This disability is literalized towards the end of *Live and Let Die*, when, in his assault on the Ouroboros Worm and Bait Shippers (Mr Big's cover organization), Leiter falls through a trap door in the floor and is half eaten by a shark. He survives the encounter, minus a leg and an arm. In the post-war climate, Britain's declining imperial position was counterpointed by the rise in political influence of the United States. Fleming's sketch of Anglo-American relations – in which his British agent Bond always inevitably bests the second-rate Leiter – represents a particular form of geopolitical wish fulfilment and national triumphalism that disregards the economic and political realities of Britain's weakened global position. In the first screen adaptation of a James Bond adventure (the 1954 live broadcast of *Casino Royale*, produced as an episode for the first series of the CBS anthology series *Climax!*), American actor Barry Nelson played James Bond as an American, while the Australian actor Michael Pate played Felix Leiter as British, a combination that just did not fit with the tone and style of Fleming's original texts. For further contextual information on Anglo-American geopolitics in Fleming's work, see Cannadine (2002), especially the chapter on 'Ian Fleming and the Realities of Escapism'.

2 Daas's assertion that Jamaica is 'foreign to Bond' is less accurate. Fleming makes it clear within his novels that Bond's relationship to Jamaica predates the adventure described in his first novel, *Casino Royale*: 'Bond knew Jamaica well', the reader is told (Fleming [1953] 2012a: 26).
3 For a discussion of Fleming's treatment of Harlem's urban dialect, see also Rosenberg and Harlemann Stewart (1989: 119).
4 As the narrator notes, Mr Big is so called 'because of the initials of his fanciful name, Buonaparte Ignace Gallia, and because of his height and bulk' (Fleming [1954] 2012b: 24).
5 Margaret Marshment disputes this argument on the grounds that such a view prioritizes a Eurocentric vision of global race relations. She notes, 'here we have the familiar Eurocentric version of world history, according to which all history began with the white man, so that the black world – having only entered history at all with the arrival of the white world on its shores, is now seen to be "developing" along the lines laid down by the "civilised" world' (1978: 336).
6 Mr Big is not the only character of African origin to be described in terms of his 'deathliness'. 'The Whisper' – one of Big's subordinates and the chief operator of Big's communication network, 'The Eyes' – is so called because of a debilitating respiratory illness. The narrator notes that '[Whisper] couldn't have spoken any louder if he had wished to. He had been born on "Lung Block" on Seventh Avenue, at 142nd Street, where death from TB is twice as high as anywhere in New York.' Indeed, Whisper is very much presented as a liminal figure, bordering both life and death: the reader is told that 'he only had part of one lung left' (Fleming [1954] 2012b: 48). Fleming's tendency to present the Black villains of *Live and Let Die* as cripplingly debilitated is characteristic of his approach across the whole canon of James Bond stories: often, the villains' moral decrepitude is signalled in their physical disability or repulsiveness (Le Chiffre's rotundity in *Casino Royale*; Rosa Klebb's toad-like visage in *From Russia with Love*; Dr No's metal arms in *Dr. No*).
7 Mimi Sheller notes that the 'dialectics of eating and being eaten pertain as much to the hollowing out of human agency by degraded forms of labour (the zombie) as to the actual appropriation, objectification, fragmentation, and ingestion of the physical body itself (to be cannibalised)' (2003: 145). Bond's fear of being 'devoured' by Mr Big's gaze transposes British anxieties over management of racial issues in the United States with traditional fears born of the British Empire's 'civilizing' mission in the non-anglophone world in the nineteenth century, during which the potent threat of succumbing to the 'lawlessness' and 'savagery' of Black culture was metaphorized as an act of bodily consumption – usually of being boiled alive and eaten by cannibals.
8 Of Mr Big's origins, the reader is told that 'the Big Boy had been initiated into Voodoo as a child, earned his living as a truck-driver in Port au Prince, then

emigrated to America' where he 'originated an underground Voodoo temple in Harlem' and 'established a link between it and the main cult in Haiti. The rumour had started that he was the Zombie or living corpse of Baron Samedi himself, the dreaded Prince of Darkness, and he fostered the story so that is was now accepted through all the lower strata of the negro world. As a result, he commanded real fear, strongly substantiated by the immediate and often mysterious deaths of anyone who crossed him or disobeyed his orders' (Fleming [1954] 2012b: 25–6). Vivian Halloran has argued that, much like his Chinese counterpart, Dr No, the eponymous villain of Fleming's next Jamaica-set novel, *Dr. No*, Mr Big 'promotes the idea in Jamaica that he himself is a monster of sorts' (2005: 160). Both Big and No draw on mythological entities to enforce this idea: while Big employs the myth of Baron Samedi, No exploits the legend of a dragon, which, he purports, roams the island of Crab Key. Halloran further asserts that 'both criminal agents import outside cultural artefacts to heighten the sense of reality or plausibility of these myths' (169). Though largely a work of (dubious) gnostic readings of Fleming's novels, with very little analytic or critical value, Philip Gardiner's *The Bond Code: The Dark World of Ian Fleming and James Bond* offers one particularly tantalizing point of coincidence. He contends that 'Samedi is one of the Loa or spirits of Voodoo, often referred to as mysteries of invisibles, akin to angels in Christianity. They are also known strangely as *Bondye* ("bon Dieu" or "good God"), who exist between humanity and the creator. They exist in the twilight world between waking and sleeping, between this world and the next … *bridging the gap*' (Gardiner 2008: 184–5, my italics). Thus, Gardiner seems to suggest an etymological connection, here, between the liminal being of Mr Big/Baron Samedi, who patrols the border between life and death, and James Bond (*Bondye*), who is himself configured linguistically as a 'God' of sorts, a metaphysical entity. Like Mr Big/Baron Samedi, Bond may be said to police his own borders – the racial and cultural divide between Anglo-Saxon Britain and the otherized world of the antipodean Caribbean. Finally, it should be noted that François Duvalier, the despotic president of Haiti who led the country from 1957 to 1971 (and rose to power four years after the publication of *Live and Let Die*), also claimed to be the Voodoo Baron Samedi in order to instil fear in his political opponents and to discourage dissention within his totalitarian regime. He declared that he was an 'immaterial being', a *loa* (or spirit) of Haitian Voodoo (Kofele-Kale 2006: 261). For more information on Duvalier, see Diedrich and Burt (1969); Marquis (2007); and Lemoine (2011).

9 Train journeys are an important narrative device and structural facet of the spatial mobilities of James Bond's adventures in general. See Riquet and Zdrenyk (2018) and Goodman (2016): 115–17.

10 Interestingly, Fleming never explicitly states what race The Robber is. Though the narrator offers a description of him – 'his complexion was the colour of tobacco

dust, a sort of yellowy beige' (Fleming [1954] 2012b: 170) – it is an ambiguously drawn one. For more on Fleming's ambivalent presentation of The Robber, see Early (1999: 155).

11 Bond is outraged by The Robber's murder of the pelican: '"what the hell d'you do that for?" asked Bond furiously' (Fleming [1954] 2012b: 173). Matthew Parker has noted that, while Bond never kills innocent animals, a number of his opponents are shown to do so. Apart from The Robber in *Live and Let Die*, both Von Hammerstein in the short story 'For Your Eyes Only' and Francisco Scaramanga in the novel *The Man with the Golden Gun* are seen to mercilessly kill birds (2014: 53).

12 Jason Dittmer attributes Bond's 'culture of privilege' to the forms of touristic experience which underpin Fleming's representation of Jamaica in the novel: 'Bond's mobility as a secret agent is directly paralleled by the mobility of the tourist who can fly into Jamaica with little in the way of documentation and can leave at will to return to the metropole. Second, Bond's transformative experience prior to his raid on Mr. Big's Isle of Surprise … is similar to the experience sought by many travellers to the island. Just as Bond spent a week alternately exercising and resting before going to work, the Jamaica many tourists seek is one of transformation and rejuvenation … Finally, as in Bond's "vacation", that transformation and rejuvenation is predicated on the service of "collaborationist" Jamaicans … who are constructed in opposition to the "dangerous" Jamaicans who are outside the gates of the all-inclusive resort.' (2008: 29) For more on the politics of Jamaican tourist practices, see Kingsbury (2005: 113–32).

13 Bond's physical development also coincides with Felix Leiter's bodily recovery. After an ill-advised and fateful solo assault on the Ouroboros Worm and Bait warehouse in Florida, during which he faces off against The Robber, Leiter is dropped through a trapdoor into a concealed shark tank. While Leiter does survive, the shark encounter costs him an arm and a leg. During the Jamaica sequence of the novel, Leiter is recovering in hospital. The final day of Bond's training, when his body is successfully metamorphosed in preparation for his 300-yard underwater swim to the Isle of Surprise, Bond receives the news from his Secret Service contact on the island, Commander Strangways, that 'your friend Felix Leiter's going to be all right. At all events he's not going to die. They've had to amputate the remains of an arm and a leg. Now the plastic surgery chaps have started building up his face' (Fleming [1954] 2012b: 236). Thus, the hardening of Bond's body in training, and his physical transformation at the hands of Quarrel, can be said to serve as a foil to the salvaging of Leiter's own shredded body.

14 The 'timelessness' of Fleming's presentation of Jamaica, here, also extends to the narrative structure of the novel. Bond's sojourn at the Manatee Bay house represents a forced break in narrative momentum. Ostensibly, it is a plot device: Bond must wait for Mr Big's boat the *Secatur* to arrive at the Isle of Surprise

before he can commence his assault on the island. Strangways, Bond's Secret Service contact in Jamaica, insists that Bond take the week to rest, recuperate and strengthen himself before taking on Mr Big. As such, the sequence of events relayed in the chapters 'The Jamaica Version' and 'The Undertaker's Wind' falls somewhere outside of narrative time. These chapters can be read as simple indulgences on Fleming's part, an opportunity for Fleming to demonstrate both his keen descriptive abilities as a travel writer as well as his love of Jamaica.

15 'The Undertaker's Wind' was also Fleming's working title for the novel.
16 For a discussion of the 'primal forces' of the James Bond canon, see Ferreras Savoye (2013). For a superior discussion of environmental elements in Fleming's novels and in the films, see Funnell and Dodds (2017).
17 In spite of this confusion, there is one point upon which the various intelligence agencies are agreed: the implications of race. Fleming is keenly aware of the United States' historical racial conflicts and demonstrates a conscious (if not entirely unproblematic) regard for due judicial process with respect to the authorities' handling of Mr Big. When the homicide detective Lieutenant Binswanger suggests to Bond and Leiter that they 'pull [Mr Big] in on tax evasion or misuse of the mails or parkin' in front of a hydrant or sumpn', he is upbraided for his ignorance by the FBI Captain Dexter: '"D'you want a race riot?" objected Dexter sourly. "There's nothing against him and you know it, and we know it. If he wasn't sprung in half an hour by that black mouthpiece of his, those Voodoo drums would start beating from here to the Deep South. When they're full of that stuff we all know what happens. Remember '35 and '43? You'd have to call out the Militia"' (Fleming [1954] 2012b: 44). Here, Dexter alludes to the notorious race riots of Harlem and Detroit, respectively, the former of which is one of the first modern race riots in US history. Both occurred as a result of increased social tensions and disaffection among minority communities over 'inequitable conditions and police brutality' towards people of colour (Griswold 2006: 75). Tellingly, Dexter's suggestion – that minority cultures are easily manipulated and called to fight through the invocation of Voodoo – of course elides the socio-economic factors at play behind such violent racial conflicts, which reduces the political legitimacy of these communities' claims for social equality – and which betrays another kind of ignorance on Dexter's part. Jeremy Black notes that, within the Bond canon, though 'the black population [has] been presented as varied and generally law-abiding', in *Live and Let Die*, Black power is sometimes presented as the 'threatening tool of Soviet malice' (2005: 12–13). For more information on the 1935 Harlem race riot, see Grimshaw (1969); Knopf (1975); and Greenberg (1991). For more information on the 1943 Detroit race riot, see Capeci and Wilkerson (1991); and Sugrue (1996).
18 For more information on the history of Captain Henry Morgan, see Allen (1976); Earle (2007); and Latimer (2009).

19 Lars Ole Sauerberg also points out that, 'although the legal basis of Bond's assignment is more convincing in [*Live and Let Die*]' than, perhaps, some of his other assignments, it is nevertheless clear that 'M. has taken upon him something the Americans would have had much better opportunities to handle' (1984: 151). For more on the legality of M's actions, see the short story 'For Your Eyes Only', in which Bond describes his discomfort at being ordered by M to assassinate Von Hammerstein in recompense for the latter's killing of M's close personal friends, the Havelocks.

2 Invasion, animality and bodily transgressions in *Dr. No*

1 The title of the novel's North American edition was much less subtle: in the United States, *Dr. No* was published under the title *Nude Girl of Nightmare Island* (Gilbert 2012: 197).

2 *Dr. No* evidences a number of shifts with respect to Fleming's global geopolitics. In *Live and Let Die*, Jamaica very much represented the backdrop for the text's much wider political concerns (the suppression of communist insurrections in the United States) and a staging ground for the ideological battle between Britain, the United States and the USSR for control of the Caribbean region. In *Dr. No*, Jamaica's geospatiality plays a much more significant role in the narrative, in that Bond is now actively defending the island. As Matthew Parker notes, 'there is a possibility that if Dr No is not stopped, one of the mis-guided missiles could hit Kingston' (2014: 230). Unlike *Live and Let Die*, in which the question of Britain's involvement in the events of the narrative is contingent upon the loosely conceived plot device of Captain Morgan's stolen treasure trove, Bond's active defence of Jamaica in *Dr. No* can be seen to reflect ever-burgeoning British concerns that the island would soon gain its independence from the empire and that Britain would no longer be able to retain its foreign territories. Sam Bourne has noted that *Dr. No* evidences Fleming's political astuteness. He says, 'Fleming tacitly concedes the new international hierarchy in the novel's plotting: what gives *Dr No*'s evil scheme punch is that its target is the missile programme in the mighty United States. [Fleming] knows that in 1957, a year after Suez has confirmed London's diminished global standing, a conspiracy against Britain alone would not be enough: the plot has to involve the US, ideally drawing in, as this novel does, the Soviet Union and the Cold War' (Bourne 2012: xiii). Finally, Gerald Early has argued that the 'most interesting difference between *Live and Let Die* and *Dr. No* is the landscape of Jamaica that we are given' (1999: 160). In the former text, Early notes, Jamaica is portrayed as 'a dangerous but lush, vegetative, [and] beautiful'; in the latter, it is 'a dung factory, desert-like, patrolled by a diesel "dragon" that burns Dr. No's enemies and the flora as well' (ibid.). While the

transition of Jamaica as a representative landscape from one text to the other can be read in terms of putrefaction, it could also be argued that Fleming has become less wedded (in *Dr. No*) to the orientalizing discourses which define his earlier novel and which underpin much of his travel writing. Jamaica is presented, here, not simply as an oriental tourist trap of tropical luxury, but as marshy and miasmic.

3 For a comprehensive selection of the critical responses to Fleming's writings, and to *Dr. No*, in particular, see Haining (1987).

4 Mills argues that 'the subliminal – or maybe not so subliminal – message for Fleming's 1950s' readership is clear: Third World insurrection means, among other things, nonwhites raping white women' (2010: 108).

5 For a particularly good summation of British attitudes towards race and racial crises, see Jenkinson (2009).

6 A similar issue would later land contemporary Conservative British prime minister Theresa May in hot water, when, in 2018, it emerged that, as a result of the so-called 'hostile environment policy' instituted by May during her time as home secretary (2010–16), many numbers of naturalized British citizens who had arrived during the Windrush migration were detained and some were forcibly deported from the UK. May's office was accused of destroying the landing cards and legal documents of many Caribbean immigrants who came to Britain in the aftermath of the Second World War, whose rights as naturalized British citizens became the topic of much-heated blowback against May's flailing Conservative government in the run-up to Brexit – the political agenda of which was sustained, largely, by anti-immigrant sentiment.

7 *Dr. No*, it can be argued, evidences Fleming's Anglo-Saxon superiority complex. Consider the casually racialist remarks of the Colonial Secretary, Pleydell-Smith, on the local Jamaican and Chinese populations: 'The Jamaican is a kindly lazy man with the virtues and vices of a child. He lives on a very rich island but he doesn't get rich from it. He doesn't know how to and he's too lazy. … there are the Chinese, solid, compact, discreet – the most powerful clique in Jamaica. They've got the bakeries and the laundries and the best food stores. They keep to themselves and keep their strain poor … Not that they don't take the black girls when they want them. You can see the result all over Kingston – Chigroes – Chinese negroes and negresses. The Chigroes are a tough, forgotten race. The look down on the negroes and the Chinese look down on them. One day they may become a nuisance. They've got some of the intelligence of the Chinese and most of the vices of the black man. The police have a lot of trouble with them' (Fleming [1958] 2012f: 79–80). Charles Mills has argued that 'Fleming was a racist who genuinely believed that particular races are differentially favoured with intellectual abilities and moral traits' (2010: 106). Mills also argues that, within 'Fleming's sociology of Jamaica', Jamaicans 'are poor because of their laziness and infantilism, while other races with more drive get ahead' (ibid.).

8   Jeremy Black is less convinced by the 'Fleming was a racist' argument; he sees Fleming's perceived racism as 'a pronounced theme of interwar adventure writing', arguing that Fleming's politics are shared even by such beloved writers as John Buchan, as well as a wider number of authors writing in this period (2005: 19). While this does not, of course, excuse any charges of actual racism on Fleming's part, Black is more certain about his view that Fleming must be viewed within the context of the historical period in which he was writing.

9   One need only think of the innumerable instances of white-on-white physical violence within Fleming's writings to see that this is not an endemically racist facet of the Bond novels. See, in particular, the brutally violent deaths of Auric Goldfinger (in *Goldfinger*) and Ernst Stavro Blofeld (in *You Only Live Twice*), both of whom Bond asphyxiates to death by crushing their windpipes.

10 See endnote number 7, above.

11 Charles Mills notes of this term that it is 'Fleming's personal contribution to the pseudo-science of racial determinism, one of the major ideological legacies of the European conquest of the non-white world' (2010: 106). Fleming first encountered the term from his editor, William Plomer, who suggested in a letter to Fleming (18 June 1957) this particular neologism – a portmanteau of 'Chinese' and 'Negro' (Fleming 2015: 174). Morris Cargill, Fleming's friend in Jamaica, has argued that the term 'Chigro' is, apart from being offensive, also an inaccurate one: he notes that this term would hardly have been used in Jamaica and that the correct name for members of the Black Chinese community is 'Chinee Royals' (1965b: n.p.).

12 Parker also inadvertently points to another similarity between Dr No and Mr Big, Dr No's villainous counterpart in the novel *Live and Let Die*. Like Mr Big, 'Dr No has achieved his wealth and therefore his power thanks to his success as a gangster in New York' (2014: 234). As in *Live and Let Die*, then, Fleming's anti-Americanism emerges in this novel, for, as Parker notes, 'there is a suggestion that it is the crime-ridden nature of American society that, in the end, threatens Jamaica, as well as the fact that the British have allowed American missiles to be stationed on their territory near the island' (ibid.).

13 In a later chapter, the narrator refers to the wealthy row of 'millionaire hotels' that line Jamaica's North Shore as a 'rash' on the landscape (Fleming [1958] 2012f: 44).

14 As Sam Goodman notes, in *Dr. No*, 'Fleming depicts a tropical idyll secured by British authority before graphically illustrating how fragile it is when its defenders become complacent' (2016: 151).

15 See Fanon (1961), who argues that violence is both an inevitable and necessary condition of the processes of colonial resistance and decolonization.

16 The violence in *Dr. No* is not wholly racialized; that is to say, it is not the case that those acts of violence which are to be found within the text are perpetrated solely by Black people against white people. As Goodman himself notes, 'a number of

characters suffer violent deaths or injuries throughout the novel' (2016: 151). Aside from Bond, who is electrocuted and whose body undergoes great physical trauma during Dr No's obstacle course, Honey Rider, a Jamaican Creole, is 'staked out naked to be devoured by a swarm of crabs' and Quarrel, Bond's local guide and ally from *Live and Let Die* from the Cayman Islands, is burnt alive by the flamethrowers on Dr No's swamp buggy, which is disguised as a dragon (ibid.).

17 This is somewhat ironic in the case of Strangways, whose meticulous adherence to the temporal boundaries of his own daily schedule (his insistence in recreating his own bounded temporal norm) proves fatal for the spy. As Parker notes, 'it is Strangways' "iron routine" … that proves his downfall, as it allows "the enemy" to plan his death' (2014: 232). The message could not be clearer: Strangways's own complacency is the cause of Britain's undoing on the island.

18 Alex Adams reads Bond's endurance of Dr No's obstacle course as 'an image of elite power which circulates at a time of [Britain's] international decline'; he argues that, though 'Britain may be embattled and diminished, but Bond's endurance of his physical trials reveals that in important respects it can still prevail' (2017: 144).

19 The 'Irish Frankenstein' is a piece of anti-Irish propaganda that appeared in a May 1882 edition of *Punch* Magazine, or the *London Charivari*, illustrated by John Tenniel. The image depicts a cowering Charles Stewart Parnell, the Irish nationalist politician and leader of the Home Rule League, as Victor Frankenstein, towered over by his creation, the monster, who is an embodiment of the Fenian movement, the Irish Republican Brotherhood who were dedicated to the establishment of an independent Ireland. The image appeared after the Phoenix Park murders in Dublin, during which the newly appointed chief secretary for Ireland, Lord Frederick Cavendish, and the permanent undersecretary, Thomas Henry Burke, were murdered by a radical splinter group of the Irish Republican Brotherhood. Tenniel's illustration, of course, was a pointed effort to underline the unsuitability of Irish home rule.

20 As O. F. Snelling notes, 'there is nothing ideological about [Dr No's] scheme: the profit motive is Dr. No's main concern. Already he has his eye on Communist China, who may be prepared to pay him even more than Russia' (1964: 138).

21 The 'yellow peril' is a racist, colonialist colour metaphor that classifies as dangerous to the Western world the peoples of the East Asian continent. The most popular embodiment of the myth of the yellow peril was Sax Rohmer's fictional master criminal, Dr Fu Manchu. See Rupert (1911); Marchetti (1994); and Frayling (2014).

22 For more on the transhumanist debate, see Hansell and Grassie (2011); More and Vita-More (2013); and Ranish and Sorgner (2014).

23 For more on the technologically enhanced bodies of Bond's foes, see Germaná (2019: 49–55); and Viol (2019).

24 With the exception of Tony Bennett and Janet Woollacott. Bennett and Woollacott argue that Honey's broken nose 'functions as a sign of her damaged sexuality' and of her 'anxieties that her femininity has been impaired by rape' (1987: 121–2).

3 Mobility, memory and touristic modernity in *The Man with the Golden Gun*

1 This notion had been well and truly solidified within the British consciousness by the time Fleming came to write his final novel. The defection of British diplomatic officers Donald Maclean and Guy Burgess to the Soviet Union the previous decade – along with the exposure of the so-called 'Cambridge Spy Ring' – had rocked the Intelligence community, particularly the United States' trust in British security. Both Maclean and Burgess are even mentioned in *The Man with the Golden Gun*, in the confrontation scene between M and Bond (Fleming [1965] 2012m: 20).
2 Unlike the novel *Thunderball*, the first third of which is set in the Shrublands health clinic and follows Bond's restorative treatments.
3 Not only is Mr Big evoked through those references in *The Man with the Golden Gun* to Caribbean Voodoo cults, but Scaramanga's particular habit of engaging in fornication to improve his 'eye' further invokes Big's expansive African-American spy network in *Live and Let Die*, known as 'The Eyes'. Scaramanga's prowess as both marksman and lover is therefore symbolically aligned with the extensive reach of Mr Big's ocular all-knowingness.
4 Of Scaramanga's curiously liminal status, Lisa M. Dresner notes that he is an 'overdetermined globetrotting figure: Catalan by birth, an immigrant to the United States after a tragic travelling circus incident in Berlin (during his circus act, he symbolically changed ethnicities by dressing as an Indian ... Scaramanga winds up working in the Caribbean for Cuba and the KGB' (2011: 274). Dresner further notes that 'Scaramanga's Catalan heritage itself serves as a signifier of mixing, as the Catalan language crosses parts of France, Spain, and Sardinia' (ibid.). Similarly, Robbie B. H. Goh points out that, in stereotypical terms, though Scaramanga is Catalan in origin, 'he is characterized by a (in the novel's terms) Latin posturing and treachery, together with an American arrogance and ruthlessness stemming from his years working for the American mafia' (1999: 30).
5 For more information on the Cuban revolution and the Castro–Batista conflict, see Benjamin (1992); Pérez-Stable (1998); Lievesley (2004); Sweig (2004); and Farber (2006).
6 Kingsley Amis suspects that there is, in fact, a sexual dimension to the relationship between Bond and Scaramanga throughout the novel that is not merely symbolic. He deduces that 'Scaramanga hires Bond [as his personal bodyguard] because

he's sexually interested in him' (qtd in Haining 1987: 20). This would seem to tally with some of the details in the report given to M by 'C.C.', which concludes that Scaramanga is 'a sexual fetishist with possible homosexual tendencies' (Fleming [1965] 2012m: 40–1).

7 That the cover identity of British Intelligence ('Universal Exports') has been changed in *The Man with the Golden Gun* to 'Transworld Consortium' further underlines Britain's ailing geopolitical position in the post-war period of decolonization. Where once Britain's political influence and the reach of its empire could be said to be 'universal', the use of the Latinate prefix 'trans-' is suggestive both of the new global political order through which Bond and Britain must navigate and an ironic indictment of Bond's comparative *im*mobility and political stasis within the novel.

8 Sam Goodman notes that 'Fleming's desire for the reclamation and updating of colonial space appears at once paradoxical and problematic, seeking to maintain a status quo and remain relevant in a developing international conflict. Fleming adopts the Janus-like position of looking back in order to move forward familiar to his novels' (2016: 153).

9 This is a position in which recent filmic iterations – especially *Skyfall*, *Spectre* and *No Time to Die* – have found themselves.

10 For the sake of parity, it should be pointed out that Britain's involvement in the plot to foil Scaramanga's criminal enterprise in the Caribbean is not entirely unrealistic, in this context. As Jeremy Black notes, 'in *The Man with the Golden Gun* there are threats to food products. This aspect of the plot reflects the greater interconnectedness of the world economy and the importance to Britain of trade and the honest operations of the markets' (2005: 24).

11 Scaramanga himself is something of a stage villain, with an apparent penchant for the period aesthetics of Wild West Americana. For instance, in the Thunderbird's 'saloon' bar, the narrative notes that Scaramanga 'leant against the polished mahogany bar and twirled his golden gun round and round on the first finger of his right hand like the snide poker cheat out of an old Western' (Fleming [1965] 2012m: 101–2). Scaramanga also has a preference for 'broad-brimmed white Stetson[s]', which Bond believes makes him look like a 'plantation owner in the South' (ibid.: 159). Finally, in a ploy to force Bond into revealing his cover, Scaramanga purports to tie Mary Goodnight to the railroad tracks like 'something from the good old Western movies' (ibid.: 168).

4 After Fleming: Jamaica on screen

1 For more information on the Cuban Missile Crisis, see Chayes (1974); Divine (1988); Gibson (2012); and Stern (2012).

2   The interference with American missile launches was, at the time of the film's release, a 'potentially explosive current issue' (Robertson 2015: 66). So politically flammable was the situation that, in a memorandum released by the Kennedy Assassination Records Review Board, the Pentagon issued a statement declaring that 'should [US astronaut] John Glenn fail to return from his 20 February flight to orbit the Earth, "evidence could be manufactured" to prove "electronic interference [by] the Cubans"' (qtd in Black 2005: 94).

3   This is very much in contrast with those later shots of the dark gloominess of British Intelligence services in London. Indeed, as Jeremy Black notes, '*Dr. No* begins with two views of empire – the club in Kingston that is the center of white, male society, and imperial Westminster, a night shot of Big Ben and the Thames' (2005: 93), thereby emphasizing the film's imperializing frame.

4   The film's alignment of the rapacious Black Jamaican male and the threat of Chinese insurrectionism on the island can be seen in the climactic battle between Bond and Dr No in the control room beneath Crab Key, the final shot of which shows Dr No's own black, mechanical hands sinking into the nuclear pool reactor. Cynthia Baron reads this as the moment of 'retribution promised to any "black hand" raised against the Empire, and of the impotency of any "black hands" that might try to wrest control from British "truebloods"' ([2003] 2009: 161).

5   James Chapman has argued that Bond's presence in Jamaica during the film constitutes a 'reaffirmation of white, British superiority at a time when, in reality, Britain was beating a hasty retreat from empire' ([1999] 2007: 62).

6   That said, the producers of *Dr. No* certainly did benefit from 'Fleming's behind-the-scenes efforts in opening doors' on the island for them, 'urging them to hire local actors [and] recommending Chris Blackwell, the future record mogul [and son of Fleming's lover Blanche] as their location manager'. As James Robertson notes, Fleming's support provided the film-makers with 'remarkable local entrée' in Jamaica (2015: 62–3).

7   James Robertson notes that the Jamaican Chinese community 'owned 90 percent of the dry goods stores and 95 percent of the newly introduced supermarkets, along with restaurants, laundries, and betting shops, while, as the high proportion of Chinese boys passing exams at downtown Kingston's elite St. George's College in the late 1950s and early 1960s also demonstrated, the shopkeepers' children were developing into a formidable group in their own right' (2015: 59). Local film audiences who were aware of the political and historical context of Chinese-Jamaican relations on the island would certainly register the implied threat of Dr No's Asian retinue, but by allowing the political history of these racial conflicts to go unremarked upon, the film 'evade[d] contentious concerns, both on and off the island' (ibid.). While the film certainly emphasizes the pervasiveness of the Chinese community's raciality, the issue of Honey Rider's ethnicity (she is a white

Caribbean Creole descended from seventeenth-century British settlers) is one that is played down. In Fleming's novel, Bond's ideological realignment of Honey is tied to her hybrid status as white Creole; in the film, however, Honey's Creole status is simply whitewashed (she is played by Swiss actress Ursula Andress), and the issues of racial and cultural identity politics within Bond and Honey's relationship are seemingly non-existent. Thus, while *Dr. No* plays up the racial facets of those villainous characters which populate the filmic Jamaica, it deliberately overlooks the problematic racial and cultural elements of Bond's subordination of Honey that are considerably more apparent in the novel.

8   Charles W. Mills has pointed out that 'Jamaica has been privileged to be defended by two of the most famous agents/sleuths in English-language genre fiction – Ian Fleming's James Bond (007) and Leslie Charteris's Simon Templar (The Saint)' (2010: 102), each of whom, of course, were, at one point, played by Roger Moore. James Chapman also notes that Moore's first Bond film, *Live and Let Die*, took in $15.9 million in the North American market and $32.8 million on the overseas and international markets, which is 'the biggest ratio difference between domestic and foreign earning for any film in the series since *Dr. No*' ([1999] 2007: 143) – a point which further aligns the cinematic universes of both Connery's and Moore's first Bond adventures.

9   During the conference speeches, the camera cuts to the interior of the interpreter box in which the British translator is sitting. The camera slowly pans past the translator to a bank of wires on the wall, where a black hand is shown to replace one of the wires on the console with another, attached to a detonation device with a plunger. When the black hand pushes down on the plunger, a sonic blast is sent through the sound system to the headset worn by the British ambassador, killing him instantly. The shot of the black hand emerging from the side of the frame is reminiscent of a similar such scene in the filmic *Dr. No*: just before Strangways's secretary, Mary Trueblood, is shot dead, we see a black hand swinging open the gate to Strangways's cottage, the rusting hinges of which create an ominous note of foreboding. As in this scene, the appearance of the disembodied hand of a Black male signifies to the audience a threatening presence, and the lack of any other identifying features connotes the diffusiveness of the threat of Black-on-white violence within this particular cinematic landscape.

10   Jeremy Black notes that the film is a 'harsh depiction of Caribbean independence', and that 'the implication is that western power is required in order to maintain control and free the people from the subjugation based on their fears [of Voodoo]' (2017: 117). But Black also argues that 'if western imperialism appears to be the answer [to the 'problems' of Black culture], there is also implicit criticism of the United Nations, which Kananga uses as a sounding board to denounce the West' (ibid.).

11 Enoch Powell delivered his infamous 'rivers of blood' speech in 1968 to significant approval by the British people; the 1971 Immigration Act banned the migration of non-white commonwealth citizens to England; and the 'mugging crisis' of the late 1960s/early 1970s vilified socio-economically impoverished, urban-dwelling people of colour in the UK (see McClure 2011: 293). As Adrian Daub and Charles Kronengold note, in the filmic *Live and Let Die* 'the colonial and the metropolitan subaltern strike an uncanny alliance' (2015: 98), as the link between the Black Caribbean and Harlem was one that was often exploited by British politicians of this period (McClure 2011: 292).

12 *Live and Let Die* certainly courts the aesthetics of blaxploitation films of the 1970s, which includes the use of 'racial slurs between whites and blacks', 'hip street language', 'on-location scenes in black centres such as Harlem' and stories which dealt with the drug trade (McClure 2011: 294). The most obvious difference, of course, between *Live and Let Die* and the traditional blaxploitation film is that the heroes of blaxploitation films are not white, upper-crust Englishmen. In terms of tone and style, *Live and Let Die* is the 'antithesis to the Blaxploitation genre', resembling more clearly those Hollywood films of the 1970s 'that embraced the political discourse of "law and order" by white heroes such as Dirty Harry' (ibid.), though the casting of blaxploitation stars Yaphet Kotto as Dr Kananga and Gloria Hendry as Rosie Carver did much to invite similarities and blur the boundaries between these genres.

13 As James Chapman notes, 'in its attitude towards miscegenation … the film contrives to have its cake and eat it: while sex between a black man and a white girl is beyond the pale, Bond is allowed a sexual encounter with a black woman' ([1999] 2007: 139–40). Similarly, Travis L. Wagner argues that *Live and Let Die* 'presents a double standard in which Bond's seduction of Carver is justified (within a colonial context) while Kananga's desire to sleep with Solitaire (to rid her of her powers) is deemed a threat; the white man is granted access to all bodies despite their color while the black man can only have access to other bodies of color. The film foregrounds the notion that only the white man can partake in interracial encounters, which may come by way of colonizing endeavours' (2015: 55). It was not until 2002's *Die Another Day*, the franchise's fiftieth-anniversary instalment, that Bond concludes his mission in the sexual embrace of an African-American protagonist – Halle Berry's NSA agent, Jinx. With the exception of Kissy Suzuki (Japanese actress Mie Hama) in *You Only Live Twice* (1967), Wai Lin (Malaysian actress Michelle Yeoh) in *Tomorrow Never Dies* (1997) and Nomi (Black British actress Lashana Lynch) in *No Time to Die* (2021), all other principal 'Bond Girls' have been played by Caucasian actresses. I am excluding, of course, Trina Parks's Thumper in *Diamonds Are Forever* and Grace Jones's May Day in *A View to a Kill* (1985), both of whom are antagonists, as well as Naomie Harris's Eve Moneypenny.

Bibliography

A View to a Kill (1985), [Film] Dir. John Glen, UK: Eon Productions.

Abraham, K. ([1927] 1973), *Selected Papers of Karl Abraham MD*, intro. E. Jones, trans. D. Bryan and A. Strachey, London: Hogarth Press and the Institute of Psychoanalysis.

Adams, A. (2017), '"The Sweet Tang of Rape": Torture, Survival and Masculinity in Ian Fleming's Bond Novels', *Feminist Theory*, 18 (2): 137–59.

Adamthwaite, A. (1988), 'Suez Revisited', *International Affairs*, 64 (3): 449–64.

Adolf, M. (2011), 'Clarifying Mediatization: Sorting through a Current Debate', *Empedocles: European Journal for the Philosophy of Communication*, 3 (2): 153–75.

Alexander, C. (2020), 'Cultural Appropriation and Capitalism: Co-opting Blaxploitation in the Filmic Live and Let Die', *International Journal of James Bond Studies*, 3 (1): DOI: 10.24877/jbs.55.

Allen, H. R. (1976), *Buccaneer: Admiral Sir Henry Morgan*, London: Arthur Baker.

Amis, K. (1965), *The James Bond Dossier*, New York: New American Library.

Anthony, P., and J. Friedman (1965), *Ian Fleming's Incredible Creation*, Chicago: Novel Books.

Arens, W. (1979), *The Man-Eating Myth: Anthropology and Anthropophagy*, Oxford: Oxford University Press.

Avramescu, C. (2011), *An Intellectual History of Cannibalism*, Princeton, NJ: Princeton University Press.

Barnes, A., and M. Hearn (1997), *Kiss Kiss, Bang! Bang!*, London: B.T. Batsford.

Baron, C. ([2003] 2009), '*Doctor No*: Bending Britishness to Racial Sovereignty', in C. Lindner (ed.), *The James Bond Phenomenon*, 135–50, Oxford: Oxford University Press.

Belnap, J. G. (1993), *The Post-colonial State and the 'Hybrid' Intellectual*, California: U.M.I.

Benjamin, J. R. (1992), *The United States and the Origins of the Cuban Revolution*, Princeton, NJ: Princeton University Press.

Bennett, T., and J. Woollacott (1987), *Bond and Beyond: The Political Career of a Popular Hero*, Hampshire: Macmillan.

Benson, R. (1984), *The James Bond Bedside Companion*, New York: Dodd, Mead.

Berberich, C. (2012), 'Putting England Back on Top? Ian Fleming, James Bond, and the Question of England', *Yearbook of English Studies*, 42: 13–29.

Bhabha, H. K. ([1994] 2006), *The Location of Culture*, London: Routledge.

Black, J. (2004), 'The Geopolitics of James Bond', *Intelligence and National Security*, 2 (19): 290–303.

Black, J. (2005), *The Politics of James Bond: From Fleming's Novels to the Big Screen*, London: University of Nebraska Press.

Black, J. (2017), *The World of James Bond: The Lives and Times of 007*, London: Rowman and Littlefield.

Blackwell, B. (1965), Letter to John Pearson, Pearson, J. MSS. 1964–66, 28 April, Lilly Library: Indiana University Bloomington.

Blanchard, C. (1965), Letter to John Pearson, Pearson, J. MSS. 1964–66, 26 January, Lilly Library: Indiana University Bloomington.

Bleuler, E. (1910), 'Vortrag uber Ambivalenz' [Lecture on Ambivalence], *Central Journal for Psychoanalysis*, 1: 266–8.

Bold, C. (1993), '"Under the Very Skirts of Britannia": Re-reading Women in the James Bond Novels', *Queen's Quarterly*, 100 (2): 311–27.

Bond, J. ([1936] 1960), *Birds of the West Indies*, London: HarperCollins.

Bourne, S. (2012), 'Introduction', in I. Fleming, *Dr. No*, ix–xviii, London: Vintage.

Boyd, A. S. (1967), *The Devil with James Bond*, Richmond, VA: John Knox Press.

Bradley, W. L. (1963), 'Ethics of James Bond', *Hartford Quarterly*, 7 (3): 35–46.

Brandon, H. (1965), Letter to John Pearson, Pearson, J. MSS. 1964–66, 13 October, Lilly Library: Indiana University Bloomington.

Brown, V. (2008), *The Reaper's Garden: Death and Power in the World of Atlantic Slavery*, Cambridge, MA: Harvard University Press.

Bryce, I. (1965), Letter to John Pearson, Pearson, J. MSS. 1964–66, 26 April, Lilly Library: Indiana University Bloomington.

Bryce, I. (1975), *You Only Live Once: Memories of Ian Fleming*, London: Weidenfeld and Nicolson.

Burnetts, C. (2015), 'Bond's Bit on the Side: Race, Exoticism and the Bond "Fluffer" Character', in L. Funnell (ed.), *For His Eyes Only: The Women of James Bond*, 60–9, London: Columbia University Press.

Campbell, H. D. (1963), 'An Interview with Ian Fleming', *Sunday Gleaner*, 10 February: 20.

Campbell, J. (1965), Letter to John Pearson, Pearson, J. MSS. 1964–66, 20 January, Lilly Library: Indiana University Bloomington.

Campbell, M. (1988), *The Maroons of Jamaica 1655–1796: A History of Resistance, Collaboration, and Betrayal*, Granby, MA: Bergin & Garvey.

Cannadine, D. (1979), 'James Bond and the Decline of England', *Encounter*, 53: 46–54.

Cannadine, D. (2002), *In Churchill's Shadow: Confronting the Past in Modern Britain*, London: Allen Lane.

Capeci, D. J., and M. Wilkerson (1991), *Layered Violence: The Detroit Rioters of 1943*, Jackson: University of Mississippi Press.

Caplen, R. A. (2012), *Shaken and Stirred: The Feminism of James Bond*, London: Robert Caplen.
Carey, B. (1997), *The Maroon Story: The Authentic and Original History of the Maroons in the History of Jamaica 1490–1880*, Kingston, Jamaica: Agouti Press.
Cargill, M. (ed.) (1965a), *Ian Fleming Introduces Jamaica*, London: Andre Deutsch.
Cargill, M. (1965b), Letter to John Pearson, Pearson, J. MSS. 1964–66, 22 June, Lilly Library: Indiana University Bloomington.
Cargill, M. (1965c), Letter to John Pearson, Russell, L. MSS. 1960–67, 6 December, Lilly Library: Indiana University Bloomington.
Casino Royale (1954), [TV programme] CBS, 21 October.
Casino Royale (2006), [Film] Dir. Martin Campbell, UK: Eon Productions.
Cawelti, J. G., and B. A. Rosenberg (1987), *The Spy Story*, London: University of Chicago Press.
Chancellor, H. (2005), *James Bond: The Man and His World: The Official Companion to Ian Fleming's Creation*, London: John Murray.
Chapman, J. ([1999] 2007), *Licence to Thrill: A Cultural History of the James Bond Films*, London: I.B. Tauris.
Chapman, J. (2018), 'James Bond and the End of Empire', in J. Strong (ed.), *James Bond Uncovered*, 203–22, Basingstoke: Palgrave Macmillan.
Chayes, A. (1974), *The Cuban Missile Crisis: International Crises and the Role of Law*, London: Oxford University Press.
Cleaver, E. ([1968] 1970), *Soul on Ice*, London: Panther.
Cork, J., and B. Scivally (2002), *James Bond: The Legacy*, London: Boxtree.
Couldry, N., and A. Hepp (2013), 'Conceptualizing Mediatization: Contexts, Traditions, Arguments', *Communication Theory*, 23: 191–202.
Coward, N. (1965), Letter to John Pearson, Pearson, J. MSS. 1964–66, 22 May, Lilly Library: Indiana University Bloomington.
Craton, M. (1983), *Testing the Chains: Resistance to Slavery in the British West Indies*, New York: Cornell University Press.
Cuneo, E. L. (1984), 'Introduction', in R. Benson (ed.), *The James Bond Bedside Companion*, xi–xiii, New York: Dodd, Mead.
Daas, M. M. (2011), 'Ian Fleming's Solitaire: The Voodoo Virgin Dethroned', in R. G. Weiner, B. L. Whitfield and J. Becker (eds), *James Bond in World and Popular Culture: The Films are Not Enough*, 162–8, Newcastle upon Tyne: Cambridge Scholars.
Daub, A., and C. Kronengold (2015), *The James Bond Songs: Pop Anthems of Late Capitalism*, Oxford: Oxford University Press.
Dayan, J. (1998), *Haiti, History and the Gods*, Berkeley: University of California Press.
Denning, M. (1987), *Cover Stories: Narrative and Ideology in the British Spy Thriller*, London: Routledge & Kegan Paul.
Diamonds Are Forever (1971), [Film] Dir. Guy Hamilton, UK: Eon Productions.
Die Another Day (2002), [Film] Dir. Lee Tamahori, UK: Eon Productions.

Diedrich, B., and A. Burt (1969), *Papa Doc: Haiti and Its Dictator*, London: Bodley Head.

Dietl, R. (2008), 'Suez 1956: A European Invention?', *Journal of Contemporary History*, 43 (2): 259–73.

Dittmer, J. (2008), 'Ian Fleming's Jamaica: Spaces of Legitimation and the Bond-Age of Popular Culture', *Caribbean Geography*, 15 (1): 14–34.

Divine, R. A. (1988), *The Cuban Missile Crisis*, New York: Weiner.

Dodds, K. (2014), 'Shaking and Stirring James Bond: Age, Gender, and Resilience in *Skyfall* (2012)', *Journal of Popular Film and Television*, 42 (3): 116–30.

Dr. No (1962), [Film] Dir. Terence Young, UK: Eon Productions.

Dresner, L. M. (2011), '"All Mixed Up": James Bond's World of Mixing, Displacement, and Boundary Crossing', in R. G. Weiner, B. L. Whitfield and J. Becker (eds), *James Bond in World and Popular Culture: The Films Are Not Enough*, 271–89, Newcastle upon Tyne: Cambridge Scholars.

Dutheil, M. H. (2001), 'The Representation of the Cannibal in Ballantyne's *The Coral Island*: Colonial Anxieties in Victorian Popular Fiction', *College Literature*, 28 (1): 105–22.

Durgnat, R. (1970), *A Mirror for England: British Movies from Austerity to Affluence*, London: Faber & Faber.

Earle, P. (2007), *The Sack of Panamá: Captain Morgan and the Battle for the Caribbean*, New York: Thomas Dunne Books.

Earle, R. (2012), *The Body of the Conquistador: Food, Race, and the Colonial Experience in Spanish America 1492–1700*, New York: Cambridge University Press.

Early, G. (1999), 'Jungle Fever: Ian Fleming's James Bond Novels, the Cold War, and Jamaica', *New Letters*, 66: 139–63.

Eco, U. ([1965] 1966), 'The Narrative Structure in Fleming', in O. Del Buono and U. Eco (eds), *The Bond Affair*, trans. R. A. Downie, 35–75, London: MacDonald.

Eco, U. (1979), *The Role of the Reader: Exploration in the Semiotics of Texts*, London: Hutchinson.

Edmond, R. (1997), *Representing the South Pacific: Colonial Discourse from Cook to Gauguin*, Cambridge: Cambridge University Press.

Egan, S. (2016), *James Bond: The Secret History*, London: John Blake.

Fanon, F. ([1961] 2001), *The Wretched of the Earth*, London: Penguin.

Farber, S. (2006), *The Origins of the Cuban Revolution Reconsidered*, Chapel Hill: University of North Carolina Press.

Ferreras Savoye, D. (2013), *The Signs of James Bond: Semiotic Exploration in the World of 007*, London: McFarland.

Field, M., and A. Chowdhury (2015), *Some Kind of Hero: The Remarkable Story of the James Bond Films*, London: History Press.

Fleming, A. (1965), Letter to John Pearson, Pearson, J. MSS. 1964-66, 24–25 February, Lilly Library: Indiana University Bloomington.

Fleming, F. (ed.) (2015), *The Man with the Golden Typewriter: Ian Fleming's James Bond Letters*, London: Bloomsbury.
Fleming, I. (1951), Letter to Sir William Stephenson, Russell, L. MSS 1951, 11 October, Lilly Library: Indiana University Bloomington.
Fleming, I. (1955), 'The Great Riot of Istanbul', *Sunday Times*, 11 September, Lilly Library: Indiana University Bloomington.
Fleming, I. (1956a), Letter to Raymond Chandler, Russell, L. MSS. 1908–59, 22 June, Lilly Library: Indiana University Bloomington.
Fleming, I. (1956b), Letter to Sir Hugh Foot, Russell, L. MSS. 1908–59, 26 November, Lilly Library: Indiana University Bloomington.
Fleming, I. (1957), Letter to Michael Howard, Russell, L. MSS. 1908–59, 4 February, Lilly Library: Indiana University Bloomington.
Fleming, I. (1959), 'If I Were Prime Minister', *Spectator*, 1 October: 446–7.
Fleming, I. (1963a), Letter to William Plomer, Plomer MMS. II 1960–64 I Folio, 3 April, Lilly Library: Indiana University Bloomington.
Fleming, I. (1963b), Letter to William Plomer, Plomer MSS. II 1960–64 I Folio, 6 May, Lilly Library: Indiana University Bloomington.
Fleming, I. (1963c), Postcard to William Plomer, Plomer MSS. II 1960–64, I Folio, 18 October, Lilly Library: Indiana University Bloomington.
Fleming, I. (1964a), Letter to William Plomer, Plomer MSS. II 1960–64 I Folio, 2 March, Lilly Library: Indiana University Bloomington.
Fleming, I. (1964b), Letter to William Plomer, Plomer MSS. II 1960–64 I Folio, 17 April, Lilly Library: Indiana University Bloomington.
Fleming, I. (1964c), Letter to William Plomer, Plomer MSS. II 1960–64 I Folio, 10 May, Lilly Library: Indiana University Bloomington.
Fleming, I. ([1947] 1965), 'Introducing Jamaica', in M. Cargill (ed.), *Ian Fleming Introduces Jamaica*, 11–21, London: Andre Deutsch.
Fleming, I. ([1953] 2012a), *Casino Royale*, London: Vintage.
Fleming, I. ([1954] 2012b), *Live and Let Die*, London: Vintage.
Fleming, I. ([1955] 2012c), *Moonraker*, London: Vintage.
Fleming, I. ([1956] 2012d), *Diamonds Are Forever*, London: Vintage.
Fleming, I. ([1957] 2012e), *From Russia with Love*, London: Vintage.
Fleming, I. ([1958] 2012f), *Dr. No*, London: Vintage.
Fleming, I. ([1959] 2012g), *Goldfinger*, London: Vintage.
Fleming, I. ([1960] 2012h), *For Your Eyes Only*, London: Vintage.
Fleming, I. ([1961] 2012i), *Thunderball*, London: Vintage.
Fleming, I. ([1962] 2012j), *The Spy Who Loved Me*, London: Vintage.
Fleming, I. ([1963] 2012k), *On Her Majesty's Secret Service*, London: Vintage.
Fleming, I. ([1964] 2012l), *You Only Live Twice*, London: Vintage.
Fleming, I. ([1965] 2012m), *The Man with the Golden Gun*, London: Vintage.
Fleming, I. ([1966] 2012n), *Octopussy and the Living Daylights*, London: Vintage.

Foot, H. (1956), Letter to Ian Fleming, Russell, L. MSS. 1908–59, 2 December, Lilly Library: Indiana University Bloomington.
Frayling, C. (2014), *The Yellow Peril: Dr. Fu Manchu and the Rise of Chinaphobia*, New York: Thames & Hudson.
Frenk, J., and C. Krug (eds) (2011), *The Cultures of James Bond*, Trier: Verlag.
Freud, S. ([1950] 1961), *Totem and Taboo*, trans. J. Strachey, London: Routledge & Kegan Paul.
Freud, S. (1988), *Case Histories II*, Penguin Freud Library, Vol. 9, London: Penguin.
Friesen, N., and T. Hug (2009), 'The Mediatic Turn: Exploring Consequences for Media Pedagogy', in K. Lundby (ed.), *Mediatization: Concept, Changes, Consequences*, 64–81, New York: Peter Lang.
From Russia with Love (1964), [Film] Dir. Terence Young, UK: Eon Productions.
Funnell, L. (2015), 'Objects of White Male Desire: (D)Evolving Representations of Asian Women in Bond Films', in L. Funnell (ed.), *For His Eyes Only: The Women of James Bond*, 79–87, London: Columbia University Press.
Funnell, L., and K. Dodds (2015), 'The Anglo-American Connection: Examining the Intersection of Nationality with Class, Gender, and Race in the James Bond Films', *Journal of American Culture*, 3 (4): 357–75.
Funnell, L., and K. Dodds (2017), *Geographies, Genders, and Geopolitics of James Bond*, London: Palgrave Macmillan.
Gant, R. (1966), *Ian Fleming: The Fantastic 007 Man*, New York: Lancer Books.
Gardiner, P. (2008), *The Bond Code: The Dark World of Ian Fleming and James Bond*, New Jersey: New Page Books.
Germaná, M. (2019), *Bond Girls: Body, Fashion and Gender*, London: Bloomsbury.
Gibson, D. R. (2012), *Talk at the Brink: Deliberation and Decision during the Cuban Missile Crisis*, Princeton, NJ: Princeton University Press.
Gilbert, J. (2012), *Ian Fleming: The Bibliography*, London: Queen Anne Press.
Goggin, J. (2018), '*Live and Let Die*: The Tarot as Other in the 007 Universe', in J. Strong (ed.), *James Bond Uncovered*, 143–62, Basingstoke: Palgrave Macmillan.
Goh, R. B. H. (1999), 'Peter O'Donnell, Race Relations and National Identity: The Dynamics of Representation in 1960s and 1970s Britain', *Journal of Popular Culture*, 32 (4): 29–44.
Goodman, S. (2016), *British Spy Fiction and the End of Empire*, London: Routledge.
Gopinath, P. (2013), *Scarecrows of Chivalry: English Masculinities after Empire*, Charlottesville: University of Virginia Press.
Greenberg, C. L. (1991), '*Or Does It Explode?*': *Black Harlem in the Great Depression*, Oxford: Oxford University Press.
Grimshaw, A. D. (1969), *Racial Violence in the United States*, Chicago: Aldine.
Griswold, J. (2006), *Ian Fleming's James Bond: Annotations and Chronologies for Ian Fleming's Bond Stories*, Bloomington, IN: AuthorHouse.
Hagen, K. (2018), 'The Spectre of "Bloody Morgan": Ian Fleming's Use of the Pirate Motif', *International Journal of James Bond Studies*, 1 (2): DOI: 10.204877/jbs.30.

Hall, D. (1972), 'Independent Jamaica: Ten Years after 1962', *Jamaica Journal*, 6 (7): 2–3.
Haining, P. (1987), *James Bond: A Celebration*, London: Planet Books.
Halloran, V. (2005), 'Tropical Bond', in E. P. Comentale, S. Watt and S. Willman (eds), *Ian Fleming and James Bond: The Cultural Politics of James Bond*, 158–77, Bloomington: Indiana University Press.
Hansell, G. R., and W. Grassie (eds) (2011), *Transhumanism and Its Critics*, Philadelphia: Metanexus Institute.
Heimann, P. ([1955] 1985), 'A Combination of Defence Mechanisms in Paranoid States', in M. Klein, P. Heimann and R. Money-Kyrle (eds), *New Directions in Psychoanalysis: The Significance of Infant Conflict in the Pattern of Adult Behaviour*, 240–65, London: Maresfield Library.
Hepp, A., S. Hjarvard and K. Lundby (2015), 'Mediatization: Theorizing the Interplay between Media, Culture, and Society', *Media, Culture, and Society*, 37 (2): 314–24.
Hjarvard, S., and L. N. Peterson (2013), 'Mediatization and Cultural Change', *MediaKultur*, 54: 1–7.
Holland, P., and G. Huggan (2002), *Tourists with Typewriters: Critical Reflections on Contemporary Travel Writing*, Ann Arbor: University of Michigan Press.
Huggan, G. (2001), *The Postcolonial Exotic: Marketing the Margin*, London: Routledge.
Hyde, M. (2016), 'The Name's Elba, Idris Elba – and He Must Be James Bond', *The Guardian*, 20 May. https://www.theguardian.com/lifeandstyle/lostinshowbiz/2016/may/20/idris-elba-must-be-james-bond-tom-hiddleston-daniel-craig. Accessed 25 October 2019.
James, C. L. R. (1963), *Beyond a Boundary*, London: Hutchinson.
Jenkinson, J. (2009), *Black 1919: Riots, Racism and Resistance in Imperial Britain*, Liverpool: Liverpool University Press.
Johnson, P. (1958), 'Sex, Snobbery and Sadism', *New Statesman*, 5 April.
Jones, K. P. (2010), 'The Hidden History of Llanrumney', *The Guardian*, 24 June.
Kingsbury, P. (2005), 'Jamaican Tourism and the Politics of Enjoyment', *Geoforum*, 36: 113–32.
'Kingston Premier for *Dr. No*' (1963), *Daily Gleaner*, 28 January: 8.
Klein, M. (2002), *Love, Guilt and Reparation: And Other Works 1921–1945* (Vol. 1), New York: Simon & Schuster.
Knopf, T. A. (1975), *Rumors, Race and Riots*, New Jersey: Transaction Publishers.
Kofele-Kale, N. (2006), *The International Law of Responsibility for Economic Crimes*, Aldershot: Ashgate.
Krainitzki, E. (2014), 'Judi Dench's Age-Appropriateness and the Role of M: Challenging Normative Temporality', *Journal of Aging Studies*, 29: 32–40.
Landa, I. (2006), 'James Bond: A Nietzschean for the Cold War', in J. M. Held and J. B. South (eds), *James Bond and Philosophy*, 79–93, Chicago: Open Court.
Latimer, J. (2009), *Buccaneers of the Caribbean: How Piracy Forged an Empire*, Cambridge, MA: Harvard University Press.

Leed, E. J. (1991), *The Mind of the Traveller: From Gilgamesh to Global Tourism*, New York: Basic Books.
Lemoine, P. (2011), *Fort-Dimanche: Dungeon of Death*, Bloomington, IN: Trafford.
Lestringant, F. (1997), *Cannibals: The Discovery and Representation of the Cannibal from Columbus to Jules Verne*, Berkeley: University of California Press.
Lett, B. (2013), *Ian Fleming and SOE's Operation Postmaster: The Untold Top Secret Story*, Yorkshire: Pen and Sword Books.
Licence to Kill (1989), [Film] Dir. John Glen, UK: Eon Productions.
Lievesley, G. (2004), *The Cuban Revolution: Past, Present, and Future Perspectives*, Hampshire: Palgrave Macmillan.
Lilli, L. (1966), 'James Bond and Criticism', in O. Del Buono and U. Eco (eds), *The Bond Affair*, trans. R. A. Downie, 146–73, London: MacDonald.
Lindner, C., ed. (2003), *The James Bond Phenomenon: A Critical Reader*, Manchester: Manchester University Press.
Lipschutz, R. D. (2001), *Cold War Fantasies: Film, Fiction, and Foreign Policy*, Oxford: Rowman and Littlefield.
Live and Let Die (1973), [Film] Dir. Guy Hamilton, UK: Eon Productions.
The Living Daylights (1987), [Film] Dir. John Glen, UK: Eon Productions.
Lycett, A. ([1995] 2008), *Ian Fleming*, London: Phoenix.
The Man with the Golden Gun (1974), [Film] Dir. Guy Hamilton, UK: Eon Productions.
Marchetti, G. (1994), *Romance and the 'Yellow Peril': Race, Sex, and Discursive Strategies in Hollywood Fiction*, Berkeley: University of California Press.
Marshment, M. (1978), 'Racist Ideology and Popular Fiction', *Race and Class*, 19 (4): 331–44.
Marquis, J. (2007), *Papa Doc: Portrait of a Haitian Tyrant*, Kingston, Jamaica: LMH.
Maudling, R. (1965), Letter to Christine E. P. Zewart, Russell, L. MSS. 1960–67, 17 December, Lilly Library: Indiana University Bloomington.
Merry, B. (1977), *Anatomy of the Spy Thriller*, London: Gill and Macmillan.
Miller, C. J. (2011), 'Foreword', in R. G. Weiner, B. L. Whitfield and J. Becker (eds), *James Bond in World and Popular Culture: The Films Are Not Enough*, xiii–xvi, Newcastle upon Tyne: Cambridge Scholars.
Mills, C. W. (2010), *Radical Theory, Caribbean Reality: Race, Class, and Social Domination*, Jamaica: University of the West Indies Press.
Montaigne, M. (1938), *The Essays of Michael, Lord of Montaigne, Volume II*, London: J. M. Dent & Sons.
Moran, C. (2013), 'Ian Fleming and the Public Profile of the CIA', *Journal of Cold War Studies*, 15 (1): 119–47.
More, M., and N. Vita-More (eds) (2013), *The Transhumanist Reader: Classical and Contemporary Essays on the Science, Technology, and Philosophy of Human Future*, New Jersey: Wiley.
MacCannell, D. (1999), *The Tourist: A New Theory of the Leisure Class*, London: University of California Press.

McClintock, A. (1995), *Imperial Leather: Race, Gender, and Sexuality in the Colonial Contest*, New York: Routledge.
McClure, D. (2011), 'Defining, Re-Defining Colonial Legacies in Film: *Live and Let Die*, *The Harder They Come*, and the Cultural Geographies of Early 1970s Jamaica', in R. G. Weiner, B. L. Whitfield and J. Becker (eds), *James Bond in World and Popular Culture: The Films Are Not Enough*, 290–302, Newcastle upon Tyne: Cambridge Scholars.
McCormick, D. (1993), *17F: The Life of Ian Fleming*, London: Peter Owen.
No Time to Die (2021), [Film] Dir. Cary Joji Fukanaga, UK: Eon Productions.
Octopussy (1983), [Film] Dir. John Glen, UK: Eon Productions.
Ormerod, D., and D. Ward (1965), 'The Bond Game', *London Magazine*, 5 (2): 41–55.
Pankratz, A. (2007), 'Mapping Bond and His "Little Atoll"', in J. Kamm and G. Sedlmayr (eds), *Insular Mentalities: Maps of Britain: Essays in Honour of Bernd Lenz*, 129–44, Passau: Verlag.
Parker, M. (2014), *Goldeneye: Where Bond was Born: Ian Fleming's Jamaica*, London: Penguin Random House.
Pearson, J. (n.d.), Notes Compiled on Bond's Spots and Places, Pearson, J. MSS. 1964–66, Lilly Library: Indiana University Bloomington.
Pearson, J. (1966), *The Life of Ian Fleming*, London: Jonathan Cape.
Pearson, J. (1967), 'An Evening with JFK', *Boston Globe*, 27 January.
Pearson, J. (2002), *Sir Anthony Eden and the Suez Crisis*, London: Palgrave.
Pérez-Stable, M. (1998), *The Cuban Revolution: Origins, Course, and Legacy*, Oxford: Oxford University Press.
Powell, D. (1974), 'Review of *Live and Let Die*', *Sunday Times*, 8 July.
Pratt, M. L. (1992), *Imperial Eyes: Travel Writing and Transculturation*, London: Routledge.
Pua, P. (2018), 'Iron Lady to Old Lady: The Neutering of James Bond's M', *Feminist Media Studies*, 18 (1): 94–107.
Quantum of Solace (2008), [Film] Dir. Marc Forster, UK: Eon Productions.
Ranish, R., and S. L. Sorgner (eds) (2014), *Post- and Transhumanism*, Bruxelles: Peter Lang.
Razinsky, H. (2016), *Ambivalence: A Philosophical Exploration*, London: Rowman & Littlefield.
Richards, J. (2001), 'Imperial Heroes of a Post-Imperial Age: Films and the End of Empire', in S. Ward (ed.), *British Culture and the End of Empire*, 128–44, Manchester: Manchester University Press.
Richler, M. (1972), *Shovelling Trouble*, Toronto: McClelland and Stewart.
Riquet, J., and A. Zdrenyk (2018), 'Between Progress and Nostalgia: Technology, Geopolitics, and James Bond's Railway Journeys', *International Journal of James Bond Studies*, 1 (2): DOI: 10.204877/jbs.29.
Robertson, J. (2015), 'Rewriting *Dr. No* in 1962: James Bond and the End of the British Empire in Jamaica', *Small Axe*, 19 (2): 56–76.

Rosenberg, B. A., and A. Harlemann Stewart (1989), *Ian Fleming: A Critical Biography*, Boston: Twayne.
Rupert, G. G. (1911), *The Yellow Peril; or, The Orient versus the Occident*, Choctaw, OK: Union.
Said, E. ([1978] 2003), *Orientalism*, London: Penguin.
Sanday, P. R. (1986), *Divine Hunger: Cannibalism as a Cultural System*, London: Cambridge University Press.
Sanneh, K. (2014), 'White Mischief: The Passions of Carl Van Vechten', *New Yorker*, 17 February.
Sauerberg, L. O. (1984), *Secret Agents in Fiction: Ian Fleming, John le Carré and Len Deighton*, London: Macmillan.
Schickel, R. (1973), 'Dirty Trick', *Time*, 9 July.
Sheller, M. (2003), *Consuming the Caribbean*, New York: Routledge.
Skyfall (2012), [Film] Dir. Sam Mendes, UK: Eon Productions.
Smith, J., and S. Lavington (2002), *Bond Films*, London: Virgin Books.
Snelling, O. F. (1964), *Double O Seven James Bond: A Report*, London: Neville Spearman, Holland Press.
Spectre (2015), [Film] Dir. Sam Mendes, UK: Eon Productions.
Sterling, M., and G. Morecambe (2002), *Martinis, Girls, and Guns: Fifty Years of 007*, London: Robson Books.
Stern, S. M. (2012), *The Cuban Missile Crisis in American Memory: Myth Versus Reality*, Stanford, CA: Stanford University Press.
Stock, P. (2000), 'Dial "M" for Metonym: Universal Exports, M's Office Space and Empire', *National Identities*, 2 (1): 35–47.
Strömbäck, J. (2008), 'Four Phases of Mediatization: An Analysis of the Mediatization of Politics', *International Journal of Press/Politics*, 13: 228–46.
Sugrue, T. J. (1996), *The Origins of the Urban Crisis*, Princeton, NJ: Princeton University Press.
Sweig, J. E. (2004), *Inside the Cuban Revolution: Fidel Castro and the Urban Underground*, Cambridge, MA: Harvard University Press.
Taussig, M. (1993), *Mimesis and Alterity: A Particular History of the Senses*, New York: Routledge.
Taylor, A. (2012), 'Introduction', in I. Fleming, *Live and Let Die*, ix–xvii, London: Vintage.
Tomorrow Never Dies (1997), [Film] Dir. Roger Spottiswoode, UK: Eon Productions.
Tornabuoni, L. ([1965] 1966), 'A Popular Phenomenon', in O. Del Buono and U. Eco (eds), *The Bond Affair*, trans. R. A. Downie, 13–34, London: MacDonald.
Turner, J. (2018), 'Jamaica's In', *The Times*, 6 September: 24.
Urry, J., and J. Larsen (2011), *The Tourist Gaze 3.0*, London: Sage.
Varble, D. (2002), *The Suez Crisis, 1956*, London: Osprey.
Verbeek, B. (2003), *Decision-Making in Great Britain During the Suez Crisis*, Aldershot: Ashgate.

Viol, C.-U. (2011), 'Quantum of Smoothness: Bond and Spatial Desire', in J. Frenk and C. Krug (eds), *The Cultures of James Bond*, 183–93, Trier: Verlag.

Viol, C.-U. (2019), 'Things Are Not Enough: Bond, Stiegler, and Technics', *International Journal of James Bond Studies*, 2 (1): DOI: http://doi.org/10.24877/jbs.43.

Wagner, T. L. (2015), '"The Old Ways Are Best": The Colonization of Women of Color in Bond Films', in L. Funnell (ed.), *For His Eyes Only: The Women of James Bond*, 51–9, London: Columbia University Press.

Ward, S. (ed.) (2001), *British Culture and the End of Empire*, Manchester: Manchester University Press.

Wark, W. K. (ed.) ([1991] 2006), *Spy Fiction, Spy Films, and Real Intelligence*, London: Routledge.

Warner, K. Q. (1992), 'Film, Literature and Identity in the Caribbean', in M. Cham (ed.), *Ex-Iles: Essays on Caribbean Cinema*, 44–58, Trenton, NJ: Africa World Press.

Warner, K. Q. (2000), *On Location: Cinema and Film in the Anglophone Caribbean*, London: Macmillan.

Waterman, T. (2018), 'Thailand, Highland, and Secret Island: Landscape and Power in Bond Films', in J. Strong (ed.), *James Bond Uncovered*, 185–202, Basingstoke: Palgrave Macmillan.

Williams, E. (1964), *Capitalism and Slavery*, London: Andre Deutsch.

Winder, S. (2006), *The Man Who Saved Britain: A Personal Journey into the Disturbing World of James Bond*, Picador: New York.

The World Is Not Enough (1999), [Film] Dir. Michael Apted, UK: Eon Productions.

'The World of Bond and Maigret: Fleming Meets Simenon' (1963), *Sunday Times Weekly Review*, 15 September.

Yardie (2018), [Film] Dir. Idris Elba, UK: Warp Films.

You Only Live Twice (1967), [Film] Dir. Lewis Gilbert, UK: Eon Productions.

Young, L. (1986), *Fear of the Dark: Race, Gender and Sexuality in the Cinema*, London: Routledge.

Young, R. J. C. (1995), *Colonial Desire: Hybridity in Theory, Culture, and Race*, New York: Routledge.

Zeiger, H. A. ([1965] 1966), *Ian Fleming: The Spy Who Came in with the Gold*, New York: Duell, Sloan and Pearce.

Zorzoli, G. B. (1966), 'Technology in the World of James Bond', in O. Del Buono and U. Eco (eds), *The Bond Affair*, trans. R. A. Downie, 122–32, London: MacDonald.

Index

A View to a Kill (1985, film) 198 n.13
Abraham, Karl 3
Adams, Alex 12–13, 15, 181 n.57, 193 n.18
Adamthwaite, Anthony 175 n.29
Adolf, Marion 172 n.12
airport
    as border crossing in *Live and Let Die* 64–5, 67
    as border crossing in *Dr. No* 101, 103–4, 111, 132
    as site of memory in *The Man with the Golden Gun* 132–5
Alexander, Camille 165
Allen, H. R. 189 n.18
Amis, Kingsley 39, 41–2, 44, 128, 181 n.53, 194 n.6
Andress, Ursula 167, 197 n.7
Anglo-American relations 18, 22, 53, 64, 69, 160, 185 n.1
animality 49, 59, 69, 110–14, 116, 118–19, 122, 131, 156, 176 n.35, 188 n.11
Anthony, Paul, and Jacquelyn Friedman 40, 42–3, 61, 63, 79
Arens, William 171 n.7
Avramescu, Catalin 171 n.7

Barnes, Alan, and Marcus Hearn 154
Baron Samedi 55, 58, 65, 71–2, 74–5, 81, 89, 101, 167, 187 n.8
Baron, Cynthia 15, 34–5, 45, 91, 93, 97, 110, 155–6, 179 n.45, 196 n.4
Beau Desert 55, 65, 76–7, 115, 121–2
Belnap, J. G. 171 n.3
Benjamin, J. R. 194 n.5
Bennett, Tony and Janet Woollacott 15, 44, 97, 116, 194 n.24
Benson, Raymond 20, 24, 40, 69, 77, 126–7, 165, 173 n.19
Berberich, Christine 14–15, 45, 92, 173 n.23, 175 n.29, 179 n.44, 180 n.50, 183 n.61

Bhabha, Homi K. 3–4
Black, Jeremy 42, 53–4, 57, 69, 71, 88–9, 92–3, 126, 144, 151, 164, 183 n.59, 189 n.17, 192 n.8, 195 n.10, 196 n.2, 197 n.10
Blackwell, Blanche 25, 172 n.15
Blackwell, Chris 172 n.15, 196 n.6
Blanchard, Claire 20
blaxploitation 165, 198 n.12
Bleuler, Eugene 3
Bold, Christine 118, 157, 169
bordello 50, 140–3, 147
borders (and border crossings) 12, 22, 89, 96, 101–2, 104–6, 108, 110, 130, 145, 186 n.6, 187 n.8
Bourne, Sam 86–8, 94, 116, 190 n.2
Boyd, Ann S. 86
Bradley, W. L. 183 n.59
Brandon, Henry 21
Broccoli, Albert R. and Harry Saltzman 22, 153
Brosnan, Pierce 36, 185 n.65
Brown, Vincent 172 n.16
Bryce, Ivar 18–19, 173 n.22
Burnetts, Charles 168–9
Bustamante, Alexander 28, 150, 176 n.33
Byron Lee and the Dragonaires 157, 161

Campbell, H. D. 172 n.16
Campbell, Jock 27
Cannadine, David 45–6, 125, 151, 169, 183 nn.60, 62, 184 nn.63, 64, 185 n.1
Capeci, D. J. and Martha Wilkerson 189 n.17
Caplen, Robert A. 118, 155
Carey, Bev 172 n.16
Cargill, Morris 14, 26–7, 29, 111, 127, 170, 176 n.34, 192 n.11
Casino Royale (1953, book) 13, 77, 173 n.19, 173 n.20, 186 nn.2, 6

Casino Royale (1954, TV programme) 185 n.1
Casino Royale (2006, film) 36, 179 n.48
Castro, Fidel 22, 133, 143, 174 n.24, 194 n.5
Cawelti, John G. and Bruce A. Rosenberg 31, 181 n.56
Chancellor, Henry 85
Chapman, James 13, 15, 43, 154–5, 160–2, 165, 196 n.5, 197 n.8, 198 n.13
Chayes, Abram 195 n.1
'Chigro' 97, 99–100, 106–10, 112–13, 191 n.7, 192 n.11
Churchill, Sir Winston 13–14, 21, 126, 176 n.32
Cleaver, Eldridge 55
Cold War 15–16, 19, 21, 54, 90, 126, 154, 158, 190 n.2
Connery, Sean 153, 161–2, 185 n.65, 197 n.8
Cork, John and Bruce Scivally 171 n.1
Couldry, Nick and Andreas Hepp 172 n.12
Coward, Noël 17, 23, 175 n.31
Crab Key 85, 107–8, 111–13, 118–19, 147, 155, 160, 187 n.8, 196 n.4
Craig, Daniel 36, 182 n.58, 185 n.65
Craton, Michael 172 n.16
Cuneo, Ernest 16, 19, 22, 172 n.18

Daas, Martha Mary 62–3, 70, 167–8, 186 n.2
Dalton, Timothy 185 n.65
Daub, Adrian and Charles Kronengold 164, 198 n.11
Dayan, Joan 72
Dench, Judi 36, 179 n.48
Denning, Michael 15, 100, 169
Diamonds Are Forever (1956, book) 172 n.18
Diamonds Are Forever (1971, film) 198 n.13
Die Another Day (2002, film) 198 n.13
Diedrich, Bernard and Al Burt 187 n.8
Dietl, Ralph 175 n.29
Dittmer, Jason 47, 54, 130, 132, 148, 150, 166, 188 n.12
Divine, R. A. 195 n.1
Dodds, Klaus 179 n.48
Dr No (character) 85, 92, 94, 97, 99, 104, 106–17, 119–20, 147, 154–5, 157, 159–60, 162, 186 n.6, 187 n.8, 190 n.2, 192 n.12, 193 nn.16, 18, 20, 196 nn.4, 7
Dr. No (1958, book) 2, 11, 15, 17, 33, 39, 41, 49, 50, 83, 85–7, 89–93, 96, 99–101, 103–6, 108, 110, 112–13, 116–17, 120, 122–3, 127, 129–30, 132–6, 138–9, 143–3, 147–9, 151, 176 n.35, 179 n.46, 180 n.51, 181 n.53, 186 n.6, 187 n.8, 190–3
Dr. No (1962, film) 5, 7, 50–1, 153–62, 167–8, 196 nn.3, 6, 197
Dresner, Lisa M. 14, 38, 43, 65, 71, 92, 115, 181 n.56, 194 n.4
Dulles, Allen 21, 174 n.24
Durgnat, Raymond 39, 44, 180 n.49
Dutheil, Martine Hennard 172 n.10

Earle, Peter 189 n.18
Earle, Rebecca 171 n.7
Early, Gerald 40–1, 59, 63, 69–71, 82–3, 90, 188 n.10, 190 n.2
Eco, Umberto 37, 39, 63, 182 n.59
Eden, Sir Anthony 24–6, 175 nn.30, 31
Edmond, Rod 172 n.10
Egan, Sean 171 n.1
Elba, Idris 5, 171 n.6, 179 n.47
Ernst Stavro Blofeld 126, 192 n.9
'The Eyes' 68, 109, 186 n.6, 194 n.3

Fanon, Franz 192 n.15
Farber, Samuel 194 n.5
Ferreras Savoye, Daniel 35–6, 89, 144, 147, 183 n.60, 189 n.16
Field, Matthew and Ajay Chowdhury 171 n.1
Fleming, Ann 148, 173 n.19
Fleming, Fergus 21, 28, 33, 129, 178 n.41, 192 n.11
Florida 72–7, 79, 89, 188 n.13
Foot, Sir Hugh 25, 28, 90, 175 n.30
For Your Eyes Only (1960, book) 176 n.36, 188 n.11, 190 n.19
Frayling, Christopher 193 n.21
Frenk, Joachim and Christian Krug 44, 153
Freud, Sigmund 3
Friesen, Norm and Theo Hug 172 n.12
From Russia with Love (1957, book) 17, 22, 39, 105, 174 n.25, 182 n.59, 186 n.6

From Russia with Love (1963, film) 174 n.25, 179 n.46
Funnell, Lisa 159
Funnell, Lisa and Klaus Dodds 19, 96, 101–2, 104, 159, 166, 183 n.60, 189 n.16

G. G. Sumatra 61–2, 68, 146
Gant, Richard 34
Gardiner, Philip 187 n.8
Germaná, Monica 60–2, 193 n.23
Gibson, D. R. 195 n.1
Gilbert, John 143, 178 n.40, 190 n.1
Goggin, Joyce 41–2, 68, 78–9, 167
Goh, Robbie B. H. 42, 194 n.4
'Goldeneye' 2, 14, 16, 19–20, 23–6, 35, 173 n.19, 174 n.26, 175 nn.30, 31, 177 nn.36, 39
Goldfinger (1959, book) 140, 172 n.18, 192 n.9
Goodman, Sam 30, 54, 75–7, 85, 90, 92, 96, 100, 169, 177 n.37, 187 n.9, 192 nn.14, 16, 195 n.8
Gopinath, Praseeda 44
Greenberg, C. L. 189 n.17
Grimshaw, A. D. 189 n.17
Griswold, John 90, 189 n.17

Hagen, Katharina 182 n.59
Haining, Peter 154, 191 n.3, 195 n.6
Hall, D. 154
Halloran, Vivian 11–12, 17, 31, 35, 40, 44, 46, 57, 65–6, 82, 109, 115, 172 n.14, 187 n.8
Hansell, G. R. and W. Grassie 193 n.22
Heimann, Paula 3
Hendry, Gloria 168, 179 n.46, 198 n.12
Hepp, Andreas, Stig Hjarvard, and Knut Lundby 172 n.12
Hjarvard, Stig and L. N. Peterson 172 n.12
Holder, Geoffrey 167
Holland, Patrick and Graham Huggan 171 n.5
Honey Rider 49, 112–13, 115–23, 135–6, 167, 193 n.16, 194 n.24, 196 n.7
Horizon (magazine) 26, 29, 99, 176 n.33
Howard, Michael 33, 129
Huggan, Graham 171 n.5
Huggins, Molly 28
Hyde, Marina 179 n.47

Ian Fleming Introduces Jamaica (book) 26
Isle of Surprise 55, 65, 76–7, 79–81, 102, 188 nn.12, 13, 14

James, C. L. R. 171 n.3
Jenkinson, Jacqueline 191 n.5
Johnson, Paul 86
Jones, Keith Philip 80

Kananga 163–6, 168–9, 197 n.10, 198 nn.12, 13
Kennedy, John F. 21–2, 64, 160, 174 nn.24, 25
Kingsbury, Paul 188 n.12
Kingston 5, 7, 18, 26, 28, 99–100, 133–7, 141, 144–5, 156–7, 160–1, 190 n.2, 191 n.7, 196 nn.3, 7
Kitzmiller, John 154–5, 179 n.46
Klein, Melanie 3
Knopf, T. A. 189 n.17
Kofele-Kale, Ndiva 187 n.8
Kotto, Yaphet 198 n.12
Krainitzki, Eva 179 n.48

Landa, Ishay 82, 110
Latimer, Jon 189 n.18
Lazenby, George 185 n.65
Leed, Eric J. 171 n.5
Leiter, Felix 36, 58–60, 62–3, 74–6, 78, 93, 149, 151, 159–60, 163, 166, 179 n.48, 185 n.1, 188 n.13, 189 n.17
Lemoine, Patrick 187 n.8
Lestringant, Frank 171 n.7
Lett, Brian 171 n.9
Licence to Kill (1989, film) 179 n.46
Lievesley, Geraldine 194 n.5
Lilli, Laura 86
Lindner, Christoph 14
Lipschutz, Ronnie D. 19
Live and Let Die (1954, book) 2, 11, 15, 17, 39–41, 48, 50, 53–5, 57–8, 60, 63, 65, 66, 68–70, 73–4, 78–9, 81, 83, 85–6, 89–91, 93, 95, 100, 101–2, 104–5, 109–10, 115, 123, 126–7, 131–2, 139, 146, 148–9, 171 n.10, 173 n.20, 176 nn.35, 36, 179 n.46, 180 n.51, 181 n.53, 185 n.1, 186 n.6, 187 n.8, 188 n.11, 189 n.17, 190 n.19, 190 n.2, 192 n.12, 193 n.16, 194 n.3

Live and Let Die (1973, film) 50, 161–5, 167–8, 197 n.8, 198 nn.11, 12, 13
The Living Daylights (1987) 177 n.38
Lycett, Andrew 18–19, 26, 31, 43, 110

MacCannell, Dean 171 n.5
McClintock, Anne 4
McClure, Daniel R. 163–4, 166–8, 198 nn.11, 12
McCormick, Donald 18, 35, 181 n.55
The Man with the Golden Gun (1965, book) 2, 11, 13–17, 22, 49–50, 123, 125–34, 136, 138–41, 143, 146–9, 151–2, 158, 159, 188 n.11, 194 nn.1, 3, 195 nn.7, 10
The Man with the Golden Gun (1974, film) 161–3
Manley, Norman 28, 176 n.33
Marchetti, Gina 193 n.21
Marshment, Margaret 57, 69–71, 186 n.5
Marquis, John 187 n.8
Mary Goodnight 137–8, 195 n.11
Mary Trueblood 92, 97, 100–1, 107, 156–7, 196 n.4, 197 n.9
Maudling, R. 158
Merry, Bruce 105
Miller, Cynthia J. 20, 22, 43
Mills, Charles W. 30, 86, 110, 112, 116, 149, 176 n.35, 191 nn.4, 7, 192 n.11, 197 n.8
Miss Taro 159
de Montaigne, Michel 171 n.2
Moonraker (1955, book) 32, 58, 129
Moore, Roger 161–2, 185 n.65, 197 n.8
Moran, Christopher 21, 174 n.24
More, Max and Natasha Vita-More 183 n.22
Morgan, Captain Henry 48, 59, 65, 70, 78, 80–3, 176 n.35, 180 n.51, 189 n.18, 190 n.2
Mr Big 17, 40, 48, 55, 58–9, 62–83, 89–91, 93, 101–2, 109–10, 131, 146–7, 165–7, 185 n.1, 186 nn.4, 6, 7, 8, 188 n.14, 189 n.17, 192 n.12, 194 n.3

Nelson, Horatio 18, 23
No Time to Die (2021, film) 36, 179 n.47, 195 n.9, 198 n.13

Octopussy (1984 film) 179 n.46
Octopussy and the Living Daylights (1966, book) 176 n.36
On Her Majesty's Secret Service (1963, book) 32, 39, 137, 189 n.59
Orientalism 20, 29, 33–5, 38, 61–2, 73, 75, 79, 91, 146, 178 nn.42, 43, 179 n.45, 191 n.2
Ormerod, David and David Ward 74

Pankratz, Anette 31–2, 177 n.38, 185 n.64
Parker, Matthew 2, 14, 16–17, 19, 21, 23–5, 27–8, 30, 33, 43, 56, 62, 78–9, 85, 90, 97–9, 101, 111, 127, 135, 143–5, 148–9, 153, 156, 160, 170, 172 n.19, 174 nn.26, 28, 176 nn.33, 34, 36, 188 n.11, 190 n.2, 192 n.12, 193 n.17
Pearson, John 23–4, 35, 55, 129, 174 n.24, 175 n.29, 177 n.39
Pérez-Stable, Marifeli 194 n.5
Pleydell-Smith (colonial secretary) 93, 107, 158–9, 171 n.7
Plomer, William 127, 178 n.41, 181 n.55, 192 n.11
Powell, Dilys 165
Pratt, Mary Louise 172 n.14
Pua, Phoebe 179 n.48

Quantum of Solace (2008) 36, 180 n.48
Quarrel 17, 39, 55, 75–7, 102–3, 110–13, 116–18, 122, 149, 154–5, 157–8, 162, 168, 176 n.35, 179 n.46, 180 n.51, 181 n.53, 188 n.13, 193 n.16
Quarrel Jr 162, 168–9
Queen Elizabeth 13, 25, 95, 161
Queen's Club 98–101, 149, 157

Ranish, Robert and Stefan Lorenz Sorgner 193 n.22
Razinsky, Hili 3
Rich Road 98–100
Richards, Jeffrey M. 10
Richler, Mordecai 39, 42, 170, 180 n.49
Riquet, Johannes and Anna Zdrenyk 187 n.9
'The Robber' 74, 187 n.10, 188 nn.11, 13
Robertson, James 153–4, 158, 160–1, 196 nn.2, 6, 7

Rosenberg, Bruce A., and Ann Harlemann Stewart 22, 31, 37–9, 42, 62, 116, 180 nn.51, 52, 186 n.3
Rosie Carver 165, 168–9, 179 n.46, 198 n.12
Rupert, G. G. 193 n.21

San Monique 161–4, 167
Sanday, Peggy 171 n.7
Sanneh, Kelefa 60
Satton, Lon 166, 179 n.46
Sauerberg, Lars Ole 53, 70, 127, 190 n.19
Scaramanga 50, 126, 129–41, 143–51, 159, 188 n.11, 194 nn.3, 4, 5, 6, 195 nn.10, 11
Schickel, Richard 164–5
Seymour, Jane 167–9
Sheller, Mimi 9–11, 72, 170, 186 n.7
Skyfall (2012) 179 nn.46, 48, 182 n.58, 195 n.9
Smith, Jim and Stephen Lavington 171 n.1
Snelling, O. F. 39, 63, 193 n.20
Solitaire 68, 72–4, 115, 147, 163, 167–8, 198 n.13
Spectre (2015, film) 179 n.46, 182 n.58, 195 n.9
The Spy Who Loved Me (1962, book) 129
Sterling, Martin and Gary Morecombe 76, 171 n.1
Stern, Sheldon M. 195 n.1
Stock, Paul 130, 132–3
Strangways 77, 80, 83, 85, 92, 94, 97, 100–2, 107, 132, 138–9, 156–8, 188 n.13, 189 n.14, 193 n.17, 197 n.9
Strömbäck, Jesper 172 n.12
Strutter 166, 168, 179 n.46
Sugrue, T. J. 189 n.17
Sunbeam Alpine (car) 138, 158
Sweig, J. E. 194 n.5

Taussig, Michael 171 n.3
Taylor, Andrew 33, 60
Thunderball (1961, book) 126, 153, 176 n.36, 194 n.2
Thunderbird hotel 140, 143, 147–8, 195 n.11

Tiffy 50, 140–3, 147
Tomorrow Never Dies (1997, film) 198 n.13
Tornabuoni, Lietta 22, 174 n.25
Turner, Janice 5–9, 171 n.8

Urry, John and Jonas Larsen 171 n.5

Van Vechten, Carl 59–60
Varble, Derek 175 n.29
Verbeek, Bertjan 175 n.29
Viol, Claus-Ulrich 193 n.23
Voodoo 48, 55, 58, 61, 65, 71–2, 74–5, 89, 101, 131, 164–9, 171 n.10, 186 n.8, 189 n.17, 194 n.3, 197 n.10

Wagner, Travis L. 132, 155–6, 198 n.13
Ward, Stuart 183 n.60
Wark, Wesley K. 43
Warner, Keith Q. 153, 155, 160–1
Waterman, Tim 20, 47, 162
Williams, Eric 172 n.16
Winder, Simon 2, 24, 26, 126, 172 nn.15, 17, 174 n.27
Windrush 1, 7, 14, 34, 43, 49, 57, 92, 97, 110, 181 n.56, 191 n.6
The World Is Not Enough (1999, film) 179 n.48
Wright, Jeffrey 36, 179 n.48

Yardie (2018) 5–9, 171 n.6
You Only Live Twice (1964, book) 17, 39, 127, 137, 178 n.41, 192 n.9
You Only Live Twice (1967, film) 177 n.38, 179 n.46, 198 n.13
Young, Lola 72
Young, R. J. C. 4
Young, Terence 153–5, 158

Zeiger, H. A. 7, 19, 31, 37
zombie 48, 68, 72–3, 81, 186 n.7, 187 n.8
Zorzoli, G. B. 86

www.ingramcontent.com/pod-product-compliance
Lightning Source LLC
Chambersburg PA
CBHW072234290426
44111CB00012B/2095